# Obama's Economy

# OBAMA'S ECONOMY

## Recovery for the Few

Jack Rasmus

**Pluto**Press
www.plutobooks.com

First published 2012 by Pluto Press
345 Archway Road, London N6 5AA

www.plutobooks.com

Distributed in the United States of America exclusively by
Palgrave Macmillan, a division of St. Martin's Press LLC,
175 Fifth Avenue, New York, NY 10010

British Library Cataloguing in Publication Data
A catalogue record for this book is available from the British Library

ISBN    978 0 7453 3219 2    Hardback
ISBN    978 0 7453 3218 5    Paperback
ISBN    978 1 84964 694 9    PDF
ISBN    978 1 84964 696 3    Kindle
ISBN    978 1 84964 695 6    ePub

Library of Congress Cataloging in Publication Data applied for

10   9   8   7   6   5   4   3   2   1

Designed and produced for Pluto Press by Chase Publishing Services Ltd
Typeset from disk by Stanford DTP Services, Northampton, England
Simultaneously printed digitally by CPI Antony Rowe, Chippenham, UK and
Edwards Bros in the United States of America

# Contents

# Introduction: A Systemic Crisis of Recovery

## 'The Wasted $12 Trillion'

The defining feature of the U.S. economy over the past three years since Obama took office has been its failure to achieve a sustained recovery. After three economic stimulus programs costing $3 trillion over the past three years, 2009–11, and after more than $9 trillion in bank rescues by the Federal Reserve, the faltering U.S. economic recovery of the past three years is headed toward an eventual double-dip recession by 2013.[1]

The U.S. economy entered recession in December 2007. The decline accelerated in September–October 2008 with the onset of the banking crash. The collapse set in motion by the events of September–October 2008 continued through the first six months of 2009, at a pace virtually identical to 1929–30. The economy only bottomed out by June 2009. But bottoming out does not constitute recovery. Nor does the weak and faltering economy that followed the June 2009 bottom.

Recovery means restoring the economy to levels and performance prior to the onset of recession, or at least to some 'average' historical level and performance preceding the collapse. The period from June 2009 to the present therefore cannot qualify as a recovery in either of these cases; nor can it in any otherwise normal sense of the term.

Except for financial asset prices—i.e. stocks, bonds, derivative trades, etc.—during the first year, from June 2009 to June 2010, nearly all real (non-financial) economic indicators recovered at best only part of the prior losses of 2008–09. And critical sectors of the economy, like jobs and housing, recovered virtually nothing. Moreover, many economic indicators that did partially regain some lost ground in the first year after June 2009 thereafter experienced a further 'relapse' in the summer of 2010. Meanwhile, jobs and housing experienced a bona fide 'double dip'. A second partial recovery followed in late 2010, even weaker than the first in 2009–10. In late 2011, the economy began to fade once more, as a second 'relapse' of the economy once again emerged.[2] This raises the first of three major themes of this book:

*What explains this weak, repeatedly faltering economy and failure to achieve a self-sustaining recovery after trillions of dollars in fiscal and monetary stimulus?*

By October 2011 an increasing number of economists, and even business sources, began to predict the 'relapse' might soon turn into a double-dip recession. A select few of those with the best forecasting track record to date have even begun to forewarn of a possible imminent global depression.[3]

To the extent there has been any recovery these past three years under the Obama administration, that recovery has been limited to and has benefited a relatively small segment of the U.S. economy and population. After June 2009 stock markets rose more than 100%. Bond markets did even better. Corporate profits exceeded levels even preceding December 2007. U.S. large corporations accumulated more than $2 trillion in cash on hand, while U.S. multinational corporations were able to build a cash hoard of another $1.2–1.4 trillion in their offshore subsidiaries. Both continue to hoard their more than $3 trillion in cash, not investing it in the U.S. to create jobs and contribute to sustained recovery. Not to be outdone, big banks accumulated—and then also sat on—about $1.5 trillion in excess cash reserves, mostly refusing to lend to smaller businesses to create jobs and assist recovery.[4]

Measuring 'recovery' in terms of its human dimension—not just in terms of impersonal economic indicators—yields a similar grossly unbalanced picture: CEO and senior management compensation and bankers bonuses recovered in 2010 to pre-2008 levels. The top 25 hedge fund managers did even better. Their income more than doubled in 2009 to surpass previous 2007 peaks. The wealthiest 10% of households returned to consuming luxury goods at pre-recession levels.

In contrast, more than three years after Obama took office there are still roughly 24 million unemployed. The numbers of part-time and temp jobs have increased by more than 10 million, as full-time permanent jobs are churned out and replaced by part-time and temp jobs with lower pay and hardly any benefits. Thus, not only the number of jobs but the quality and level of pay and benefits associated with jobs has also not 'recovered'. Real weekly incomes for more than 100 million non-supervisory workers are less today than two years ago due to wage cuts, fewer hours of work, and escalating inflation of basic items—like health care services, education, gasoline, and many basic food costs that have risen at double-digit rates throughout 2011.

In addition to jobs and wage income, home foreclosures have more than doubled in number since early 2009, to 11.4 million by late summer 2011. 17 million homes are 'underwater', with home values worth less than their mortgages. States and cities continue to lay off workers by the hundreds of thousands in 2010 and 2011, slash vital services and programs, and raise fees at an accelerating pace. Poverty rates in the U.S. are now at their highest levels in half a century, impacting more than 15% of the population (45 million). That includes more than 15 million children—the latter distributed more or less evenly across white, latino, and black kids. More than 50 million officially—and more in fact—are without any kind of health care coverage. Food stamp usage has more than doubled in the past two years, as has student loan debt in two years. Trillions of dollars of seniors' retirement 'nest eggs' have disappeared forever, as Congress in late 2011 nonetheless proposed to reduce their medical and retirement benefits further. The litany of conditions that have worsened is endless. That is not recovery by any stretch of the imagination.

And it's not just workers, homeowners, students, and the 100 million plus working- and middle-class households who have not 'recovered'. Hundreds of thousands of small businesses have gone under since the bottom of the recession in June 2009, more failing than are being created, as banks continue to starve them (and households) of basic loans and credit as the banks continue hoarding more than $1 trillion in cash reserves on hand. Even banks themselves have been divided into 'haves' and 'have-nots'. The 'too big to fail' largest 20 or so banks have in part recovered, propped up by $9 trillion in U.S. Federal Reserve liquidity injections, zero-interest loans and direct subsidies, and hundreds of billions in direct grants from the U.S. Treasury and taxpayers. Meanwhile, more than 500 small community and regional banks have either failed outright or have been forced into mergers by government regulators to protect what little depositors' assets remain on their books. In short, a small layer of wealthy households, professional speculators and investors, big banks and multinational corporations, CEOs and senior managers, have indeed 'recovered'. But virtually no one else. The preceding undisputable facts lead to the second major theme of the book:

*How to explain this historically unprecedented lopsided economic recovery enjoyed so much by so few at the expense of so many?*

The Obama team has introduced no fewer than three economic recovery programs over the past three years. One each year in 2009, 2010 and 2011. This does not include Obama's election year proposals he offered in 2008 as a program for economic recovery. This book will look at each of the three recovery programs and his pre-election promises and analyze each in depth.

Each of Obama's economic recovery programs share certain similarities, no doubt in large part explaining why all have similarly failed. They are all composed of a particular mix of tax cuts, spending stimulus, Federal Reserve monetary policies, and lesser efforts to expand manufacturing exports and trade. Each subsequent economic recovery program, however, has been less in magnitude and scope than the preceding. In turn, each recovery program's impact on the economy has therefore been weaker and of shorter duration. Obama's first economic recovery program (2009) produced a brief and weak recovery of barely twelve months. The second (2010) recovery program produced an even weaker and shorter nine months' recovery. And this writer predicts the third (2011) recovery program, in development since September 2011, will be weaker still than the preceding two.

The book is about the evolution of Obama's economic recovery programs and policies from 2008 through 2011, why they were so 'lopsided' in favor of the wealthiest few and their corporations and why they failed to generate sustained economic recovery. The book not only describes those programs and policies in some detail, but also provides a critique and an analysis of why they failed at recovery as well as benefited just a wealthy few. The book therefore constitutes an indictment and critique of traditional fiscal and monetary policies at the heart of the Obama programs and policies.

The book argues that Obama's economic programs and policies have been both ineffective and inefficient. Ineffective because they have failed to generate sustained recovery. Inefficient because a mountain of trillions of dollars in tax cuts, spending, and money injection into financial institutions has brought forth a molehill recovery—a recovery that appears to be faltering yet again.

The current economic crisis has always been global and never just a U.S.-centric event. As 2011 draws to a close, not only is there evidence that the U.S. economy underwent a second 'relapse' in the summer of 2011— leading perhaps to an even more serious double-dip recession by 2013—but also that it may have entered an evolutionary trajectory toward eventual global depression.

The global economy itself is clearly slowing and heading toward growing instability. While the U.S. economy hovers somewhere between economic relapse and double dip, many economies elsewhere are already experiencing a double-dip recession. The Eurozone periphery economies are already there. So is Japan. The main engines of the Euro economy, France and Germany, are near zero growth as of October 2011 and may well soon slip into recession by the fourth quarter should the Euro debt crisis not be resolved soon—which in all likelihood it appears it will not. The U.K. economy is slowing rapidly, to less than 1%, and approaching stagnant growth much like Germany and France. All are on the cusp of a double dip. Meanwhile, economic growth is rapidly slowing in China, India, Brazil and other key emerging economies that over the past two years were able to grow robustly and temporarily to help dampen the global contraction of 2007–10 in part somewhat. But now they too are slowing rapidly. There are no remaining props to offset the worsening condition in the core capitalist economies of North America, Europe and Japan.

The eventual slipping into global double dip was predicted by this writer in late 2009 in a prior work, *Epic Recession: Prelude to Global Depression*, which was written at that time, as others were predicting recovery coming in only a few more months.[5] As others predicted a 'V-shape' rapid recovery from the June 2009 recession bottom, this writer was warning that a long stagnation would follow the June 2009 recession bottom. That stagnation would take the form of a series of short, weak recoveries followed by short, mild downturns (relapses) or even double dips. The policies introduced in early 2009 by the Obama administration were rejected as inadequate for generating any sustained, true economic recovery. Not only were those policies, it was argued, insufficient in magnitude of stimulus, but the composition and timing of the stimulus were even more incorrect. And so far as Obama's and the Federal Reserve's monetary policy was concerned, it would prove ineffective in whatever form it assumed, given the massive debt that was allowed to remain on bank, general business, and household balance sheets. In other words, *Epic Recession* argued the 'system was still fragile' and would remain so since the Obama economic recovery program of 2009 did not address this key condition affecting banks, businesses, and household balance sheets.

Unlike *Epic Recession*, however, *Obama's Economy: Recovery for the Few* will not address such issues of economic theory. The former work is about how and why the current economic crisis occurred. *Obama's Economy* is about how and why recovery from the crisis has failed these past three years and why similar policies will continue to fail to generate a sustained recovery.

But *Obama's Economy* goes further, beyond just describing, analyzing and critiquing the Obama economic recovery policies of the past three years. Describing and explaining today's failed recovery is only half the task. If the Obama policies of the past three years have failed, what alternative policies may perhaps prove successful? The most important part of this book therefore is its final chapter—'An Alternative Program for Economic Recovery'. For the most important question of the day is not answering 'How did we get here?' It is not even explaining 'Why did recovery fail?' The most important question is: 'How do we get out of the crisis; what will it take?' Thus the third major theme of this book, in addition to *Why has recovery failed?* and *Why did so few benefit so much at the expense of so many?*, is:

> *What alternative policies and programs are necessary to ensure a full recovery for all?*

This book therefore concludes with recommendations of policies and programs needed to generate a sustained economic recovery. The proposals for recovery described in the final chapter of this book are of three kinds. The first are immediate policy proposals designed to check the tendency of the economy to continue on its current 'stop–go'. The second type of proposals address more intermediate level demands. They are institutional in character and are designed to lead to sustained economic recovery. The third set of policy proposals are more long term, deeply structural and even transformative of the economy, They are designed to make changes that would prevent a future recurrence of today's continuing systemic crisis in the U.S. economy.

# 1
## The Weakest, Most Lopsided Recovery

'Who Recovered, Who Didn't, and Why'

With less than a year remaining before the November 2012 elections, the policies that have come to define Obama's economy have been largely implemented. The results and consequences are mostly known or predictable. Significant further economic stimulus in 2012 beyond that introduced in late 2011 is highly improbable or likely to prove token and ineffective. It is appropriate at this juncture therefore to assess the performance of Obama's economy over the past three years; to understand why its policies and programs have failed to generate a sustained economic recovery; and to explain why the uneven recovery has benefited only the wealthy and powerful few at the direct expense of the rest.

Economic recovery under Obama's economy has been the weakest recovery on record of all the eleven recessions in the U.S. since 1945. It has also proven the most lopsided recovery of all the postwar recessions—benefiting investors, corporations, and the wealthiest 10% of households, but not workers, homeowners, small businesses, or the remaining 'bottom' 80% of households in the U.S.—more than 100 million. Furthermore, as of late 2011 the economy now appears on its way to a second contraction, or 'double dip', if not in 2012 for certain sometime in 2013.

Important sections of the economy—jobs and housing—had already experienced a 'relapse' in 2010 and by 2011 appeared headed for yet a second 'relapse'.[1] After a collapse of employment of historic dimensions from mid 2008 through June 2009, the U.S. jobs market underwent a relapse in the summer of 2010. For a second time, employment levels fell. The jobless numbers continued to rise for four consecutive months, from June to September 2010. That was followed by a modest growth of employment for a short period, from the early fall of 2010 into the spring of 2011, after which job growth slowed sharply once again. A similar scenario describes the housing market. Residential housing—which experienced a deep collapse from 2007 through 2009 not seen since the Great Depression of the 1930s—recovered briefly in late 2009. It subsequently declined again in the summer of 2010, recover briefly once more, and retreated yet again.

Other key sectors of the economy also showed significant weakness twelve months after the official end of the recession in June 2009. Twelve months after the June 2009 low, many had regained at best only half their losses from the deep contraction of 2008–09.

6

Retail sales recovered only half of their 2008–09 losses by summer 2010. Business spending rose only 3% in the first half of 2010, after having fallen to a postwar record of –6.7% in 2009. Industrial production was still off 30% by mid 2010, as were durable goods orders. After rising to 58 in the first quarter of 2010, the index for manufacturing activity had fallen once again to 50 by July 2010, indicating 'no growth'.

Following the June 2009 recession low point, the broader U.S. economy entered its first relapse in the summer of 2010. That first relapse was followed by an even briefer recovery of six months. But the economy soon began to weaken again in 2011. Gross domestic product (GDP), the measure of total economic output, fell from 2.3% in the closing quarter of 2010 to roughly one-third (0.8%) that level in the first six months of 2011. Both jobs and housing markets slowed even more, both headed for yet a 'third' dip. By late 2011, it became increasingly clear that the U.S. economy was not even close to achieving self-sustaining recovery, and was possibly headed toward a double-dip recession.[2]

The unprecedented weakness of the U.S. economy today—four years after the recession began in December 2007 and more than two years after the recession was officially declared over in June 2009—is illustrated by a comparison of the current faltering, 'stop–go' recovery with the two previously most severe recessions of 1973–75 and 1981–82.

## THE WEAKEST RECOVERY SINCE 1945

Comparing the Obama 'recovery' to the two other worst recessions since 1945—those of 1973–75 and 1981–82—the track record to date since 2009 offers a dramatic contrast.

Thirty-nine months after the 1973–75 recession, GDP had risen 4.8% over pre-recession levels. Thirty-nine months after the 1981–82 recession, GDP rose by 9.8% over pre-recession levels. In stark contrast, GDP 39 months after the start of the 2007–09 recession was still below pre-recession levels. This comparison of recoveries is summarized in Table 1.1.

*Table 1.1*  Post-recession recoveries compared, GDP index
(Seasonally adjusted; index 100 = 2005)

| Recession | Recovery 39 months after start of the recession |
|-----------|------------------------------------------------|
| 1973–75   | 4.8%  |
| 1981–82   | 9.8%  |
| 2007–09   | –0.1% |

*Source*: U.S. Commerce Department, National Income and Product Accounts, Table 1.1.3, June 24, 2011, and National Income and Product Accounts, Table 1.1.3, December 22, 2011.

## The Jobs Picture

Comparing the recovery of jobs in the three recessions is even more dramatic than comparing GDP figures. Following both prior recessions in the 1970s and 1980s, total employment had *risen* by 5–6% over pre-recession levels after 39 months. In today's recession, jobs are still 5% *below* 2007 pre-recession levels by the most conservative estimates. And if workers who have left the labor force are counted, it's 8–10% below. As of the fourth quarter of 2011, there are a minimum of 25 million still without work nearly four years after the current recession officially began in December 2007.

To get back to the 7.1 million unemployment level of December 2007 before the recession began would take more than ten years of creating 300,000 jobs a month, every month, for more than a decade. Thus far, for the first nine months of 2011, the average net new job creation has been well less than 100,000 a month.

Since 2000 the rate of new job creation in the U.S. has been historically weak even in good times. For nearly three years following the prior mild recession of 2001, jobs for non-supervisory wage and salary workers hardly grew at all until 2004. Thereafter jobs grew mostly as a result of the unhealthy over-expansion of the financial and construction sectors of the economy during the decade. And when the financial crisis and recession hit in late 2007, jobs collapsed even faster in those two sectors than in the rest of the economy.

For example, the number of wage and salary workers employed at the end of 2001 was 100,343,000. By the bottom of the recession in June 2009 that number had fallen to 100,033,000. All the jobs created in the intervening years, 2002–08, had been wiped out. By June 2011—two years after the end of the current recession in June 2009—total employment was still only 100,397,000. That's a net long-term gain of jobs of only 54,000 after ten years. In short, the economy had not only regressed to job levels where it was in 2009, but retreated all the way back to where it was a decade ago![3] The comparison of the Obama recovery period with prior recessions is depicted in Figure 1.1.

There are three great 'mini-crises' within the general crisis of the U.S. economy today, which explain, in significant part, why the general economy has been unable to generate a sustained recovery. The three mini-crises are: jobs, housing foreclosures, and the fiscal crisis of state and local governments. Tables 1.2 and 1.3 show a comparison of the Obama recovery with the two prior worst recessions, 1973–75 and 1981–82, in terms of housing and local governments.

## The Housing Picture

There has never been a sustained recovery from a recession since 1945 without a recovery in housing and construction. A comparison of the Obama recovery with prior recoveries shows that construction recovered sharply from recession lows in both 1973–75 and 1981–82 after 39 months. After 39 months, construction was up by more than 30% from the start of the recession in both

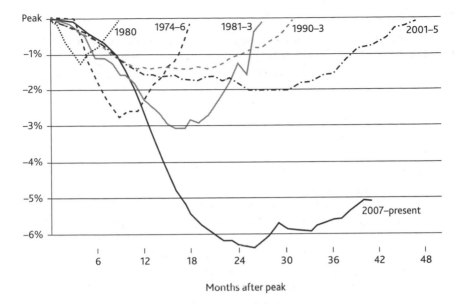

*Figure 1.1*   Comparing recessions and recoveries: job changes

*Notes*: Horizontal axis shows months. Vertical axis shows the ratio of that month's nonfarm payrolls to the nonfarm payrolls at the start of recession. Because employment is a lagging indicator, the dates for these employment trends are not exactly synchronized with the NBER's official business cycle dates.

*Source*: Federal Reserve Bank of Minneapolis, www.Minneapolisfed.org.

prior recession recoveries in the 1970s and 1980s. In contrast, construction fell by more than 30% during the recent 2007–09 recession and subsequently has fallen by another 11%. Construction is not only not recovering, it is already in what is called a 'double dip', i.e. second recession.

*Table 1.2*   Construction sector recoveries compared, residential plus non-residential structures ($ billions, seasonally adjusted; index 100 = 2005)

| Recession | Recovery 39 months after start of the recession | Recovery from official end of the recession to 39 months |
|---|---|---|
| 1973–75 | 23.2% | 34.7% |
| 1981–82 | 27.3% | 31.9% |
| 2007–09 | −36.9% | −5.4%* |

* 27 months from the end of the recession.

*Source*: U.S. Commerce Department, National Income and Product Accounts, Table 1.1.3, June 24, 2011, and National Income and Product Accounts, Table 1.1.3, December 22, 2011.

More dramatic still is the condition of residential housing. According to the leading industry research source, RealtyTrac, more than 11.4 million homes have already foreclosed.[4] The number is undoubtedly larger, since many have lost their homes through 'short sales' and by just 'walking away' from their mortgages without having gone through the legal process of foreclosure.[5]

Other sources predict 13–14 million, or about one in four homeowners, will have eventually faced foreclosure before the housing sector bottoms out. As home prices began falling a second time (i.e. double dip) in 2011, the number of homes in 'negative equity' (i.e. home values worth less than the mortgage) rose to approximately 16–17 million. Foreclosures and negative equity comprise nearly half of all the 54 million mortgages in the U.S. After nearly four years of Obama recovery, the housing sector remains mired in what can only be described as a deep 'depression'. New home construction is off 75% from prior peak levels, home price declines average almost 40% and, except for minimal apartment construction, there are no signs whatsoever of recovery on the horizon.

Figure 1.2 shows clearly that foreclosure activity not only peaked under Obama in 2009–10 but remained consistently high until the 'robo-signing foreclosure' scandal that erupted in summer 2010, in which banks foreclosed and repossessed many homes illegally. That scandal precipitated a public reaction on the eve of the November 2010 midterm Congressional elections. The banks then temporarily backed off processing foreclosures and home repossessions at their prior record rate during the summer of 2010. By mid 2011, foreclosure and bank repossession rates rose sharply once again.

As James Saccacio, CEO of RealtyTrac, commented on the temporary slowdown in foreclosures in late 2010 due to the robo-signing scandal, "Total properties foreclosure filings would have easily exceeded 3 million in 2010 had it not been for the fourth quarter drop in foreclosure activity—triggered mainly by the continuing controversy surrounding foreclosure documentation and procedures that prompted many major lenders to temporarily halt some foreclosure proceedings." And as RealtyTrac senior vice-president Rick Sharga

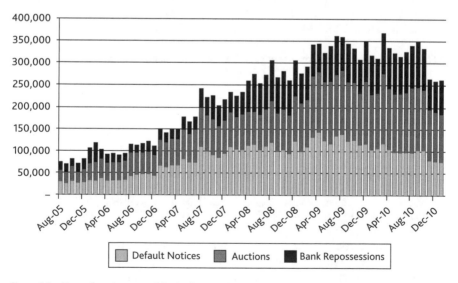

*Figure 1.2*   Home foreclosure activity in the U.S., 2005–11

*Source*: RealtyTrac.

added, concerning the summer 2011 resumption of foreclosures: "We're on track for a record year for homes in foreclosure and repossessions...There is no improvement in the underlying economic conditions."[6] By late summer 2011, foreclosures were once again rising at a 2.5 million annual rate.

### State and Local Government Picture

In the two prior worst recessions of 1973–75 and 1981–82, state and local government spending grew through the recessions and continued thereafter into the recovery period. State and local government spending thus offset the sharp declines in private sector spending and job loss. This moderated the depth and cut short the duration of those prior recessions, and allowed recovery to occur more rapidly. This has not happened in the current Obama recession. For the first time, the state and local government sector has not taken up the slack in the private sector during the downturn. State and local government has thus played no role in offsetting the decline in the private sector of the economy, during the recession or after. In fact, state and local governments are now a major contributing factor to job loss and a major drag on recovery. This job trend and drag on the economy will continue in 2012 and beyond, it appears.

*Table 1.3*   State and local government recoveries compared
($ billions, seasonally adjusted; index 100 = 2005)

| Recession | Recovery 39 months after start of the recession | Recovery from official end of the recession to 39 months |
|---|---|---|
| 1973–75 | 36.3% | 11.3% |
| 1981–82 | 25.6% | 15.0% |
| 2007–09 | –4.4% | –4.6%* |

* 27 months from the end of the recession.

*Source*: U.S. Commerce Department, National Income and Product Accounts, Table 1.1.5, June 24, 2011, and National Income and Product Accounts, Table 1.1.3, December 22, 2011.

As Tables 1.1–3 and Figure 1.1 illustrate, the Obama recovery is different from the two worst recession recoveries in three ways. First, job creation is stagnant at best and periodically relapses after very brief and modest gains. Second, the construction sector and residential housing continue to decline without even a modest temporary recovery. Third, state and local government has not performed its normal offsetting stimulus role, as in previous recoveries, and is in fact now a contributing factor preventing economic growth. Given these three distinct characteristics of the Obama period, it is no wonder that there has not been any sustained recovery for the past three years.

### THE MOST LOPSIDED RECOVERY

In addition to being the weakest recovery from recession on record since 1945, the second major distinguishing characteristic of the Obama recovery is that it has been the 'most lopsided' recovery in the post-1945 period; 'lopsided' in terms of who has benefited. It has been a recovery in which investors in stock and bond markets have realized historic record returns, in which corporate profits have snapped back to record highs not seen in decades, in which bank and corporate CEOs have achieved record income gains once again, and in which the wealthiest 10% of households in the U.S.—including millionaires, multimillionaires, and billionaires—have experienced surging incomes on a par with the best post-recession years since 1945. For the wealthiest few, the current recession was historically short, 'V-shaped', and their recovery fully complete after barely a year.

## Stocks and Bonds

For example, the Dow Jones index of U.S. stocks rose between June 2009- and June 2010 more than 90% from its prior lows. The bond markets have done better. After a 30% increase in returns in 2009, high yield bonds returned an additional 57% in 2010. Compounded, that's more than 100%.

## Corporate Profits

Corporate profits have done still better. Having experienced the fastest recovery in 31 years by late 2011, corporate profits were higher than they were in December 2007 prior to the start of the recent recession. The average annual rate of increase of profits in the U.S. since 1948 has been around 10%. But as Table 1.4 shows, pre-tax corporate profits nearly doubled in just a little more than two years, from their recession lows of $971 billion in December 2008 to $1,876 billion by March 2011. They were even 47% higher in March 2011 than their previous pre-recession highs in 2007. Similar gains occurred for after-tax profits recovery. The 43–49% pre- and after-tax profits recovery in the first two years following the 2007–09 recession compares to a similar two-year profits recovery of 28% in 2001–03 and 11% in 1991–93 following the two most recent recessions of 2001 and 1990–91. So profits recovery after recessions has been accelerating, and profits recovery from the 2007–09 has been the most rapid.

*Table 1.4*  Corporate profits recovery: 2007–11, pre-tax and after-tax
($ billions)

|  | *Recession begins* <br> *2007 (IV)* | *Profit low-point* <br> *2008(IV)* | *Recession ends* <br> *2009(II)* | *+ 2 Years* <br> *2011(I)* |
|---|---|---|---|---|
| Pre-tax | $1,460 | $971 | $1,262 | $1,876 |
| After-tax | $989 | $746 | $1,017 | $1,454 |
| Corporate tax | $445 | $272 | $244 | $422 |
| Corporate tax <br> as % pre-tax profits | 30% | 28% | 19% | 22% |

*Source*: U.S. Department of Commerce, Bureau of Economic Analysis, National Income and Product Accounts, News Release July 29, 2011, Tables 11A, 11B, also 12 and 13.

However, the profit surge shown in Table 1.4 still does not reflect total corporate profits. It only includes profit from corporations' sale of goods and services. It should be further increased by including corporate depreciation allowances, which are essentially profits as well, but earmarked and set aside for only future capital spending. And a third source is portfolio profits, which are profits from financial securities realized by non-financial corporations— i.e. from capital gains, returns from speculating in derivatives, dividends paid to them by other corporations, interest earned on foreign investments, and other pure financial activities. Large, multinational corporations, in particular, realize significant portfolio-financial profits. Their portfolio profits as a share of their total (non-portfolio) profits have been growing significantly over time. The large multinational corporations are thus financial institutions as well, at least in part. They are the 'deep-shadow' banks of the corporate world.[7] Neither depreciation nor portfolio profits show up in the profits totals in Table 1.4, so the profit gains indicated in the table are conservative, low estimates of true total corporate profits.

A good example is the General Electric Corporation (GE). GE reported a 77% increase in its first-quarter 2011 profits.[8] GE Capital, the company's financial arm, saw profits triple from $583 million to $1.8 billion over the previous year. GE's 2010 total worldwide profits amounted to $14.2 billion. But the company still paid no tax on those profits whatsoever. In fact, it received a $3.2 billion tax refund check from the government.[9]

Finally, for a view of how well the really big corporations did in terms of profits and recovery, data for the 500 largest companies, the S&P 500, show that their profits surged by 206% in 2009 alone and another 37% in 2010. All that compares to their average annual profits gain of 10% a year from 1998 to 2007.[10]

Yet another way to look at profits is profit margins. While profit levels rose to their highest levels in 31 years, profit margins reached levels not achieved in 80 years. Profit margins are defined as that percentage of revenue left over after expenses—i.e. profits as a percent of operating costs. Therefore if costs are cut, profit margins rise whether or not sales and revenues increase. Normally in recessions profit margins fall because sales revenues typically decline and costs rise. But not so during the recession that began in 2007. As the chief U.S. economist for investment bank Goldman Sachs, David Kostin, remarked: "In the downturn, companies managed to maintain higher profit margins than ever before."[11] What that means is that businesses cut costs even faster than their sales revenue dropped. Record profit margins during the recession means the record profits recovery was due to cost-cutting—labor cost-cutting in particular. In other words, the record gains in profits have been largely achieved at the direct cost of workers' wages, jobs, hours of work, benefits, and the rapid productivity gains achieved after June 2009 that have not been shared by companies with their workers.

## CEO and Executive Pay

After leveling off or slightly declining for one year during the worst of the 2008-09 economic collapse phase, top U.S. executives' paychecks rose significantly in 2010. Median pay for top executives at 200 big companies rose 23% to $10.8 million in 2010.[12] Average pay was of course higher, as averages generally exceed medians.

Cash bonuses as a component of executive pay rose even more, by 38%, according to a study by Equilar, an executive compensation research firm.[13] The biggest payouts were for oil, commodities, and technology companies. These figures, moreover, do not include the cash-outs of very large stock options that were granted in 2008–09 when stock prices were low and thereafter rose by large margins. Those stock cash-outs will take place in 2011–12 when the stock market will have peaked. It will no doubt show up in 2011 executive pay results. The 2010 CEO pay gains of 23% compare to the same companies' median revenue gains of only 7%. So executives in effect awarded themselves bonuses of more than three times the sales growth of their companies.

## Bankers' Bonuses

Despite the near collapse of many of their banks, bankers did even better than non-bank CEOs and executives during the recovery period. The average pay for the CEOs of the 15 largest banks rose by 36% in 2010, according to a study carried out by Equilar. Those same 15 banks' revenue rose by an average of only 2.9%. Seven of the 15 banks actually reported a loss, but their CEOs still got bonuses. The 36% is a low-end estimate, moreover. The 36% does not include contributions to CEOs' retirement plans or stock accumulation. Nor does it include realized capital gains in 2010 derived from sales from stock awards granted before 2010. For example, JP Morgan Chase bank CEO Jaime Dimon was paid $21 million in 2010 but also received another $35 million in 2010 from prior stock and option awards before 2010. That $35 million is not counted in the 36% general pay increase for bank CEOs in 2010.[14]

Shadow bank CEOs did even much better than their commercial bank cousins. Quoting an *Absolute Return + Alpha* magazine survey of the top 25 hedge fund managers, one academic source reported that hedge fund managers' profits more than doubled in 2009, surpassing even previous 2007 historical highs.[15]

## Dividend Payouts and Stock Buybacks

The record surge in corporate profits of the past two years resulted not only in big compensation and bonus increases for the top managers of those corporations. It also resulted in a massive income 'pass-through' from corporations realizing record profits to their shareholders. This income pass-through occurs in two ways: first, in the form of increased dividend payments to stockholders and, second, in the form of corporations buying back their own stock. The surge in stock buybacks in turn drives up the price of the stocks held by the corporation's shareholders, enabling huge capital gains once the stocks are sold by those shareholders at the higher prices generated by the buybacks.

Concerning dividend payouts, a recent 2011 study by professors at the Wharton School of Finance at the University of Pennsylvania showed that dividend payouts kept rising right through the recent 2008–09 recession. As the author of the study noted, "dividend growth in the last two years [2009–10] has averaged over 10% per year, more than twice the long-term dividend growth rate." The author added, "Today the aggregate dividends paid by the non-financial sectors are about 20% higher than they were at the 2007 peak...Despite the sluggish economy, the corporate sector is churning out record profits and increasing dividend payments."[16]

Concerning stock buybacks and consequent capital gains, for the largest U.S. corporations, the S&P 500, stock buybacks began surging from the low point of the recession in June 2009. The total value of stock buybacks were about $25 billion at that June low point, according to the corporate research company Standard & Poor's. As of mid 2011, two years later, the value of stock buybacks rose to $90 billion—a nearly 200% increase. According to the global business periodical the *Financial Times*, "More U.S. companies are set to buy back shares this month [August 2011] than in any month since the peak in 2007."[17]

It is important to note that for both the 2002–07 period and the more recent 2009–11 period, the huge income pass-through from corporations to shareholders was made possible by the dividend and stock buyback payouts that occurred in both periods. But the income pass-through could also not have happened without the massive cuts in dividends and capital gains taxes made possible by the Bush tax cuts of the last decade, which significantly lowered taxes on both dividend and capital gains—from the 70% tax rate that existed for both in 1980—to only 15% in 2003. Between $2 trillion and $3 trillion was 'passed through' in this manner between 2001 and 2010. It has been estimated, moreover, that if the Bush tax cuts of the past decade were continued through 2020 they would amount to an additional $4.2 trillion in lost tax revenue, according to the Congressional Budget Office.

## The Wealthiest 10% of Households

There are approximately 115 million taxpaying households in the U.S. The wealthiest 10% of households in the U.S. own the vast majority of all common stock outstanding, about 80%, and are therefore the prime recipients of the huge gains from both dividend and stock buybacks. Among the top 10%, the wealthiest 1% own nearly half—38%—of that 80%.[18] They are the greatest beneficiaries of the dividend payouts and stock buybacks. Their share of all the income generated each year in the U.S. has risen from 8% in 1980 to 24% in 2007.[19] If you live in New York City, the share of the top 1% is 44% of all income in that city. They also own $39 trillion in total assets. In the next decade their assets are forecasted to grow to $87 trillion.

During the expansion years of 1993–2000 the income of the wealthiest 1% grew on average every year by 10.3%. During the expansion of 2002–07 their incomes grew another 10.1% per year. In the 1993–2000 period they captured 45% of all the increase in national income. But by 2002–07 they captured 65% of all the income gains during those years. While their incomes did decline, as did everyone's, during the recession years of 2008–09, their incomes quickly 'snapped back' within a year of the end of the recession and resumed their 10% annual growth rate—while just about all other households in the 'bottom' 80% either stagnated or declined.[20]

## 100 Million Workers' Earnings

In contrast to the historic, lopsided recovery after June 2009 in favor of the wealthy and their corporations, the 'bottom' 80% of American households had an average income in 2008 of only $31,244 a year. Conservatively estimated, their income grew in the 1990s by less than 2.7% a year, then fell by more than −3.3% in the 2001 recession. Their situation then got worse. During the expansion years of 2002–07 their income grew by less than 1.3%, and then collapsed in 2007–08 by more than −6.9% a year. In other words, their gains last decade were less than half their gains in the 1990s, but their losses in the recent recession were almost three times their losses in the 2001 recession. With each business cycle upturn they recover less, and with each downturn they suffer greater income losses.[21]

Given that trend, it is not surprising that income inequality in the U.S. has been intensifying rapidly since the 1980s, and at an accelerating rate.

In addition to slowing and declining income gains for the 'bottom' 80%, since the recent recession began 11.4 million have lost their homes. Sixteen million families are experiencing 'negative equity' with their homes worth less than they owe on them. More than 50 million are without any kind of health insurance coverage. More than 40 million have no full-time permanent job and earn on average 70% of full-time pay as temp and part-time workers. Forty-seven million Americans live below the official poverty level. And 45 million are now living on food stamps, including more than15 million children.

Table 1.5 shows that median weekly earnings of all wage and salary workers in the U.S., adjusted for inflation, *declined* by about 2.4% between June 2009 and June 2011.[22]

The middle and working classes in the U.S. are a subset of the above 99% and even 80% households. They are the category called 'non-supervisory production and service workers'. The average weekly earnings for non-supervisory production and service workers fell as well, as also indicated in Table 1.5.

*Table 1.5*   Real weekly earnings ($, 1982–84)

|  | Median weekly earnings All wage and salary workers | Average weekly earnings Non-supervisory production and service workers |
| --- | --- | --- |
| June 2009 | $345 | $299 |
| June 2011 | $337 | $295 |

*Sources*: Bureau of Labor Statistics, *Usual & Weekly Earnings of Wage and Salary Workers*, Table 1, July 19, 2011, and *Real Earnings News Releases*, Tables A-2, July 2009–July 2011.

These numbers contrast sharply with the historic gains for profits and executive pay previously noted that exploded during the post-June 2009 recovery period. A summary comparison of profits, executive pay, and workers weekly earnings (median and averages) is given in Table 1.6.

*Table 1.6*    Profits and executive pay versus wages and earnings in the recovery, June 2009–June 2011

|  | *June 2009* | *June 2011* | *Change* |
|---|---|---|---|
| Median weekly earnings | $345 | $337 | –2.4% |
| Non-bank CEO pay (2010) | $8.8 million | $10.8 million | 23% |
| Bank CEO pay (2010) | $7.1 million | $9.7 million | 36% |
| Pre-tax profits | $1.262 billion | $1.876 billion | 49% |
| After-tax profits | $1.017 billion | $1.454 billion | 43% |

*Sources*: For median weekly earnings see Bureau of Labor Statistics, *Usual & Weekly Earnings for Wage and Salary Workers*, July 29, 2011. For CEO pay see the two Equilar surveys, as reported in *New York Times* (non-bank CEOs), July 2, 2011, and *Financial Times* (bank CEOs), June 15, 2011. For both pre-tax and after-tax profits see U.S. Department of Commerce, Bureau of Economic Analysis, *National Income and Product Accounts, News Release* July 29, 2011, Tables 11A, 11B, also Tables 12 and 13.

## SEVEN REASONS WHY THE OBAMA RECOVERY HAS FAILED

Why then has the current recovery been so weak and faltering? That central question can only be answered by an examination of the character of the policy responses by the Obama administration, Congress, and the Federal Reserve since the economic crisis began and, in particular, since 2009. The economic recovery has been the weakest on record—with multiple relapses in key economic sectors and a double dip looming on the horizon—because the policy responses by the Obama administration since 2009 have failed in at least seven important ways.

First, Obama recovery programs have all been insufficient in terms of magnitude. The government spending stimulus initiated in early 2009 was grossly insufficient in terms of level of spending. It was less than $400 billion in short-term spending during the 2009–10 period. An additional $300 billion of the stimulus was tax cuts, mostly business tax cuts, that would prove to have little impact on recovery given the nature and depth of the current 'epic' contraction. The remaining roughly $100 billion was very long-term infrastructure spending that had barely any effect in the first two years and not much more over a decade. The $400 billion short-term spending represented less than 3% of total output of the economy, or GDP. In retrospect, it is now known that the U.S. economy was contracting for six months in late 2008 to early 2009 at an annual rate of 7.8%—i.e. about two and a half times the rate of the Obama immediate spending stimulus.

In contrast to Obama's weak stimulus, other economies like China and Germany introduced far more fiscal stimulus when the late 2008 economic collapse occurred. China's stimulus was approximately 17% of its GDP. Germany's was also significantly more than that of the U.S. Both the German and Chinese economies fared among the best in terms of recovery.

Mainstream liberal, or 'Keynesian', economists typically argue Obama's first recovery program in 2009 simply did not spend enough. But that is only part of the story. There is a second reason for the failure of the Obama recovery that contemporary Keynesians ignore: the stimulus was insufficient not only in terms of its magnitude of spending but even more so in terms of its composition of spending. Spending was not focused on immediate job creation. It was composed largely of subsidies of various kinds. Most of the $400 billion short-term spending assumed the form of subsidies to state and local governments, to schools, to cover accelerating costs of unemployment insurance as millions lost jobs, subsidies for health insurance for the unemployed, to fund a doubling of food stamps, and for other similar 'safety net' spending programs. At first Obama declared that these subsidies would provide 3–4 million jobs. He then quickly reframed this to proclaim that millions of jobs would be 'saved' by the subsidies.

But once subsidies are spent, their economic impact is gone. And that's exactly what happened a year later in 2010. In contrast, job creation results in a continued stream of spending by those now employed. But Obama never remotely considered immediate job creation programs by the government. His program always counted on the private sector to create jobs, with hiring, picking up about the time that the subsidies would run out, mid 2010. But in one of the greatest failures in U.S. economic policy history, the corporate sector did not create jobs after the stimulus ran out in 2010. Corporations ended up hoarding record levels of cash and not investing it in the U.S. to create jobs. To the extent they invested at all, it was in offshore markets or in financial securities globally—neither of which produced jobs in the U.S.

Obama's fundamental strategy was to provide a cushion, a floor, to the collapse of consumption for a year. Once the stimulus ran out, the private sector and business spending and investment was supposed to kick in. Banks were also supposed to lend to small businesses. Bank lending and big corporations investing their recovered profits would generate longer-term job recovery, reduce foreclosures, and restore state and local government tax revenues. Much depended on private sector investment and job creation, but that didn't happen as anticipated.

The third failure of Obama's recovery program was its heavy weight given to tax cuts for business and investors. Obama counted on tax cuts to boost corporate profits and in turn result in investment and jobs. Nearly half of Obama's 2009 fiscal stimulus was tax cuts, and mostly tax cuts for business and investor households. But businesses and investors simply hoarded most of it, used it to pay down debt, or to invest abroad in emerging markets. Or they held it for the purposes of anticipated stock buybacks and dividend payouts to their stockholders. By mid 2011 the 'cash hoard' amounted to more than $2 trillion, and stock buyback programs were in full swing.[23]

Obama's response to this third failure of a recovery program overweighted in tax cuts was to provide even more tax cuts to business to entice them to invest and create jobs. Small businesses got tens of billions of dollars, big and small companies got faster depreciation write-offs, and the Bush tax cuts were not rescinded and were instead extended for two more years. Obama from the very beginning of his election campaign had a strong preference for tax cuts as a main policy tool, and for business cuts in particular. This preference became clearly evident in all his three economic recovery programs, that were increasingly tax-cut heavy in each successive form.

The fourth great failure of Obama's recovery programs was his lack of an effective approach to the three great 'mini-crises' in the U.S. economy: immediate job creation, foreclosures and spreading homeowner negative equity, and the ever-deepening fiscal crisis of state and local governments. Obama's recovery programs never included a real jobs creation program, apart from tax cuts and nonsense about 'saving' jobs in the public sector by providing local government subsidies. He never had a foreclosures program of any significance. And aid to local government was essentially limited to one year. When the recovery slowed sharply after just one year, the states and local government were essentially 'cut loose' on their own.

A fifth failure was Obama's inability to extend the bailout of big businesses and big banks and financial companies to 'Main Street'. The summer and fall of 2010 would prove a critical historical juncture. As a subsequent chapter will argue, Obama's failure to act aggressively and move to a higher stage of stimulus and program mix doomed him and his party in the November 2010 midterm elections. Obama failed to seize the moment and opportunity to expand the recovery program in the fall of 2010. Having therefore lost the Congressional elections badly, he resorted to a weaker dose of monetary policy and still more business tax cuts in the closing months of 2010. The economy would relapse once again by early 2011. With the entry of Tea Party radicals in the House of Representatives, future stimulus in 2011 was effectively blocked, and with it any possibility of seriously confronting the three mini-crises of jobs, housing, and state and local government finances.

This raises the sixth, and most recent, program failure by Obama: his succumbing to policies of his opponents focusing on austerity—i.e. on deficit and debt cutting. Instead of learning the lessons of the fall of 2010 and the midterm elections, Obama retreated further into the policy initiatives of his opponents. He lost control of the policy agenda. Cutting deficits and debt—i.e. focusing on austerity solutions to the crisis—became Obama's policy centerpiece by late 2011. But no economy ever recovered from a deep contraction by means of austerity programs. In fact, such programs all but ensure greater deficits and a more serious economic relapse, or worse.

A seventh reason is that the Obama bank bailout program did not require the banks to rid themselves of bad assets on their books, thus laying the groundwork for sluggish bank lending, subsequent future credit crunches, and a further banking crisis. Despite a $9 trillion injection of cash and liquid assets into the banks since the 2008 crisis by the Federal Reserve, and hundreds of billions more by Congress and the U.S. Treasury, a good part of the banking system in the U.S. remained financially 'fragile'—in particular major institutions like Bank of America, Citigroup, Morgan Stanley and others. The Obama policy only offset those bad assets with corresponding cash injections. The theory was that such massive offsetting liquidity injections into the banks would free-up bank reserves for lending to small and medium-sized businesses dependent on bank loans. But just as the boosting of large business profits resulted only in cash hoarding without investing or job creation, so, too, banks simply hoarded the record cash injection and refused to loan to small businesses and consumers. Bank lending actually continued to fall for 15 months after June 2009.[24]

To summarize, Obama's three economic recovery programs have failed to generate a sustained recovery and the economy has experienced repeated 'relapses' since 2009 as it drifts toward a double dip by 2013, for the seven fundamental reasons:

- insufficient magnitude or level of fiscal stimulus
- government spending that was erroneously focused on subsidies instead of jobs
- over-reliance on business tax cuts that were hoarded instead of invested
- failure to require bank lending as a condition of the $9 trillion-plus bank bailouts
- basic disregard of the three core 'mini-crises': jobs, housing, local government
- weak, traditional policy response to the first economic 'relapse' of summer 2010
- tail-ending opponents' focus on deficit cutting and austerity solutions in the face of the second economic 'relapse' in 2011.

## SOME KEY QUESTIONS

The key questions raised by this book are:

- What have Obama's basic economic recovery programs and policies actually accomplished?
- Why have those programs and policies failed to generate a sustained recovery, resulting in two economic 'relapses' in the summer of 2010 and 2011 and the growing prospect of a double-dip recession in 2013?
- Why have fiscal and monetary policies implemented under Obama produced such a lopsided and unequal recovery in terms of who has benefited?

After the Federal Reserve's $9 trillion in cash injections into the banks, zero interest rates, and successive experiments of 'quantitative easing', has monetary policy reached a dead end? The increasing bickering and growing differences within the Federal Reserve itself as of late 2011 appear to suggest so. Banks are flush with cash, so there's no need to inject more. Yet there is little lending going on and the prospect of less in the future. So Fed policy has failed by lowering rates to zero and injecting trillions of dollars into the system. It has only stimulated stock, bond, and commodity futures bubbles that have now begun to collapse. It has not stimulated the housing market. It has lowered the dollar's value, making U.S. exports more attractive, but the slowing of world trade that began in 2011 will mostly offset lower-cost U.S. exports. In net terms, therefore, monetary policy has largely failed.

On the fiscal side, the pressing question is why more than $3 trillion in tax cuts and spending from 2008 to 2012 has produced such an anemic, faltering recovery. Has the dismal performance of Obama's economy neutralized and made impossible further fiscal stimulus? Should further fiscal stimulus occur in 2012, it will certainly be less in terms of magnitude than even the previous two attempts in 2009–10. Moreover, if it happens it will likely take the now familiar form of tax cuts, subsidies, and long-term infrastructure spending. Therefore it is reasonable to ask, has the U.S. economy in 2012 reached a spending and tax policy dead-end?

The Obama administration's increasing willingness throughout 2011 to become a 'partner in deficit slashing' with the Republicans and their radical half-cousins, the Tea Party brigade in Congress, represents yet another phase in the evolution of Obama administration programs and policies. A new phase of deficit cutting and austerity, but not a phase that can be characterized as a recovery program. Deficit cutting and austerity do not constitute a recovery program; they represent a retraction or reversal of prior recovery programs. After a weak, insufficient, poorly composed and badly timed series of economic recovery programs introduced between 2009 and 2011, Congress and the president at year-end 2011 appear intent on continuing more of the same failed programs and policies.

The Congressional Supercommittee's decision in November 2011 not to cut more than the legally required $1.2 trillion represents not the end of social program cuts but rather just another decision point on the road to still further trillions of dollars in social program spending cuts after the 2012 elections. Both political parties will continue to spar over what to cut further during the 2012 election year. Regardless of who is elected in November 2012, both parties will then return to massive program spending cuts immediately after the November 2012 elections. This new round of cutting will add a further major drag on the economy in 2013 and thereby contribute significantly toward the drift to double-dip recession.

# 2
# From Tax Cuts to Tactical Populism

'Obama's 2008 Campaign Promises'

The recent recession began in December 2007.[1] But critical sections of the economy had begun deteriorating well before.

Residential housing had already peaked in 2006 and was well on its way in decline by 2007. The financial sector was also in trouble well before December. In early 2007 several large mortgage companies failed—a clear warning of the crisis to come. By early summer the mortgage companies were followed by several large hedge funds—a kind of unregulated investment company for wealthy investors that speculated in risky financial securities. Then the bottom fell out of the housing markets in August 2007 with the subprime mortgage market implosion. The financial contagion spread rapidly to other sectors of the financial system within a few months. By December 2007 the situation was severe. Even banks stopped loaning to each other, not knowing which of their industry counterparts were insolvent—i.e. technically bankrupt. Meanwhile, the U.S. Federal Reserve after August 2007 responded slowly and did little to address the growing financial crisis while the U.S. Treasury did virtually nothing at all.

By January 2008 the economic crisis train had left the station and there was no calling it back. Enter now presidential candidate Barack Obama, contesting for the nomination of his party in an intense competition with the other two candidates, Hillary Clinton and John Edwards.

## OBAMA THE CONTENDER: JANUARY–JUNE 2008

As the year progressed and the economic crisis deepened, it became virtually impossible for presidential candidates not to propose measures to address the growing crisis. Obama's main Democratic Party competition—Hillary Clinton and John Edwards—had developed their own recovery programs before Obama. As late as January 2008, he was still 'tail-ending' both Clinton and Edwards with the least defined proposals for dealing with the crisis.

In a public 'economic stimulus debate' between the three candidates held in early January 2008, Obama's recovery program focused on what he called 'targeted tax cuts'. In contrast, Edwards proposed aid to the unemployed, aid to states and cities, and public investment in alternative energy. Clinton too focused more on spending as stimulus than on tax cuts, calling for $25 billion in home heating assistance and $110 billion to aid states, homeowners, and the unemployed.

Obama's tax-centric program cost $75 billion, divided between a tax rebate of $250 for everyone plus other business-specific tax cuts. Conspicuously absent from his January program were specific proposals to create jobs or save homeowners, now foreclosing at a rate of 2.3 million a year. As *New York Times* economic columnist Paul Krugman noted at the time, "Mr. Obama's top economic advisor claimed that the long term tax cut plan the candidate announced months ago is just what we need."[2] Obama's program was thus tax-centric from the very beginning.

Candidate Hillary Clinton jumped on Obama for focusing primarily on taxes. Obama quickly adjusted, as he would throughout the 2008 election campaign, adopting the measures proposed by his opponents to outflank and co-opt their more populist appeal. But from the beginning, tax cuts were Obama's true focus—as they would prove to be once elected.

In response to Clinton's criticism that his proposals failed to address jobs and homeowners, in February 2008 the Obama team revised the candidate's 'Economic Plan'. It's total cost now rose to $140 billion. Nonetheless it was still 'tax top-heavy'. It included a $1,000 tax credit per family, $4,000 in student college credits, an increase in the child care credits for low-income families, a $500 savings credit, and tax credits for seniors earning less than $50,000 a year, plus various business tax credits.

Clinton also criticized Obama's program, arguing that his health care plan did not include everyone and he did not explain how it would be paid for. In response, in February candidate Obama explained his health insurance plan, costing about $65 billion a year, would be funded from saving by allowing the Bush tax cuts of the previous eight years to expire, raising between $50 billion and $85 billion a year. For a jobs program, Obama then simply absorbed nearly verbatim John Edwards' proposals. In a speech to a General Motors plant in Janesville, Wisconsin in February Obama proposed to create jobs by constructing solar, wind, and other alternative energy infrastructure. He proposed $150 billion in alternative energy infrastructure spending over ten years, and a national infrastructure bank costing $60 billion. Obama claimed the alternative energy spending and infrastructure bank would create 2 million jobs. The $210 billion cost ($150 billion plus $60 billion) would all be funded by ending the wars in Iraq and Afghanistan and by ending corporate tax loopholes. Ending the wars, the Bush tax cuts, and closing tax loopholes were thus Obama's main proposals for his various economic recovery programs. But as subsequent chapters will show, none of these funding measures would be implemented once he was elected, jeopardizing the size and composition of his 2009 stimulus programs.

Clinton criticized Obama's proposals, pointing out they did not create jobs in the short run. Jobs were needed now. That was an accurate assessment, given that jobs were being lost in the economy at the rate of more than 100,000 a month during February and March 2008, and that rate would soon accelerate to more than 200,000 a month from April to June.[3] But proposals for immediate job creation by the Obama team were not forthcoming. Nor would they be during the rest of the election campaign; nor at any time during Obama's first three years in office. Programs and proposals designed to immediately create jobs were simply not a priority on Obama's political radar at the time; nor would they be later when in office.

In response to Clinton's critique that he had no immediate jobs program, Obama replied he would address the need for jobs by fundamentally overhauling the NAFTA (North American Free Trade Agreement) originally passed by Bill Clinton in the 1990s. In a visit to the National Gypsum Plant in late February, Obama declared to his worker audience: "We can't keep passing unfair trade deals like NAFTA that put special interests over our workers' interests."[4] This of course resonated with workers since more than 10 million U.S. workers had lost jobs to free trade deals or other preferred trade concessions since 1994.[5] But Obama's opposition to free trade was more a political tactic at the time than a fundamental principle. It enabled him to paint his main opponent, Hillary Clinton, with the brush of her ex-president husband, Bill Clinton, who had championed the passage of NAFTA in 1993, pushed through its passage by Congress that year, and thus set the trade-related job loss juggernaut in motion, eventually costing millions of jobs over the next 15 years.

Obama's true position on free trade was evident years earlier when, in 2006, he was one of only twelve Senate Democrats who voted for free trade with Oman, and then supported the free trade pact with Peru in 2007. Once elected, Obama would turn aggressively to champion free trade agreements with Panama, South Korea, and Colombia—arguing the exact opposite from his campaign promises in 2008. As president, Obama's active intervention and support would result in the passage of free trade deals later in these three countries in 2011.

Obama's populist rhetoric against free trade and NAFTA in his campaign speeches at the time set off a political flap with free trading partner Canada. In a particularly embarrassing revelation, the story hit the press in late February that, as he was blasting NAFTA in his speeches, his staff was writing memos telling Canadian trade officials "not to worry about his views on free trade" and to take them "with a grain of salt."[6] Obama's economic advisor, Austin Goolsbee, himself an avowed 'free-trader,' assured the Canadians that his candidate's talk about renegotiating NAFTA was just "political positioning." The story soon blew over, however. Clinton and Edwards did not press home the hypocrisy of Obama's statements and his staff's actions. For Clinton it was difficult to push this issue since she, like Obama, had also supported free trade agreements on various occasions in the past as a Senator.

Despite the Canadian flap, candidate Obama continued to publicly oppose NAFTA, in particular the still unenforced element of that treaty that called for allowing 'open trucking with Mexico.'[7] If allowed, it would cost the U.S. Teamsters union significant job losses. Teamsters leaders were understandably opposed. And they contributed millions to Obama's election campaign in 2008. Obama took their campaign contributions, continued his rhetoric about Mexican trucking during the campaign, and then subsequently in 2010 approved the introduction of Mexican trucking into the U.S.

In February 2008 Clinton addressed the rising home foreclosures problem and accused Obama of sitting on the sidelines on that issue as well. She called for a 90-day moratorium on foreclosures and a five-year freeze on adjustable mortgage interest rates that were now beginning to balloon and were driving homeowners into foreclosure. She also proposed a $30 billion fund for local governments to use to assist homeowners facing foreclosure.

It is interesting to note Obama's counter to these housing crisis challenges. It revealed his fundamental attitude toward assisting homeowners facing foreclosures. Obama retorted that Clinton's proposal "rewards folks who made the problem worse"—as if the homeowners were the cause of the foreclosures crisis and not the bankers, mortgage brokers, and real estate salespersons who pushed their 'liar loans,' offered no down-payments to borrowers, introduced 1% adjustable one-month 'teaser rates', balloon loans—while making trillions of dollars reselling shaky subprime mortgages into secondary markets. Obama argued Clinton's more homeowner-friendly plan would "dry up credit." In short, Obama was clearly less concerned with the plight of the homeowner and more with the mortgage lenders, servicers, and investors. Obama attacked all of Clinton's housing measures—the moratorium, the five-year freeze on adjustable rates, the $30 billion rescue fund—as "reckless." His alternative was a $10 billion fund to help get new owners into the foreclosed homes, but not to try to stop foreclosures in any meaningful way.

Candidate Obama continued to hammer home his differences with Clinton and Edwards on the housing and foreclosures crisis, reiterating that the solution to the growing foreclosures problem was to increase tax credits to homeowners and to issue bonds to assist first time homebuyers. But tax credits do nothing for homeowners facing immediate foreclosure. And issuing bonds to assist first time homebuyers is in effect admitting that those in foreclosure should lose their homes and let new buyers take them over. Getting homeowners facing foreclosure out of their homes and getting new buyers in is a much more lucrative proposition for mortgage companies and mortgage servicers who earn fat fees from reselling the homes but nothing from modifying loans to help current homeowners avoid foreclosure. Indeed, in a number of cases it appeared that mortgage lenders actually made money from pushing foreclosures if they took out insurance contracts on defaults, as many in fact did at the time.

By March 2008 the lid blew off the financial side of the crisis. That same month, investment bank Bear Stearns collapsed. Despite a $29 billion bailout of the company by the Federal Reserve (Fed), and hundreds of billions additionally thrown into other investment banks at the time by the Fed, the financial crisis continued thereafter to deepen below the surface, spreading contagion in all directions.

Deepening financial crises mean contraction of credit to the 'real,' non-financial side of the economy. This 'real' economy was progressively weakening throughout 2007 and into 2008, as credit began to dry up. Then, in the spring 2008, another major factor hit the real economy: inflation driven by commodity speculation, in particular driven by oil price speculation. Crude oil prices shot up to nearly $150 a barrel—compared to $50 a barrel pre-crisis. Oil price hikes soon translated into rising consumer prices for food, other forms of energy, and of course gasoline. The general commodities surge led to rising costs for raw materials and semi-finished goods, raising product prices for consumers in general.

The oil and commodities inflation significantly reduced real wages and thus consumption, which represents 71% of the total U.S. economy. It resulted in businesses reducing spending on investment. That meant more layoffs. Third, it covered up growing underlying problems in the economy, making it appear as if it was growing more than it in fact was. Beneath the surface, in other words, both the financial side and the real side of the economy were weakening fast by March–April 2008.

Obama's key advisor, Rahm Emmanuel, announced a new economic program for recovery. It was called "A New Deal for the Economy."[8] Emmanuel pointed out that the median annual income for workers had fallen $1,000 since 2001, that health insurance premiums had doubled to $12,000 a year, and that college costs were up 64%. Nevertheless, there was little fundamentally new in it; mostly Obama's previous positions through March.

In his next major speech at Cooper Union college in New York City, candidate Obama added a measure to his program: he would now allow the Federal Housing Administration (FHA) to increase its loan guarantees to mortgage lenders. Behind in the primary polls, Hillary Clinton then upped the ante on housing. Instead of merely providing more money to mortgage lenders, she called for the FHA to buy up the mortgages of the 3 million homeowners now in foreclosure, as well as the mortgages of those 8.9 million at the time with their mortgages in 'negative equity.'

In contrast, Obama's proposal was far closer to that of Republican candidate John McCain, who opposed such direct government action suggested by Clinton to save homeowners under duress. McCain proposed 'voluntary action' by banks to modify mortgage loans. Obama agreed and proposed the same. As Obama himself put it at the time, "It's premature to start talking about taxpayer funded bailouts."[9]

By now both the 'style' and fundamental philosophy of candidate Obama was becoming increasingly clear. As *New York Times* columnist and Nobel Prize-winning economist Paul Krugman wrote at the time: "Policy proposals offer a window into candidates' political souls." Krugman added, with regard to Obama's housing proposals, that "He wants to nudge private lenders into restructuring mortgages rather than having the government simply step in and get the job done." Krugman was one of the first to foresee early where candidate Obama might be headed as an eventual president. The direction was quite different from the 'liberal mystique' then beginning to build around the candidate. As Krugman noted, "Mr. Obama is widely portrayed, not least by himself, as a transformational figure who will usher in a new era. But his actual policy proposals, though liberal, tend to be cautious and relatively orthodox."[10] By late 2011 Obama's policies for attempting to rescue a still faltering economy three years after election would, in many respects, appear even more corporate-mainstream in content and form.

With the further eruption of the financial crisis with the collapse of Bear Stearns investment bank in March 2008, candidate Obama added proposals to restore financial stability. He called for more powers to be given to the Federal Reserve and for a Financial Market Oversight Commission. Absorbing proposals from his Democratic opponents once again, he announced a $10 billion fund to assist cities and states facing burgeoning deficits—originally an Edwards idea—and a modest $10 billion for the long-term unemployed—a Clinton proposal. But he still offered no proposals for immediate job creation and no change to his conservative, mortgage-lender-friendly housing measures.

Obama and Clinton then faced off in the strategic Pennsylvania primary in late April. Once again Obama co-opted his opponents and adopted Clinton's $30 billion fund to help local governments buy up foreclosed homes. While the debate raged over the $30 billion, both candidates announced their support for the Fed's request for an additional $400 billion to bail out the banks.

About the same time, Congress passed a Bush fiscal stimulus package amounting to about $168 billion. Most of this was tax cuts. But like tax cut-heavy stimulus packages in general, it proved to have little effect on the economy which continued to weaken. The problem with tax cuts in an economy heading into a deep recession is that the cuts are mostly pocketed and do not result in investment and hiring. The money is simply 'hoarded.' This would prove a problem not only with Bush's own 2008 tax-heavy stimulus, but later with Obama's 2009 also tax-heavy fiscal stimulus and his even more tax-centric follow-on tax cuts of 2010.

By late May, Obama's recovery program was focused on taxes more than ever, in a mix of both cuts and hikes. It included raising the capital gains tax rate to 28% from the current 15%, a change estimated to produce an extra $85 billion a year in funding.[11] Other May proposals included extending the Bush era tax cuts only for households with annual incomes under $250,000 but ending it for those with incomes of more than $250,000. The proposal to discontinue tax cuts for the wealthiest 1% was an Edwards idea from earlier in the campaign. Now it became Obama's. His other tax proposals included relieving the Alternative Minimum Tax (AMT) impact on the upper middle class, sales tax rebates for middle-class households, tax credits to buy health insurance, and other measures. So there were initially at this point a decent mix of consumer-related tax cuts, not just for business. But this was a campaign package, not a legislative one.

Apart from raising capital gains taxes and closing tax loopholes, other funding for his proposed spending programs was to come from ending the wars in Iraq and Afghanistan now costing well over $100 billion a year. Another funding source was to sell 'carbon credits,' which he estimated would also produce $100 billion a year in new revenues. But conspicuously absent was any suggestion of imposing an oil company windfall profits tax, even as oil and energy companies were enjoying record profits from the $150 a barrel oil prices of that spring 2008. Both Clinton and the Republican candidate,

John McCain, had proposed such a windfall tax. But Obama did not, and actively spoke against it.

Apart from savings from wars, carbon credits, and tax loopholes, ending the Bush era tax cuts, scheduled to expire at year-end 2010, was by far the biggest potential source of revenues. War spending had ballooned the Pentagon budget by a cumulative $2.1 trillion during the decade.[12] But this $2.1 trillion was still less than the loss of revenue from the Bush tax cuts. Over the preceding decade the Bush tax cuts reduced federal government revenues by as much as $3.4 trillion.[13] And 80% of that went to the wealthiest 20% of households and corporations. The Congressional Budget Office, the respected research arm of Congress, estimated that the continuation of the Bush era tax cuts from 2011 to 2018 for another decade would cost the U.S. Treasury another approximately $4.6 trillion.[14] Once elected, none of these major funding sources for a recovery program would survive the campaign period. None would materialize, as the future President Obama would either be denied these funding sources by Congress or would himself decide to shelve them.

## THE SHIFT TO THE RIGHT: JUNE 2008

By early June 2008 candidate Obama had amassed enough support from the Democratic primaries to be assured of the nomination. By mid June he began a shift to more conservative positions. In an interview with the *Wall Street Journal* he declared he was "open to a corporate tax rate cut." The corporate rate cut was, in his view, a tradeoff for reducing tax loopholes. In other words, he was for ending tax loopholes but for cutting corporate top tax rates. He offered no numbers as to whether the tradeoff of tax rates for loopholes resulted in a net corporate tax cut. Obama indicated these cuts should take place as part of a major change to the U.S. tax code overall—a formula and approach he would resurrect in 2011. In a CNBC interview in June 2008 he emphasized his pro-business tax cut perspective, saying to his host: "Look, I'm a pro-growth, free market guy. I love the market."[15]

At this juncture, mid June 2008, finance, real estate, commercial banks and hedge funds had already together contributed more to Obama's campaign than they had to Republican John McCain's. The corporate contributions gap would grow over the next six months. As conservative business columnist David Brooks noted on July 1, the big investment bank "Goldman Sachs gave more to Obama than workers of any other employer. Goldman was followed by the next biggest three contributors, the mega-banks J.P. Morgan-Chase, Citigroup, and UBS."[16]

This abrupt about-face on corporate taxes prompted the conservative *Wall Street Journal* editorial column on July 2, 2008 to remark:

> Barack Obama keeps protesting so vigorously against the prospect of George Bush's third term. Maybe he's worried that someone will notice that he's the candidate running for it...Mr. Obama isn't merely running for

the center. He's fleeing from many of his primary positions so markedly and so rapidly that he's embracing a sizeable chunk of President Bush's policy.[17]

In July 2008 the financial crisis intensified even further, spreading to the giant quasi-government mortgage companies Fannie Mae and Freddie Mac. The collapse of investment banks like Lehman Brothers, Merrill Lynch, and other commercial banks quickly followed by September 2008. The banking crash was on.

Candidate Obama quickly met with his chief economic policy advisors to determine his position with regard to the now emerging banking panic. These advisors were Robert Rubin, ex-Citigroup senior manager and Clinton era Treasury Secretary; Larry Summers, also Clinton Treasury Secretary and ex-Citigroup and now president of Harvard University; William Daley, top manager of J.P. Morgan Chase; Robert Wolf of UBS Bank; Ken Griffin of the big hedge fund, Citadel; and Penny Pritzker, heiress to the Hyatt Hotel chain headquartered in Chicago and early financier of Obama election campaigns since his first Senate run.

By mid August, candidate Obama had successfully raised $340 million from large donors. The most successful sources were Wall Street and real estate interests, in particular various New York hedge funds and the global superbank, UBS. Up there as well were the Chicago billionaire families, the Crowns and Pritzkers, as well as California high-tech and venture capitalist companies. These corporate campaign funding sources would play a key role in influencing his positions and proposals on the growing financial crisis, as well as his forthcoming first economic recovery program in early 2009.

His economic policies at this juncture were best summed up in a joint article written by his main economic advisor, Austan Goolsbee, and Jason Furman. The title of the piece was 'The Obama Tax Plan,' revealing clearly that tax policy was the centerpiece and most important element of Obama's economic recovery program. Goolsbee made an emphatic point that Obama's proposed tax changes were less burdensome on corporations and investors than those during Clinton's administration in the 1990s—and were even less burdensome still than under George Bush Sr. and Ronald Reagan in the 1980s. Goolsbee made assurances that any increase in capital gains or dividend taxes under Obama would not exceed 20%, compared to the current 15%, which he stressed was less than under Bush Sr. or Reagan when it was 28%. Goolsbee failed to note, however, that Obama's early 2008 position was to raise capital gains and dividends back to the Reagan period 28% and not 20%. Obama thus signaled with this proposal his future willingness to back off his proposals to raise investors' taxes.

Goolsbee further noted that Obama was in favor of additional tax cuts for small businesses and the total elimination of capital gains taxes for small businesses and business start-ups. This 'small business tax cut' did not mean 'mom and pop' small businesses with a dozen or so employees. Small business officially defined by the U.S. government is any company with 500 or fewer employees, and business start-ups could be even larger, such as divisional 'spin-offs' from a larger conglomerate. For example, Microsoft Corp. could create a division pursuing social networking, split off from the original company, and be considered a 'start-up' for tax-cut purposes. The taxpayer would thus be giving money to giant Microsoft to expand its business.

Obama's plan, according to Goolsbee, also included a 'simplifying of the tax code'—which is generally a codeword in policy circles signifying lowering top income tax rate brackets. Goolsbee noted that that included making permanent Bush cuts for the estate tax. In other words, Obama proposed to exempt the estate tax from any future general repeal of the Bush tax cuts of 2001–04. Once elected, his estate tax proposal would prove even more generous than Bush's.

So far as the payroll tax for social security was concerned, Obama's advisor clarified that the candidate did not support raising the 'cap' on the payroll tax above the $106,800 a year ceiling, so that the wealthier 15% households would no longer be exempt from paying the tax on all their salary and bonus income above that ceiling.[18]

## BACK TO THE CENTER: SEPTEMBER 2008

By late August Obama was still in a statistical dead-heat with Republican candidate, John McCain. Nominee Obama consequently supplemented his tax-centric campaign policies, that had been steadily shifting toward favoring corporate interests since June, with what he called his 'Urban Agenda Program.' This called for an increase in antipoverty program spending, a new White House Office of Urban Policy, a national infrastructure bank that would spend $60 billion over the next decade, full funding for Bush's 'No Child Left Behind' Act and community block grants, and a raise in the minimum wage to $9.50 an hour. In other words, a little for everyone in the Democratic Party urban establishment.

Absent still was any specific plan for immediate job creation. His jobs program still amounted to a call for very long-term infrastructure spending on capital-intensive alternative energy projects and to his suspect view on reforming NAFTA and free trade. However, the latter free trade point was now increasingly de-emphasized after having defeated his primaries opponent, Hillary Clinton. By the fall election period it was hardly referenced in his speeches.

Regarding the housing-foreclosure crisis, Obama's September proposals were limited to calls to change the bankruptcy laws to allow judges to 'write down mortgages' and a proposal for restructuring the Fannie Mae/Freddie Mac government mortgage loan guarantee companies that had been bailed out and were now under federal control. In other words, Obama's immediate pre-election day housing program was to 'pass the buck' to the courts when it came to saving homeowners in foreclosure. In contrast, even his opponent, McCain, proposed in September that the government create a Resolution Trust Corporation (RTC) to address the housing crisis. The RTC idea was a more aggressive solution to the crisis. It was adopted during the previous housing crises in the 1980s and in an even more pro-homeowner aggressive form in the 1930s to resolve that period's housing crisis. Both worked. The RTC concept forced consolidations among the mortgage lenders, and the government housing agencies bought up homeowners' mortgages, rewriting the terms and reducing them to lower homeowners' monthly payments. Obama's response to an RTC-like solution was this kind of forceful measure was "premature." His many and generous bank and real estate campaign donors were no doubt pleased.

In a major pre-election speech in Clearwater, Florida, in late September Obama responded for the first time in a comprehensive way to the banking panic and crash that was then accelerating, and to the $700 billion check just given by Congress to Treasury Secretary Paulson for the explicit purpose of bailing out the banks. Obama called for the payback of the $700 billion to taxpayers, a bipartisan board to oversee the money, and limits on bankers' bonuses. Years later, in 2010, the director of the $700 billion TARP (Troubled Asset Relief Program) program, Neil Barofsky, would reveal that the $700 billion was granted by Congress only with the understanding that it would be used to assist homeowners in foreclosure, not just banks. But that original intent for the $700 billion TARP fund was strongly resisted by the banks which considered TARP to be a bailout source earmarked for their rescue alone. Their resistance continued well into 2009 every time the point was made that the intent was to rescue homeowners, not just banks. Nonetheless, according to the banks, that was 'their' money and they didn't want to share it with anyone, especially homeowners in distress.

## THE JOBS AND HOUSING CRASH OF 2008

By October not only were the banks crashing, but jobs were in full collapse and home foreclosures were spiraling. Between September and December 2008 a total of 522,000 workers were added to the unemployment rolls. These numbers, moreover, do not reflect the half-as-large-again surge in part-time jobs as full-time workers were reduced to part time. More than 260,000 were thus added to the employment rolls—i.e. an equivalent of another 130,000 full-time jobs lost. Nor did the unemployment data reflect the nearly 1 million additional workers who became jobless and then dropped out of the labor force altogether in the second half of 2008.[19]

The banking crash may have gotten most of the headlines and attention but an equivalent crash of the labor market did not get similar attention. No emergency jobs program was proposed in the weeks and months immediately following the November national elections by the president-elect. Nor was any direct attention paid to the similar collapse of the housing market and the surging foreclosures. By December 2008 home foreclosure rates doubled to 7.56% from 4.5% in January of 2008, most of which occurred after September. Meanwhile, the pipeline of future foreclosures also jumped, as mortgage delinquencies accelerated from 14.43% to 23.17%.[20] A total of 1.3

million homes entered foreclosure in 2007 and then rose another 2.3 million in 2008. It would grow still higher, much higher, in 2009–11.

In one of his last major pre-election speeches delivered in Toledo, Ohio in mid October, candidate Obama revealed his final and most comprehensive economic program to date. His prior proposals cost $115 billion in spending and tax cuts. The new total rose to $175 billion. Once again, however, the main focus was on taxes for the short run as well as the longer term.[21] In addition to tax measures already announced, in October Obama proposed to give all businesses a $3,000 tax credit for new hires, at a cost of $40 billion of the total $175 billion. Once again, tax cuts and a jobs program were synonymous. Tax cuts were the main way to create jobs in the short run and alternative energy infrastructure spending in the very long run. At this juncture, however, his infrastructure proposals amounted to spending only $25 billion, a paltry sum not likely to create many jobs even in the longer run. His immediate job creation program was to cut business taxes and not much more.

Obama continually insisted his tax cuts would create 2 million new jobs in the short run. For the longer term, spending on alternative energy over the next decade would create another 5 million additional green jobs. Prospective voters were left with trying to figure out how business tax cuts, $25 billion for repairing roads, and $15 billion a year on alternative energy would create 7 million jobs.[22] Meanwhile, the U.S. Labor Department reported in September 2008 that jobs had declined by 886,000. Another nearly 2 million would lose their jobs before the year's end.[23]

The Obama approach to the housing crisis was equally timid in the face of a fast deteriorating housing and foreclosure situation at the time. In his October 14 Toledo speech, Obama proposed allowing a 90-day moratorium on foreclosures—a measure borrowed directly from Clinton and strongly ridiculed by the Obama team earlier in the year. Combined with his prior proposal to permit bankruptcy judges to modify mortgages, the moratorium proposal constituted the main element of his housing recovery program at the time. There was essentially no plan to save homeowners facing foreclosure.

Right up to election day Obama continued to reject any kind of more aggressive action to rescue homeowners. As he himself put it on the eve of the election in his editorial piece in the *Wall Street Journal* of November 3, 2008. In response to McCain's more aggressive proposal to re-establish the 1980s 'Resolution Trust Corporation' agency to clean up the housing crisis, Obama retorted "It's not change...to address our housing crisis that puts another $300 billion of taxpayer money at risk" (i.e. the cost of another 1980s-like Resolution Trust Corp. solution to the housing crisis).

Massive layoffs and exploding foreclosures portended an equally serious crisis of state and city budgets on the eve of the election. Borrowing costs for states and cities in the municipal bond markets were rising fast, as the general financial crisis spread and deepened after September 2008. The Obama team's answer to head off a general fiscal crisis of the states and cities was a cautious package of aid to the states in the amount of $25 billion.

Obama's proposals for addressing the short-term and rapidly deteriorating financial and economic crisis in general—and in particular in the three critical problem areas of jobs, housing, and local government—were thus quite limited given the depth and magnitude of the emerging economic crisis at the time. Measures responding to the banking crisis were simply what Congress and the Federal Reserve were already proposing at the time.

## ASSESSING OBAMA'S CAMPAIGN PROMISES

A number of important conclusions may be reached from the evolution of candidate Obama's proposals for dealing with the growing economic crisis during the election period of 2008.

First, Obama was clearly not the most 'liberal' of the three Democratic Party candidates. In fact, a reasonable case can be made he was the most pro-business. Moreover, much of the mildly populist elements he embraced were co-opted directly from his opponents, Hillary Clinton and John Edwards.

Second, at no time did he propose a jobs program apart from more business tax cuts. Proposals for long-term alternative energy infrastructure spending were modestly funded, very long term, and capital-intensive in any event. Other infrastructure spending of a more immediate character was ridiculously poorly funded at only $25 billion. Creating jobs by overhauling NAFTA was a tactical maneuver. For Obama, the primary means for short-term job creation was tax cuts, in particular business tax cuts. That placed him in the camp of traditional 'supply side' economics advocates and the policies of Reagan and George W. Bush before him. Supply side is sometimes referred to as 'trickle down' economics. It proved not to create jobs for the George W. Bush administration, despite more than $3 trillion cuts in capital gains, dividends, estate taxes, and various corporate tax reductions. It would prove no more successful under Obama, as corporate America from 2009 through 2011 would pocket and hoard its tax cuts and not invest and create jobs.

Obama's program for resolving the equally serious housing-foreclosures problem never focused on directly assisting homeowners in foreclosure. The focus was always on assisting either states and local governments to buy up the foreclosed homes as they came onto the market or to assist mortgage lenders to resell the foreclosed homes as the foreclosures mounted. He strongly opposed even the moderate suggestions by Clinton, and even McCain, for the government to play a more direct, active role in the housing crisis as it had before in the 1980s and 1930s, in both cases successfully.

Another clear conclusion from the campaign period was that once Obama had all but sewn up the nomination, he began a shift even further to the right. This was not unnoticed, even by the ultra-conservative editorialists at the *Wall Street Journal*, not to mention liberal economic columnists like Krugman. To the extent that candidate Obama's election period programs were 'populist' in any sense, they were positions largely borrowed from his Democratic opponents in the primaries. Most of these populist elements were de-emphasized in the fall election period, or soon after the election. Few would appear in his eventual 2009 first economic recovery program.

Finally, from the very beginning candidate Obama surrounded himself with banking, corporate and market-oriented economic advisors. This was not surprising, since Obama's main fundraisers were big financial institutions, along with other representatives of 'big industry money' and other key corporate sectors like West Coast technology companies, venture capitalists, and Midwest billionaires.

The national election campaign necessarily muted awareness of these not so liberal characteristics of how candidate Obama viewed solutions to the growing economic crisis. Populist rhetoric served a pragmatic purpose, especially when it was borrowed from his opponents. It neutralized the differences between himself and them. It mobilized previously disenchanted and alienated elements of the Democratic Party base. Thereafter his superior fundraising, his relatively greater corporate (and media) support, and his ability to appear as a 'new' liberal—and even at times as a potential progressive—made an electoral difference. But a closer inspection of candidate Obama's positions in 2008, and the shifts in these positions, would have clearly revealed to voters that he was the most pro-business of the Democratic primary candidates.

Behind the liberal persona lay a decidedly pro-business policy emphasis— backed up by far more corporate funding and support than any other candidate in the 2008 presidential races, whether in the primaries or in the final phase of the national presidential election.

# 3
# Obama's Jobless-Homeless Stimulus

'The First Economic Recovery Program (2009)'

On November 7, in his first press conference following the November election, president-elect Obama declared "my priority is going to be how do we grow the economy. How do we create more jobs."[1] But no specific proposals for creating jobs were offered. With regard to foreclosures, he noted his new Treasury Secretary would address the issue, "but stopped short of calling for any new initiatives."[2] And nothing as yet was offered about assisting state and local governments facing fiscal implosion.

October 2008 employment statistics were released that same day, Friday, November 7, as Obama held his press conference. The Department of Labor report showed that October employment levels had fallen by 372,000. They would fall another 513,000 in November and another 806,000 in December.[3] A similar accelerating collapse of the housing market was also underway. That same October a total of 279,561 homeowners received foreclosure notices. Another 582,295 would receive notices in November–December 2008 and a total of more than 2.3 million for 2008—an 81% increase over 2007.[4] Simultaneously it was reported that "States are facing a great fiscal crisis. At least 44 states faced or are facing shortfalls in their budgets…Combined budget gaps for the remainder of this fiscal year and state fiscal years 2010 and 2011 are estimated to total more than $350 billion."[5]

To this initial lack of specific proposals to address jobs, housing, and states and cities, defenders of the president's apparent 'go slow' approach replied 'give it time.' However, given the accelerating collapse of the economy at the time in terms of jobs, housing, and local government, one might have also reasonably argued for bolder early action. But boldness and getting ahead of the crisis curve were not Obama's strong points. Nor would they prove to be once elected. As will subsequently be shown, none of the three great problems of jobs, housing, and local government fiscal crises were to receive particularly high priority from the new president after the November election—neither during the transition period from November to January nor in the president's initial 2009 stimulus package.

## THE DRIFT FROM POPULISM: FROM ELECTION TO INAUGURATION

During the closing months of 2008, the Obama team offered vague references about creating 2.5 million jobs. Most would come in some way from green energy infrastructure investment. The 2.5 million was a pared down estimate from the early campaign period prediction of 5 million jobs from such investment. There was some talk of grants to the states, but no more than $140 billion—that is, less than half their projected shortfalls. Nor was there any statement from Treasury Secretary Timothy Geithner on his newly assigned task of addressing the growing flood of foreclosures.

The failure of the Obama team to say much about the deepening housing-foreclosures crisis prompted Congressman Barney Frank, chair of the House Finance Committee, to call in early December for the new administration to spend the remaining TARP $350 billion to implement a 'foreclosures prevention program.' His call was all but ignored.[6]

There were other notable indicators at the time of the president-elect's retreat from earlier campaign promises. The president's populist promise that once elected he would immediately raise taxes on the wealthiest households earning above $250,000 a year was announced as now shelved for an unspecified period. Obama's key advisor, David Axilrod, indicated in early November that the plan was now to just let the Bush tax cuts expire as scheduled by law on December 31, 2010.[7] That same month, Obama indicated that his campaign promise to reform the NAFTA, was also now on the 'back burner'. Obama also backed off from implementing an economic stimulus immediately before the year's end. There would be no immediate stimulus until next February at the earliest—despite the loss of 1.3 million jobs in November–December, 800,000 more foreclosures, and the now accelerating decline of state and local government finances.

Ending the wars in Iraq and Afghanistan and immediately rescinding of the Bush tax cuts for the rich were repeatedly emphasized during the 2008 election campaign period as the primary means by which to raise revenue necessary to fund the economic stimulus going into 2009. Ending the Bush tax cuts in January 2009, two years earlier than scheduled, would have saved the U.S. Treasury about $450 billion, according to estimates. Promptly ending the wars in 2009 saved approximately another $341 billion.[8] That's a total of $791 billion, or just about what Obama's would eventually spend ($787 billion) for his 2009 economic stimulus. Obama's election promise to shift funds from war spending and end the Bush tax cuts would thus have avoided the necessity altogether of raising the deficit to pay for the 2009 stimulus.

Yet a third potential major source of revenue to fund economic stimulus and recovery was the unspent $350 billion remaining from the $700 billion TARP that Bush's Treasury Secretary, Hank Paulson, received from Congress earlier in September 2008 during the depths of the banking crash. Paulson distributed only half the $700 billion TARP allotment and then simply held on to the remaining $350 billion, refusing to allow the Obama administration to apply the remainder to a general economic stimulus until Obama took office in January 2009. Bankers and the Federal Reserve thereafter insisted the remaining $350 billion be held in reserve for bank bailout use only. In January 2009 Congressman Barney Frank again raised the proposal to spend TARP funds to staunch the foreclosures bloodletting, now at a much reduced $40 billion.[9] The Obama team opposed the idea openly at that time, just as it had ignored Frank's earlier proposal in December for funding to save homeowners.

The Obama team also continued to reject the idea of having the government buy up mortgages and reset principal and interest payments to help foreclosed owners stay in their homes. As he revealed in an interview in early January, when asked specifically how he would limit foreclosures, his answer was: "my preference would be that the private sector was doing this all on their own."[10] His solution a few months later in 2009 would be in sync with this 'private sector' approach in the form of a totally voluntary program, run by the banks themselves, to modify homeowners' mortgages.

Given the Obama team's reluctance to aggressively take on the foreclosures issue, once Congress gained control of the TARP funds in January it refused to allocate any of the remaining $350 billion to the Obama administration without assurances some would be used to help homeowners facing foreclosure. A compromise was brokered. The Obama team agreed to apply $50 billion for foreclosure aid. In exchange, $50 billion more was given in bailouts to the mega-banks, Citigroup and Bank of America. The rest was given back to the Treasury.[11]

The $50 billion for foreclosure aid was used to fund a program called HAMP (Home Affordability Modification Program) that focused largely on providing subsidies to mortgage lenders and mortgage servicers—the latter dominated by the big six banks—in exchange for their lowering mortgage rates. Mortgage rates declined by less than 1% in exchange for the $50 billion, and did very little to help those facing foreclosure to remain in their homes.

A fourth major potential source of funding Obama promised to raise during his election to pay for economic recovery programs was to require U.S. investors and corporations to pay taxes on offshore income that was being hoarded outside the U.S. Between $1 trillion and $1.4 trillion had been accumulated offshore since 2004 by multinational corporations in their foreign subsidiaries. That amount was subject to the normal 35% corporate tax rate. That's about $350 billion in lost tax revenue. In addition to offshore tax avoidance by multinational corporations, tax experts estimate another $11 trillion was held in offshore accounts by U.S. wealthy individual and institutional investors. That represented, according to experts, a tax revenue loss to the U.S. Treasury of another $225 billion annually.[12]

In 2009 the Obama administration initiated an effort to recover some of these offshore sheltered funds, in particular from Swiss banks. But the effort soon faded. Reportedly only $30 billion was recovered from U.S. investors sheltering money in Switzerland alone as of mid-year 2011.[13]

The $350 billion remaining TARP funds, plus the estimated $450 billion savings from a prompt rescinding of the Bush tax cuts, the estimated $340 billion savings from ending war spending, and the repatriation and taxing of the offshore hoarded $575 billion together amount to more than $1.7 trillion. That's an amount that not only would have fully funded the 2009 stimulus but also would have paid for the administration's $900 billion health care program that eventually passed in 2010.

For whatever reasons, Obama refused or failed to pursue these revenue sources as he had promised during his election campaign. As a result, both the stimulus and the health care plan were eventually financed out of deficit spending—thus creating a 'hammer' issue for Republicans and Tea Party conservatives that would come back to politically haunt the president in just two years. Had Obama done what he said during the campaign concerning rescinding the Bush tax cuts for the wealthy, ending the wars, closing tax loopholes for the rich and corporations, and had he insisted on applying the TARP funds to the stimulus, there would have been no deficit issue dominating politics and the economy in 2011. A second, more effective stimulus would consequently have been possible in 2011. In short, the roots of the failure of Obama economic recovery programs throughout his first term can be found not only in how his economic recovery programs were structured, but also in how he chose to finance those programs.

Obama's November to January transition period revealed not only the president's steady backtracking on his populist campaign pledges, but also his steady shift after the election toward more conservative, more cautious, and business tax-friendly approaches to addressing the general economic crisis. This retreat and shift was foreshadowed and predictable, given his selection of economic advisors soon after the election.[14]

## OBAMA'S AMERICAN RECOVERY AND REINVESTMENT PLAN (ARRP)

Early indications of what Obama's first economic recovery program might look like began to leak out in early January. Recalling Obama's campaign period, his recommendations for economic recovery early in 2008 were predominantly tax-centric. A year later, in early January 2009, there were rumors Obama's stimulus was again to include mostly tax cuts. Specifics included faster depreciation write-offs. Retroactive tax refunds for business reaching back five years. Small business tax credits. And of course the continuation of the Bush tax cuts for another two years. For workers, the tax mix was rumored to include a 'make work pay' tax credit, a kind of delayed tax rebate by another name. Some aid to the states and schools and unemployment insurance extensions were also rumored in the mix. But direct job creation programs or specific measures to halt foreclosures were not in the early recovery program draft.

Economists at the time indicated between $800 billion and $1.3 trillion in spending alone was needed to ensure economic recovery. Any tax cuts would be additional. Council of Economic Advisors (CEA) chair, Christina Romer, polled various well-known economists in late December–early January 2009 for their recommendations. At the low end of the spectrum, conservative Martin Feldstein proposed only $400 billion would be necessary—all in tax cuts—plus a modest $30 billion increase in defense spending as well. Moderate Keynesian economist and former Labor Department Secretary, Robert Reich, recommended $900 billion. In the same camp as Reich, liberal Keynesian economist Paul Krugman argued that Obama's likely $800 billion, low-end stimulus package, being composed 40% of tax cuts, "will do little for the economy." Krugman added, "that's not enough."[15] Business economist Mark Zandi of Moody's Inc. predicted that without at least $800 billion the unemployment rate in 2010 would reach 10.8%. It would reach nearly that a year *earlier*, in 2009, *with* the $800 billion.

As the Reich and Krugman recommendations illustrate, the Keynesian position focused on ensuring a sufficiently large absolute magnitude of stimulus. Their error was not paying equal attention at this early stage to the 'composition' of the stimulus as well as the magnitude. How and on what the stimulus was spent was crucial—not just the amount that was spent.

On January 8 in a speech at George Mason University in Virginia, Obama provided a first summary look at his economic stimulus package, which was introduced as the American Recovery and Reinvestment Plan.[16] He promised that the ARRP would 'create or save' 3 million jobs. Now for the first time emphasis was on preventing further job loss, not primarily on creating jobs. It is one thing to create jobs. Those numbers can be identified. But 'saving' jobs is virtually impossible to verify. Nonetheless, the magic number for jobs was now 3 million, down from 5 million during the campaign. This 3 million represented 2.4 million private sector jobs actually created over the next two years plus 0.6 million public sector jobs 'saved'. The 'saved' jobs would come from the subsidies given to states and school districts as part of the spending portion of the upcoming stimulus plan. The subsidies would thus 'save' the jobs of teachers, police officers, firefighters and others who would otherwise face layoffs, given the deteriorating fiscal crisis of local governments.

Private sector jobs were to grow from spending on rebuilding roads, bridges, and other infrastructure projects, and from various alternative energy-related projects like upgrading the national electrical grid system and refitting federal buildings for energy efficiency. Tax cuts would stimulate jobs in manufacturing and elsewhere, adding to the construction related jobs. Clean energy, Obama predicted, would create 500,000 jobs. Repairing infrastructure, another 400,000. And somehow computerizing health records would create an amazing 200,000 jobs. It was all based on economists' models that assumed 1 million jobs would be created automatically for every 1% increase in GDP. Those models, of course, would prove to be wrong.

On January 9, 2009, using this same model, the administration's CEA chair, Christina Romer, released the CEA's report entitled *The Job Impact of the American Recovery and Reinvestment Plan*.[17] The report predicted that without the recovery plan, the ARRP, unemployment would rise to 9% by mid 2010. With the plan, unemployment would decline to 7.5% by mid 2010 and decline further to 6.5% by mid 2011. History now shows that unemployment remained consistently between 9% and 10% in 2009–10 with the plan, and still exceeded 9% by year-end 2011 three years later.

With regard to jobs created, Romer's report estimated that a total 3,675,000 jobs would be created, assuming an economic stimulus of $775 billion. The Romer report predicted that "construction and manufacturing are likely to experience particularly strong job growth." Construction jobs were projected to increase by 678,000 in the report as a result of the $775 billion stimulus. Manufacturing jobs were forecast to rise by 408,000 jobs.[18] Contrary to the report's predictions, however, more than a million additional jobs were instead lost between December 2008 and June 2010 after Obama's $787 billion stimulus was introduced. Construction jobs declined—not rose—from 6.83 million in December to 5.78 million by June 2010, a loss of 1.05 million jobs. Similarly, manufacturing jobs over the same 18-month period fell from 12.98 million to 11.60 million, for a decline of 1.38 million instead of a rise of 408,000. In other words, instead of gaining 600,000 jobs in construction, more than a million were lost. And instead of gaining 400,000 jobs in manufacturing, nearly 1.4 million were lost. That represents a combined 'swing,' of difference, of about 3.4 million jobs. The report's predictions concerning job creation were thus no more accurate than its forecast of unemployment. Why then were the report's projections for job creation and unemployment so far off what happened?

The simple answer is that there was essentially no actual jobs creation program in Obama's initial economic recovery proposals of January 2009, or in the final version that was eventually passed by Congress in February 2009. There were just assumptions—i.e. if so much was spent and/or so much in taxes were cut, jobs would automatically appear based on an erroneous GDP to jobs creation formula and model. The economic stimulus relied overwhelmingly on a level of private sector job creation that simply did not happen. On the public sector side, instead of even 'saving' 600,000 public sector jobs, nearly half a million public sector jobs were nevertheless lost over the next two years.

## THE STIMULUS: THE AMERICAN RECOVERY AND REINVESTMENT ACT (ARRA)

The House of Representatives' initial version of Obama's original ARRP proposals amounted to $825 billion. The Senate then voted on its version as well in January. A joint version was finally voted up by both Houses of Congress in mid February and Obama signed the bill into law on February 17, 2009.

The final version voted into law provided $787 billion in spending and tax cuts.[19] About $288 billion, or 38% of the stimulus total, were tax cuts for households, for businesses, and relief for upper-middle-class taxpayers in the amount of a $70 billion one-time exemption from the Alternative Minimum Tax, AMT. Another 38% was composed of 'Aid' spending, the largest elements of which were $40 billion in subsidies to schools, $87 billion for temporary subsidies to states to cover Medicaid, $27 billion for jobless benefits, and $31 billion for education tax credits and tuition aid. The 'tax cuts' and 'aid and subsidies' thus amounted to $576 billion of the $787 billion total. Neither would have much immediate, direct effect on jobs over the next 18 months. The tax cuts would be 'hoarded' by businesses and households alike or used to pay down debt. The subsidies aid would keep states and schools afloat temporarily for another year or so. Essentially nothing of the total was allocated to address the housing foreclosures crisis.

The remainder of the $787 billion, 24% and $213 billion, was composed of spending programs—the major elements of which were alternative energy projects ($30 billion), road and bridge infrastructure ($29 billion), and public transit and water infrastructure projects ($34 billion). But these spending programs were long-term or very long-term so far as job creation was concerned—notwithstanding the administration's hype that most were 'shovel ready.' Had these construction projects been in fact 'shovel ready', there certainly would not have been an additional loss of more than a million construction jobs over the next 18 months. An additional $75 billion in supplemental programs were added later in 2009–10 as the recovery faltered, raising the total cost of the Obama first recovery program to approximately $862 billion.

## STIMULUS CRITIQUE 1: INSUFFICIENT MAGNITUDE

As noted, the $787 billion cost came in below the 'low end' consensus recommended by most economists outside the administration. Cautiously once again, Obama chose less than even the low-end recommended number. In order to get even that $787 billion, Obama conceded on significant items to Republicans in the House and Senate, especially on business tax cut programs. He also agreed to reduce the total stimulus amount—from the Democratic-controlled House's $825 billion to $787 billion. His concessions were to no avail. In the final vote tally, the House voted 246–183 for the bill and not a single Republican voted for it. In the Senate, only three crossed over and voted for the first recovery program.

It was not really necessary for Obama to concede at all—whether on particular items or on the magnitude of the stimulus—in order to placate the Republicans. The Democrats certainly had sufficient votes to push through the House's original $825 billion proposal, the larger $920 billion Senate package, and undoubtedly a stimulus even much larger. But when the administration's OMB (Office of Management and Budget) director, Peter Orzsag, publicly commented that the $787 billion was "about the right size," the administration signaled its willingness to accept the much smaller $787 billion stimulus package. Obama then met with Republican Senators and conceded to the Republican demand to cut out $140 billion from the Senate proposal of $920 billion. Most heavily impacted were consumer tax cut proposals, education spending, and a $40 billion cut in aid to the states.

The Republicans' unanimous rejection of the stimulus package despite getting numerous concessions should have been a clear warning shot for the president as to what he could expect going forward. But it apparently made little impact, as he would seek time and again the next three years to placate Republican opposition with concession after concession, only to face unified rejection of his proposals and programs repeatedly every time concessions were made.

Another way to consider the 'insufficient magnitude' question is to compare the Obama $787 billion stimulus to other countries' recovery programs at the time. The $787 billion stimulus amounted to roughly 5.7% of U.S. GDP. China's stimulus of $560 billion was about 16% of its $3.5 trillion GDP. Something similar, though proportionately less, was Germany's response. Both countries were hardly impacted by the global downturn.

Still another way to view the insufficient magnitude issue is to consider it in relation to the rate of collapse of the U.S. GDP at the time. Revised estimates of GDP released in 2011 show that GDP for the U.S. economy plummeted by a postwar record −8.9% in the fourth quarter of 2008, followed by another successive drop of −6.7% in the first quarter of 2009. As Obama was therefore putting together a stimulus package of $787 billion, equal to about only 5% of GDP, GDP was collapsing at a rate of nearly three times that. In short, the spending side of the first recovery program needed to be in the range of $2 trillion, with at minimum two thirds taking effect in the first year, a stimulus of about 15% of GDP.

A further way to consider the 'insufficient magnitude' point is to recognize that even the $260 billion or so of the $787 billion stimulus that was dedicated to subsidize the states and local government was not sufficient to offset the projected decline in state and local government spending and tax revenue loss for the next two years.

## STIMULUS CRITIQUE 2: POOR COMPOSITION

Criticisms of the legislation by mainstream economists focus on arguments that the $787 billion stimulus was insufficient in magnitude. This is of course true. But the most important criticism of the stimulus is that the composition of the $787 billion Obama stimulus represents its greatest failure. By 'composition failure' is meant that the stimulus focus was top-heavy on tax cuts and short-term subsidies spending ($576 billion). This left essentially no funding for immediate job creation programs or programs to save homeowners facing foreclosure or to develop permanent solutions to local governments' financial crises.

Tax cuts normally have less of an effect on the economy than spending increases. In severe recessions such as in early 2009, tax cuts have an even less effect on stimulating the economy.[20] And business tax cuts in particular have the least stimulus effect on the economy under such conditions. Committing nearly 40%, i.e. hundreds of billions of the $787 billion stimulus, to tax cuts was to reduce the impact of the already insufficient stimulus by nearly half. The barely 3% of GDP represented by the $787 billion stimulus was effectively less than 2%, since the tax cuts were either hoarded, used to pay down debt, invested abroad, or just saved by business and households alike. Tax cuts of the size introduced in the first recovery program represented a serious problem of composition.

A similar problem of composition was the temporary aid to states, schools and the unemployed. The hundreds of billions in aid to states and schools in Obama's 2009 recovery program did not require that jobs must be created first before disbursement of funding. Subsidies have a short term and temporary effect. They dissipate quickly. They may temporarily prevent some job loss but don't create new jobs.[21] Like the tax cuts, subsidies of nearly $300 billion in the first recovery program did nothing for job creation or solving the housing crisis. Even for states and local government, the effect lasted hardly more than a year and then only partially so since states and local governments continued to reduced spending and lay off public workers despite the subsidies.

## STIMULUS CRITIQUE 3: BAD TIMING

Another problem with the 2009 recovery program was its 'timing' impact. What the economy needed was a major initial 'shock' of a $2 trillion stimulus. But over the first nine months of 2009, only $85 billion in direct spending occurred in fact and another $65 billion in tax cuts. That's a total of only around $150 billion. That was less than the $168 billion combined tax-spending fiscal stimulus passed under Bush in the spring of 2008. That $168 billion had little effect on the economy. Now the economy was immeasurably much worse, but roughly only the same small amount of immediate stimulus was implemented in 2009. In the second fiscal year, October 2009 to October 2010, only $108 billion in direct spending was projected. In contrast, nearly twice that, $180 billion in tax cuts, took effect in the second year with virtually no effect on job creation.[22]

Another example of bad timing was the longer term infrastructure investment, about $100 billion in direct spending in alternative energy, water projects, electric grid, high speed rail and such. But that $100 billion was distributed over the next ten years. That's only $10 billion or so a year. Yet Obama over-hyped the job-creating potential of these longer-term spending projects, which produced very few jobs in the first two years. Expectations of millions of such jobs from alternative energy, upgrading the national electrical grid, bringing broadband to rural areas, etc., and even many 'shovel ready' projects were just too long term. So far as getting the economy on a sustained recovery path was concerned, the money spent on infrastructure in the first recovery program represented money spent that was badly timed for purposes of engineering recovery.

What was needed was immediate job creation not delayed job creation, not subsidies that temporarily 'saved' jobs but did not create jobs, and certainly not business tax cuts that would be pocketed, distributed to shareholders, or invested abroad and thus create no jobs.

The timing factor in the broader context of Obama's fundamental strategy was also in error: it was to buy time with subsidies in the short run, have the tax cuts create jobs after a year in the intermediate term, and have the longer-term infrastructure projects keep the recovery ball rolling after the second year. But Obama's assumptions about timing failed on all three levels: the subsidies weren't enough to buy more than a year's time to get the economy going at most, business did not invest and create jobs after the first year despite the tax cuts, and the infrastructure projects were just too long, too little funded, and too capital-intensive rather than labor-intensive.

## OBAMA'S STRATEGIC ERROR

Obama relied excessively on tax cuts, temporary subsidies that soon dissipated, token housing recovery measures, and on having the Federal Reserve commit $9 trillion in bailing out the banking and financial sector. The latter Fed bailouts assumed that bailing out the banks would simultaneously result in banks lending to small and medium-sized businesses that would in turn invest and also create jobs. The return of jobs would then subsequently resolve the housing foreclosure problem. And jobs, investing, and corporate profits recovery would restore state and local government tax revenues. But it didn't happen that way. Big corporations instead hoarded the cash, or else invested offshore in emerging markets, or in foreign currencies or financial securities, or disbursed the cash hoard in stock buybacks, mergers and acquisitions of competitors, or dividend payouts. They didn't spend on investment and jobs in the U.S. Making matters worse, banks refused to lend to small businesses despite their $9 trillion bailout and despite, by 2011, still sitting on $1.7 trillion in excess cash reserves. So that engine of job recovery—and in turn housing stabilization and local tax revenue recovery—did not materialize either.

Not only was there no job creation of any meaningful magnitude forthcoming from the private sector; there wasn't any job creation in the short and medium term forthcoming from the government. Continuing fiscal crisis at the state and local government level resulted in hundreds of thousands of job losses, not job hiring.

To summarize with regard to the first recovery program's $787 billion fiscal stimulus, it had little impact on the economy. At most, it perhaps helped to slow the collapse that was underway in early 2009. But it was not a 'recovery' program, if recovery is defined as programs that restore the economy to a sustained growth path and recover the level of economic activity that existed prior to the collapse. The stimulus' was grossly insufficient in terms of magnitude or level of spending. The $787 billion was probably a third of what was needed. Secondly, it was tax-cut top heavy and tax cuts in steep contractions have virtually little effect on stimulating the economy. The cuts are hoarded and not spent, or used to retire debt, or invested offshore in safer recovering economies like China, Brazil, etc. Thirdly, the barely $100 billion in potential job-creating infrastructure spending was very long-term infrastructure in focus, amounting to a meager average of $10 billion a year. What was needed desperately was to put the unemployed back to work quickly, to do something about the collapse of the housing sector and the millions facing foreclosure and falling equity. Fourthly and not least, a permanent restructuring of state and local government finances was needed, not just a temporary one-year subsidization policy.

## OBAMA'S OTHER RECOVERY PROGRAM: BANK BAILOUTS

As the $787 billion fiscal stimulus was being finalized in February 2009, the second major element of the first recovery program was being debated. Behind closed doors, and far from the spotlight of Congressional legislative debate on the stimulus, the parallel bailout of the banking and financial sector of the economy was being formulated. This task was not allocated to Congress. It was not even relegated to the administration alone. It was developed in a series of confidential meetings in February–March, led by Obama's Treasury Secretary, Tim Geithner, in conjunction with the Federal Reserve chairman, Ben Bernanke. The big 19 banks themselves were also directly involved. Other relevant government agencies, like the Federal Deposit Insurance Company (FDIC), which was responsible for the then 8,100 or so small regional-local banks, was also involved indirectly—as were mortgage lending and servicing companies, and peripheral government agencies like the Securities & Exchange Commission. Key U.S. House and Finance Committee chairmen, in particular House chairman, Barney Frank, were kept in the loop.

At the top of Obama's economic recovery priority list was the bank bailout—not job creation, not housing, not even rescue of local governments. It was considered far more important than the $787 billion fiscal stimulus. As he himself put it at the time, the top priority was to 'get credit flowing again.' That meant bank bailouts. After that, the task was to ensure a constant availability and flow of money to the financial sector in general, without which lending to non-financial businesses was not going to happen. It was no accident that the banking and finance industry was the single largest campaign contributor to Obama's 2008 election.

The approach to bank bailout in 2008 was the Troubled Asset Relief Program, or TARP. TARP was $700 billion in funds provided by Congress to the U.S. Treasury to buy banks' bad assets. But TARP was virtually stillborn. It clearly didn't work. The banks wouldn't sell those assets at market rates. The bad assets remained on their balance sheets, and bank lending to non-banks collapsed and didn't recover. Neither did the banks. What prevented the banks in late 2008 from completely imploding was the Federal Reserve providing special auctions for the banks, at which they were able to borrow funds from the Fed at below market rates in order to keep themselves from becoming technically insolvent—which means bankrupt. But the auctions from September–October 2008 were a temporary fix. Bank assets continued to collapse and the Fed found itself pumping hundreds of billions into the worst performers, like Bank of America and Citigroup. A more permanent fix was required.

The TARP approach to bank bailouts proved ineffective and politically risky. Firstly, the $700 billion directly impacted the U.S. budget deficit and thus raised taxpayer ire. TARP was too visible and thus was dangerous politically for administration and Congress alike. Using the Federal Reserve to bail out the banks was far less visible and preferable politically.

The advantages of a Federal Reserve-led approach to bank bailout were several. Firstly, the public need not know how much the Fed spent on the bailouts. For almost two years this was the case. It wasn't until July 2010 that the Fed was required to report how much it spent. Only then did it become public the Fed had spent $9 trillion on the bank bailouts up to that date.

Another advantage of the Fed approach is that it didn't have to answer to the public. The Fed was insulated from electoral—and therefore Congressional—pressure to a large extent. That, of course, was one of the reasons for its initial creation back in 1913: to allow periodic bailouts of banks and the banking system itself (called acting as a 'lender of last resort') without having to have the U.S. Treasury borrow from Congress to bail out the banks whenever they got in trouble, which was the case before 1913 and the creation of the Fed.[23]

An even bigger advantage of the Fed approach to bank bailout was the Federal Reserve could simply print money in the worst situation, if necessary, to bail out the financial sector. This was doubly easy for the Fed so long as the U.S. dollar remained the accepted international currency, which it has been since 1944 and continues to be to this date.

Given the messy problems with the Treasury and TARP approach in 2008, by February 2009 the consensus in the Obama administration, and within the banking and finance sector and Federal Reserve as well, was that the second half of Obama's second recovery program—i.e. the bank bailouts—was assigned to the Federal Reserve. The Fed would be the primary implementing institution, not Congress or even the Treasury.

By March 2009 the Fed faced several strategic tasks. First, the big 19 banks had to be more permanently stabilized—in public perception if not in fact. Several of the major banks were technically insolvent, or bankrupt, and had been now for months. Bank of America and Citigroup, two megabanks, in particular. They were 'too big to fail'. At least half a trillion dollars had been committed to keep the two afloat. Other big 19 banks were in serious shape, though not as bad. How to restabilize these megabanks and the others was the Fed's first key task. The government could keep pumping money, i.e. liquidity, into them as it had for the past six months. But that was not a long-term solution. The banks needed to 'recapitalize', as it was called, i.e. they had to raise money capital themselves to offset their massive bad debts and assets still clogging their balance sheets. One way was to help them raise their stock prices. But to raise stock prices, they had to convince would-be public stock buyers that they were again profitable. A series of measures were undertaken to achieve this.

Another major task was what to do with the 8,100 or so smaller, regional banks in the U.S. They traditionally relied upon local small-medium business loans, especially in the residential and commercial property sectors of the economy—both of which were now in a state of collapse. It was decided the task of rescuing the 8,100 'tier 2' banks was the responsibility of the FDIC. It would undertake a consolidation of the worst-off banks into larger regional banks. The FDIC's other important function was to ensure retail depositors, John and Jane Q. Public, were protected from losses. Otherwise, depositor bank runs would occur. The deposit guarantee had already been raised from $100,000 to $250,000. Initial concerns during the banking crash of September–October 2008 had been stabilized. The FDIC now began a staged process of local community-regional bank consolidations. Within two years more than 400 would be seized and processed, although as of the summer of 2011 more than 850 'in danger of failure' banks were still on the FDIC's 'troubled bank' list.

Another major Fed task going forward in 2009 was to determine what policy approach was appropriate for stabilizing the 'shadow banking' sector. The shadow banks were that grouping of financial institutions that were, up to 2008, not regulated commercial institutions under the purview of the Federal Reserve. This was a long list of financial institutions—from investment banks like Bear Stearns, Lehman Brothers, Goldman Sachs, Morgan Stanley and others, to insurance companies like AIG, to thousands of hedge funds, mutual funds, finance companies, private asset banks, private equity firms, and dozens of other such entities.[24]

The shadow banks (sometimes called 'financial intermediaries') had become as large as the big 19 and 8,100 commercial banks in terms of assets.[25] Moreover, they were especially unstable in times of crisis. As the leading edge of global financial speculation, they had also become a major force creating financial bubbles and busts, and played a major role in the subprime market crash of 2007, as well as the collapse of the rest of the banking sector thereafter. Like the big commercial banks—e.g. Bank of America, Citigroup, etc.—they too were in many cases loaded up with bad assets and deadweight debt.

Both the big banks and shadow banks had pushed a boom in what were called 'secondary markets' where financial instruments were easily bought and sold among investors, including various forms of derivatives like mortgage backed bonds, collateralized debt obligations (CDOs), and credit default swaps (CDSs). The secondary markets enabled the accelerated expansion of mortgage-housing and commercial property markets. With the bank crash of 2008, however, by 2009 these secondary market traded securities, once worth trillions of dollars in value, had collapsed. If housing, commercial property, auto, and the like, were to revive, these 'secondary markets' had to be revived as well somehow. That too was left to the Fed to figure out.

A fourth Fed task was what to do about the residential housing itself, specifically the growing problem of foreclosures, and collapsing home prices and 'negative equity.'

Obviously the Fed could help with lowering interest rates for prospective home buyers. But that still did not resolve the problem of foreclosures. The housing-foreclosure problem therefore required more than just Fed action on mortgage interest rates. The Obama administration would have to play some kind of direct role if it seriously wanted to stem the rise in foreclosures. There were several choices. It might require banks to modify the terms of existing mortgage loans, principal or interest or both. This could be done voluntarily, by providing incentives to mortgage lenders and banks that serviced the loan payments. Or the administration could issue mandatory directives to lenders and servicers to modify mortgages and enforce those directives by penalties if they did not modify. The quasi-government agencies Fannie Mae and Freddie Mac already held millions of mortgages since they were required by law to buy private lenders' mortgages if sold to them. Fannie and Freddie could start the process of mandatory modification of principal and interest for the mortgages they held. The administration might also push for legislation that would allow judges to decide on modification of mortgage principal and interest in bankruptcy court. To recall, that was a proposal by Obama during the 2008 election. An even more direct, aggressive form of intervention by the Obama administration was possible—along lines similar to the 1930s and the Home Owners Loan Corporation, HOLC, during that period. The HOLC simply took over the mortgages and it—not the banks or servicers—renegotiated new principal and interest terms despite banks and mortgage investors' objections.

Not surprising, the Obama administration chose once more the path of least resistance to the housing-foreclosures element of the financial crisis. It chose a completely voluntary approach to foreclosure prevention, administered by the banks and mortgage servicers themselves. There were no penalties if they failed to remodify mortgages, no specific mandatory minimum national standards for loan modification, no bankruptcy court participation in the modification process, and only token funding for the entire voluntary modification program. That program was called the Home Affordability Modification Program, or HAMP, more on which shortly.

## 'BAD BANKS' AND BANK NATIONALIZATION DEBATES

In February 2009, as the $787 billion fiscal stimulus was being finalized, debate grew within bank and administration-political circles as to what approaches to take to stabilize and revitalize the banking system—the big 19, the second tier 8,100, the 'shadow banks' and secondary markets, and the mortgage banking sector.

One wing of the debate argued for some form of bank nationalization. Nationalization had several possible meanings and could assume various forms. Not all nationalizations are the same. Some argued that the insurance giant, AIG, was already nationalized. But government oversight of decisions made by the corporate team remaining in place does not constitute national-ization. Neither does majority government stock ownership per se.

Another form of nationalization debated at the time was the experience of the Swedish government with its own banking crisis in the early 1990s. A bank crisis happens when the bank becomes insolvent. Insolvent means its liquid and other assets are worth less than its debt and the bank has no way of raising further funds to pay the principal and interest on the owed debt as it comes due. Technically, debtors in such situations can then go to court and proceed with the seizure of the company and its assets and the resale of those assets on the market to recover the debt principal owed. Bad assets means assets that have collapsed in market value well below the level at which they were purchased.

The Swedish solution to the bad assets on private bank balance sheets was to have the government buy them up and put the bad assets in a 'bad bank,' a government-owned bank. The government over time sold off the assets to buyers and recouped some of the cost of having initially bought the bad assets from the banks. The private banks therefore no longer had the bad assets on their books. Theoretically, their good assets would exceed the remaining fewer bad assets. They would now have reserves to lend to non-bank businesses.

But the 'bad bank' Swedish approach to resolving banks' insolvency and getting them to lend again was rejected in the U.S. by the Obama administration. The bad bank approach was also firmly ruled out by both Fed chairman, Bernanke, and Treasury Secretary, Geithner, who delivered a 'one-two' punch on the same day, February 25, 2009. In testifying before Congress that day, Bernanke stated "There are other ways to exert adequate control" of the banks. In an interview of the PBS *News Hour* that same day Geithner declared it (bank nationalization) was "the wrong strategy for the country."[26] The option of a 'bad bank' was intensely opposed by the banks themselves, and their lobbying power both within the administration and the Congress was still immense. The big 19 U.S. banks were only willing to sell their 'bad assets' at full market purchase prices, not at lower market prices—as was the case in Sweden. This refusal to sell at anything but top prices—i.e. refusing to accept any kind of even minimal loss—was the political wall Treasury Secretary Hank Paulson had also run into in 2008. That wall was still firmly in place in February 2009.

## THE OBAMA-TREASURY SOLUTION: PIPP, TALF, AND HASP

The administration proposed three financial bailout programs. The first was called the Public Private Investment Program, or PIPP. Announced on March 23, 2009, PIPP was designed to buy up the bad assets clogging bank balance sheets. But not directly buy up, as in the case of TARP. PIPP was 'TARP with a twist.' Geithner estimated that about $500 billion to $1 trillion in government funding was needed. The idea of PIPP was to subsidize both the new investor-buyers of the bad assets as well as the bank-sellers of the bad assets. The government funding, in other words, would guarantee the buying and selling of the bad assets for both sides of the exchange—the banks and the investors.[27]

PIPP targeted what were called 'legacy loans'—i.e. real estate loans held by banks and other securities backed by such loans. The true market value of these mortgage and related loan assets were now no more than 10–20 cents on their original purchase price. The banks nonetheless were carrying them on their books at 95–98 cents of their value. If the banks simply sold these loans to the government at their true, and now much lower, market price, the banks would have to take an accounting loss of 75–85 cents on the dollar. The banks were already 'under water' and technically insolvent. So to sell the collapsed assets at their true price would have increased their losses even more. They would agree to sell only at their original price or not at all.

But unlike TARP, PIPP was designed to get investors to buy the loans from the banks, with the guarantee that the government, the Treasury, would put up public funds to ensure up to 50%, i.e. half, of the investors' purchase cost. The investors then owned and controlled the asset once purchased even though the Treasury paid for half of it. Conversely, government funding would ensure the banks selling the loans were paid nearly what they wanted. The plan was simple: the Treasury would pay and subsidize both investors and banks to sell and to buy the loans. It would guarantee a price for both and pay the difference.

The markets and the business press quickly panned the idea as soon as it was announced. The flawed major premise of the PPIP was that enough investors would enter the market and buy the bad assets if the government subsidized half of their purchase price; and that the banks would agree to sell at whatever the auctions determined the market price might be, with the government guaranteed $6 of every $7 dollars of the sales price. Since the program was voluntary, there was little to compel the banks to sell or even participate in the PIPP. This was not the Resolution Trust Corporation (RTC) of the 1980s. It would have forced the sale of the bad assets. This was the Obama administration, with close ties to the banking and shadow banking institutions. No one was going to force the banks to do anything, and they damn well knew it.

As the savvy *Financial Times* columnist, Gillian Tett, wrote at the time, "The PIPP plan can only fly if banks take part. But no banker wants an auction that produces asset prices lower than on bank books...So some banks are—unsurprisingly—adopting a policy of quiet foot-dragging."[28]

The PIPP program limped along with few takers until June 2009. On June 3, 2009, the *New York Times* reported that the voluntary program had few takers, since "many banks refuse to sell their loans because doing so would crystallize book losses...the prices that banks were demanding have remained far higher than the prices that investors were willing to pay." A report by the Treasury in January 2010 indicated only $24.8 billion of bad loan assets had been purchased under the program to date. That was about $975 billion short of its announced goal. The program simply faded from view.

The second major financial bailout program was called the Term Asset Backed Securities Lending Facility, or TALF. Whereas the PIPP was administered by the FDIC, under the direction of the Treasury, the TALF was the administrative responsibility of the Federal Reserve. The goal of TALF was similar to PIPP. But instead of government subsidizing the purchase of loans and securities, TALF was designed to resurrect the collapsed 'securitization' markets. Once worth about $2 trillion in 2006–07, and generating $200 billion a year in new credit, the selling of bundled packages of securities involving property, auto, student, small business, and credit card loans had declined to $160 billion in 2008 and by early 2009 to less than $10 billion. To get economic activity going again in commercial building, autos, education, and credit card sales, the securitized markets behind them needed to recover. Shadow bank financial institutions like hedge funds, pension funds, insurance companies, etc., had been particularly instrumental to the securitized markets before 2008. And TALF was designed to largely subsidize the same shadow banking institutional investors, and to get them once again to start buying up securitized packages of auto, commercial property, student, and other loans.

TALF was initially funded in late 2008 by $200 billion provided by the Fed. But the program was postponed and then reintroduced in March 2009 as part of the financial bailouts. Commitment to funding was raised to $1 trillion, $900 billion from the Federal Reserve and another $100 billion from the Treasury. But the same problems facing PIPP applied to TALF as well. Why should investors bother with taking any risk of loss by purchasing what were already 'dog' assets, or buying assets from companies that were barely solvent, when safer and more profitable investment opportunities existed offshore in emerging markets like China, Brazil, or by speculating in foreign currencies or other financial securities?

By August 2009 the Fed had helped issue TALF loans worth only $29.6 billion. By the end of 2009, about $48 billion. The program was discontinued for consumer loans (auto, student, credit card) in March 2010, but continued until June 2010 for commercial property loans. Like PIPP, the TALF program thereafter faded away with little net effect on either the securitized consumer loan markets (auto, student, credit card) or the commercial property market.

The third official financial bailout was the administration's Home Affordability and Stability Plan (HASP). Announced on February 18 by the Treasury, less than a week after Obama signed the fiscal stimulus bill into law, HASP was designed to "help up to 7 to 9 million families restructure their mortgages to avoid foreclosure," according to the U.S. Treasury's executive summary of the plan. It was thus the centerpiece of the administration's plan to save homeowners facing foreclosure, as well as to assist millions more whose mortgages were now worth more than the value of their homes after the 25% fall in home prices since the recession began.

From late 2006 to the end of 2008, 4.35 million homes had entered foreclosure by the end of 2008. In the first half of 2009, an even greater number, an additional 1.9 million, homeowners were foreclosed. HASP was supposed to stop the hemorrhaging of foreclosures, now accelerating in 2009 even faster. It was composed of three elements that were together designed to check this rising flood of foreclosures hitting the economy—foreclosures that in turn were driving down housing prices, and causing a major dampening effect on consumer spending and thus economic recovery.[29] Since 1945 there had never been a recovery from recession without housing leading the way; housing was now leading—but not toward a recovery. It was leading in the other direction. It had become a major anchor and drag on the economy.

The first element of HASP was aimed at getting 4–5 million 'responsible homeowners,' as they were called by the Treasury, to refinance their mortgage loans at lower rates. These were homeowners that could still pay their mortgages but whose homes were in what is called 'negative equity.' They owed more than the homes were now worth after two years of plummeting prices. It was feared that if they could not refinance, many would eventually choose to walk away from their loans, creating a second 'wave' of foreclosures that would add to the first wave of owners with 'subprime' mortgages who could not pay their monthly mortgage. These were owners whose loans were either held, or guaranteed, by the government mortgage agencies, Fannie Mae and Freddie Mac.

To enable Fannie and Freddie to help refinance the 4–5 million owners under water, the two agencies would need more funding. HASP provided another $200 billion to the agencies to enable them to continue to buy private investor-owned mortgages being dumped on them by the banks and other mortgage lenders as required by law.

The second element of HASP targeted another group of an additional 3–4 million homeowners—i.e. the second group with mostly subprime loans who were not able to pay their mortgage. This second element of HASP was sometimes called the 'Home Affordability Modification Program,' or HAMP. Most homeowners eligible for HAMP were already in foreclosure, or in later stages of delinquency in making mortgage payments and thus were facing imminent foreclosure as well. HAMP was allocated $75 billion in the first recovery program of early 2009. The main objective was modification of existing loans—primarily by lowering interest payments—to permit owners facing foreclosure to remain in their homes. The $75 billion was to be used as follows: if a mortgage lender agreed to lower the owner's monthly mortgage payment to 38% of the homeowner's monthly income, the Treasury would subsidize the next 7% reduction to 31% of the owner's monthly income. This reduction was for no more than five years, however. After that, the mortgage payments rose back to original level. Generous incentives were also provided out of the $75 billion directly to mortgage servicers. Servicers were paid $1,000 a year for three years when they agreed to modify the loans to 31% of the owner's income. A further incentive of $500 was paid to servicers if they modified before the homeowner became delinquent in his payments. Another $10 billion was allocated to discourage mortgage lenders from foreclosing. So most of the $75 billion was targeted to mortgage lenders and services, not to homeowners facing foreclosure. HAMP was really a lenders' subsidization program.

Originally HASP proposed to empower bankruptcy court judges themselves to modify mortgages for the worst case foreclosures. Bankers' opposition to the provision immediate arose during the 2008 campaign by the mortgage bankers association. That opposition intensified as soon as the HASP was announced in February 2009. The mortgage bankers association argued existing laws did not permit bankruptcy court judges to unilaterally change contract terms for mortgages. A 1993 Supreme Court decision following a prior housing bust in the late 1980s explicitly prevented mortgage modifications, the bankers cited. Additional legislation was therefore required by Congress, they argued. The enabling legislation was successfully blocked.

Mortgage lenders and the big five bank mortgage servicers also argued that the original legislation establishing Fannie Mae and Freddie Mac required an 80% loan-to-value for refinancing of loans. Since HASP permitted owners 'under water' to refinance up to 105% loan to value, this too was illegal, the bankers' association noted. This too required Congressional legislation to change the law, they argued.

The mortgage bankers association, the big three mortgage servicers,[30] U.S. Chamber of Commerce, and other business groups all came out strongly against HASP provisions allowing 'under water' homeowners to refinance at lower rates, and homeowners in foreclosure having their mortgage principal and interest rates lowered. The 10 million homeowners at the time with negative equity amounted to mortgages valued at $500 billion. Lowering rates meant significantly less profits, even when limited to no more than a five-year modification period.

There were many problems with HASP. One problem was that it was totally voluntary on the part of mortgage lenders and servicers. They did not have to participate. Fewer than 500,000 of the targeted 9 million homeowners had their loans 'modified' during the first two years of the Obama administration, and then only temporarily and only in terms of interest rate reduction (no principal reduction) almost exclusively. Secondly, the incentives provided by HASP to get servicers to lower mortgage rates were insufficient. There was no government subsidy if the owners' loan to value was already more than 38%. Thirdly, only mortgages held by Fannie Mae and Freddie Mac were eligible for modification. This amounted to a potential of only 2.7 million, it turned out. Fourth, the big three bank mortgage servicers were making big fees on delinquencies and foreclosure processing, more than the HASP subsidies of $1,000 and $500 offered to them. Finally, in many cases mortgage lenders had taken out insurance contracts (credit default swaps) to insure against foreclosure. If a foreclosure went through, they got to collect the full amount of the mortgage. This was a great incentive to push foreclosures, not to try to prevent them.

Congress refused to pass legislation to allow bankruptcy court judges to decide mandatory changes to principal and interest for owners in foreclosure. This left the program totally voluntary, and self-administered by the banks themselves. Violations of the loan modification guidelines by lenders and services resulted in no penalties for lenders or servicers. This voluntary and penalty-free approach predictably resulted in foot-dragging and slow-roll processing by mortgage servicers. Had the U.S. government undertaken the task of modification itself directly—as it did in the 1930s—easily 5 million or more homeowners would still be in their homes today.

As late as March 2011, only 540,000 loan modifications out of the target 9 million had been accomplished. Of the $30 billion of the original $75 billion set aside for loan modifications, only $1 billion had been spent to actually subsidize homeowners.[31] The rest went to mortgage lenders and servicers or was unspent. HASP proved totally ineffective. It did not stop foreclosures, which eventually rose to more than 11.4 million by mid 2011.[32] Nor did it reduce the number of homeowners with mortgages in negative equity. The 10 million 'under water' at the time of the HASP announcement in February 2009 grew to 15 million by year-end 2010, and to more than 17 million by mid 2011. The special federal investigator general assigned to evaluate how the TARP funds were spent, Neil Barofsky, evaluated the HASP-HAMP program. In his 2011 report he concluded "that program has been a colossal failure."[33]

## THE REAL BANK BAILOUT: MARK-TO-MARKET ACCOUNTING, ZIRP, AND QE

From the foregoing it is clear that none of the four major programs introduced by the Obama administration in February–March 2009 designed to stabilize the banking, shadow banking, or mortgage markets had any significant effect. In fact, it is hard to find another example of a package of programs announced at one time that virtually all failed to have an effect. Nonetheless, financial institutions were stabilized—if only imperfectly and temporarily in 2009. So what was responsible, if PIPP, TALF, and HASP were in fact failures?

The real 'bailout' of the banking and finance sector began in April of 2009, after the above three failed official bailout programs were announced. The first key to the bailout was the decision by Congress to force the Financial Accounting Standards Board, FASB, to suspend what was called 'mark-to-market accounting' practices by the banks. Mark-to-market accounting meant the banks had to value their bad assets on their books at true current market prices. Suspending it meant they could now value those assets at their 'hold to maturity' purchase price instead of current market price. With assets valued at their once highest price, instead of actual price, banks appeared more profitable than they actually were simply due to an accounting change. It was estimated at the time that by suspending mark-to-market accounting, "some analysts predict an upside in bank profits of up to 20% upon accounting rule change."[34]

With higher asset values, banks now looked more appealing to investors who began buying their stock once again. Stock purchases raised in turn the value of the banks' stock. More cash on hand further improved their total assets' value. More cash on hand from stock sales also meant more to invest in speculative ventures like foreign currencies and commodities and thus further possible earnings that would raise stock sales and prices.

Fed chairman Bernanke came out strongly in favor of suspending mark-to-market accounting in March. Congress picked up the matter quickly. Even House Financial Services Committee chairman Barney Frank, once opposed to the idea, came around to support it. Under growing pressure from Congress, within a week after the House hearings the normally very slow moving FASB voted to change the rule on April 2. Bank stocks immediately surged in price. The U.S.-based FASB accounting change was quickly globalized, as the international IASB accounting body followed suit. As former IMF economist Willem Buiter commented at the time, "the FASB's encouragement of marking-to-myth is likely to increase future financial instability."[35]

The suspension of the rule had a particularly negative effect on the PIPP and TALF programs and contributed to their premature 'stillborn' fate: if banks could value their bad mortgage and other assets at purchase price, what incentive would they have to sell those bad assets at anything less? By leaving them on their books, they at least didn't have to register further losses. However, by participating in PIPP and TALF they might have to sell them at lower, market (even if partially subsidized) value and register some degree of loss on the assets. In other words, suspending mark-to-market all but ensured that the PIPP and TALF programs would fail to have any appreciable effect. Longer term was an even more serious strategic consequence: bad assets would remain on the books, 'offset' by the huge liquidity injections by the Fed, but never really expunged or removed in the final analysis—as they might have been with a 'bad bank' approach, with some form of true bank nationalization, or as they were in the 1930s. That left the basis for future bank instability still in place down the road.

In support of the accounting rule suspension, the U.S. government undertook simultaneously at the time what were called 'stress tests' of the banks. These were largely phony auditing exercises designed to make the banks appear more solvent than they actually were and thus potentially profitable, when in fact many were still technically insolvent—in particular Citigroup and Bank of America. The bank stress tests undertaken in March by the government were necessary to support the suspension of mark-to-market accounting by Congress and together artificially boost bank stock prices and assets. Together they quickly led to a steady rise in bank common stock prices and stock sales.

With more capital on hand from the stock appreciation and offerings, the banks loaned out the additional funds—not to small businesses in the U.S. but to speculators like hedge funds, private equity firms, and the like. The latter were busy speculating in Chinese property, foreign currencies, derivatives, swaps, and similar investments. The banks that loaned them the funds in turn made nice profits, which further boosted their stock prices. Banks thus turned once again to the speculative investing that got them in trouble in the first place. The government turned a blind eye to the practice. It was preferred from the Treasury's point of view to having to pump even more bailout money directly into them from the government.

As this accounting rule change plus stress tests scenario was developing, the Federal Reserve was providing near zero interest loans to the banks as well—a policy sometimes referred to as ZIRP. The Fed charged the banks a mere 0.25% for banks to borrow funds from it. The banks then lent the money to speculators globally and received returns of 6–10% on average. Free money from the Fed for above-average market returns. Bank profits and stock prices moved still higher as a result. In fact, it was more than just 'free money' from the Fed. The Fed added the feature that, while the banks were deciding to which speculators to loan the free money, the Fed would pay the banks interest while they parked the Fed money with the Fed. Very little of the free money ended up in loans to U.S. small businesses. In fact, bank lending to small business would decline every quarter for the next 18 months in the U.S.

While mark-to-market accounting suspension, stress tests, and ZIRP were occurring, at the same time the Fed was pumping $1.45 trillion into the financial system in the form of its 'quantitative easing 1' (QE1) policy, buying up mortgage and long term treasury bonds. QE1 meant the Fed simply printed money, eliminating the need to ask Congress for funding, and used the money to buy up mortgages. The Fed also directly repurchased another $300 billion in 30-year Treasury bonds from the market—i.e. from banks and other investors. Within 18 months the banks were sitting on more than $1 trillion in excess reserves. The bank bailout has thus succeeded—albeit perhaps temporarily and at the cost of $1.75 trillion or so of direct Fed-printed money injected into the economy.

So the method by which the banks and other financial institutions were effectively 'rescued' or bailed out was not via the official Obama bank bailout programs—PIPP, TALF, and for the mortgage sector, HASP. It was via the massive liquidity injection by the Fed, through means of near zero cost loans, with interest paid to the banks on those loans, and via measures that artificially boosted banks stocks and recapitalization such as phony stress tests and suspension of reasonable accounting rules.

## SHORT- AND LONG-TERM CONSEQUENCES OF THE BANK BAILOUTS

If banks were allowed to let the overvalued assets sit on their books, if the Fed provided 0.25% loans to the banks and then actually *paid them* interest, and if the banks were allowed to lend their new-found excess liquidity to offshore hedge funds and speculators—why should the banks bother to loan to small-medium enterprises (SMEs) that desperately needed the capital to invest and to expand employment? Given these more attractive profit options, bank lending to real SMEs might simply stagnate or even decline. As economist Willem Buiter predicted, "banks with large amounts of undeclared crud on their balance sheets will act like zombie banks, engaging in little new lending or new investment in the real economy."[36] And, unfortunately, that is exactly what happened after June 2009.

Despite banks' cash tripling over the last six months of 2009, bank lending to small-medium businesses declined every month for the remainder of 2009.[37] The banks' cash hoard was now higher than any time previously in U.S. bank history, measured as a percentage of GDP, as the banking industry reported a net profit of $2.8 billion for the third quarter of 2009. Nevertheless, in the third quarter of 2009, total bank loans fell by $210 billion, or 3%, the biggest decline since 1984.[38] And for the full year 2009, bank lending fell by its steepest decline in 67 years. Not since 1942 was the collapse as great. The most important source of loans for small businesses, Commercial & Industrial loans (C&I), fell every month from June to December 2009, as did residential mortgage and credit card loans for consumers and households.[39]

The problem with the Fed's 'massive liquidity injection' approach to bank bailout was that the original bad assets were not expunged from bank balance sheets. They were still there. The Fed simply 'offset' the bad assets with a massive money injection. This meant the bailout would be only temporary. For the moment, the banks were indeed bailed out. But the potential for another banking crash and panic remained so long as the mountain of bad assets and debt also remained on banks' balance sheets.

The bank bailouts were originally supposed to 'get credit flowing again,' as Obama liked to say as a justification for the trillions of dollars pumped into the financial sector. But the way it was done only boosted profits and didn't lead to lending that would have created jobs. Small businesses, where half the jobs are created, remained starved into 2011 for commercial and industrial loans. The banks simply preferred to invest short term to speculators, rather than longer term to real businesses that created real investment and jobs. Nor, as has been shown, did they really want to rescue homeowners. It was more profitable to foreclose or leave the mortgages on their books at inflated prices than mark them down and refinance principal or interest for homeowners.

Just as the Obama fiscal stimulus plan of 2009 was temporary in its effect, boosting non-bank profits via tax cuts, while leaving three key areas of the crisis—jobs, housing, and local governments—without an effective solution, so too were the administration's bank bailout measures—PIPP, TALF, and HASP—no less ineffective.

The true measures by which the bank bailout was engineered created in turn two problems of major dimensions that would play a key role in preventing recovery in the short term while continuing the probability of a renewed financial crisis in the longer term: the bailout measures resulted in a collapse and continued stagnation of bank lending in the short run and ensured a return to financial instability over the longer term.

As this writer pointed out in great detail in his 2010 book, *Epic Recession: Prelude to Global Depression*,[40] the Obama second recovery plan of 2009 was a classic case of applying policies that could not resolve a 'Type I' epic recession. In a 'Type I' the banks get bailed out by massive government liquidity support, but a fiscal stimulus for the rest of the economy is insufficient in magnitude, and suffers from bad timing and poor composition. The result of a Type I and such a bailout is that sustained economic recovery does not follow. The result is a short, shallow and temporary recovery that is followed by a series of relapses of the economy or 'double dip' contractions that are also relatively short and shallow. The relapse and double dip provokes a second fiscal stimulus that is also insufficient, typically even less in terms of magnitude. The economy recovers even more weakly and more briefly. This 'bouncing along the bottom' can go on for years, in a kind of long-term stagnation of the economy. Or, the stagnation eventually confronts another major banking-financial implosion somewhere, in which case the 'Type I' can deteriorate into a 'Type II' epic recession and subsequent bona fide depression.

# 4
# A Record Short, Faltering Recovery

'The First Economic Relapse of 2010'

With most of Obama's $787 stimulus scheduled to take effect in 2010 instead of 2009, with the bank bailouts failing to produce the anticipated lending, and business in general intent on hoarding profits instead of investing, it wasn't surprising that the economy for the first six months after June 2009 did not immediately recover as strongly as the administration predicted.

Even when measured in terms of GDP, an imperfect measure at best of the overall condition of the economy, the second half of 2009 was not all that great. After collapsing for four straight quarters from July 2008 through June 2009, including consecutive drops of −8.9% and −6.7% from October 2008 through March 2009, GDP 'recovered' by only 1.7% and 3.8% in the final two quarters of 2009. That's an average annual GDP growth rate in the first six months following the end of the recession of only 2.7%.[1] A GDP growth rate of at least 4% is needed to begin reducing the level of 25 million unemployed.

The recovery for the first six months following the 2007–09 recession's June 2009 end was less than half the rate of GDP recovery for a similar six-month period in the two earlier recessions in the 1970s and 1980s. Both the 1973–75 and 1981–82 recessions 'snapped back' with average annual GDP growth rates of 5.0% and 7.3%, respectively.[2] In other words, more than twice as fast and strong. As a central theme of this book maintains, the reasons for the weak, hesitant and faltering recovery after June 2009 were the failure of Obama's three recovery programs to create jobs, to stem foreclosures and decline of house values, and to conclusively resolve the crisis in state and local government finances.

## JOBS, FORECLOSURES AND THE STATES: JUNE–DECEMBER 2009

During the first six months of official recovery after June 2009, total employment fell by more than 2 million. The Labor Department's narrowly defined U-3 unemployment rate rose from 9.5% to 10.0% and the broader, more accurate U-6 unemployment rate rose from 16.5% to 17.3%.[3] Nearly all other job indicators worsened as well. The long term duration unemployed— those out of work for 27 weeks or more—escalated from 4.3 million in June to 6.1 million in December 2009.[4] The involuntary part time, or underemployed, rose by 300,000 to 9.1 million in the second half of 2009, while the number of workers with full-time jobs fell by nearly 2 million more.[5] Many of those who found full-time jobs after June were employed as temporary-status workers, at 70% normal pay and 10% normal benefits. By December, 6.2 workers were looking for every one job available.[6]

Despite this dismal condition in the jobs market, the Obama administration nonetheless claimed that the $787 billion stimulus 'saved' 640,000 jobs in 2009.[7] That would have represented a cost of $1.3 million per job saved.

Of the three 'mini-crises' of jobs, housing, and state and local government finances, jobs creation was the key. The jobless numbers remained consistently around 25 million for the remainder of 2009. It would remain stuck around that level throughout 2010. As of mid 2011, it was still 25 million.[8]

Foreclosures also continued to rise monthly for the rest of 2009, by an additional million. In 2010 foreclosures accelerated further, adding another 2.8 million.[9] By the close of 2009 the foreclosures problem was now increasingly driven by the growing ranks of unemployed, discouraged, and record long-term jobless workers. Unable to make mortgage payments, this third 'wave' of jobless-induced foreclosures added to the first 'subprime' borrowers wave and the second 'negative equity' wave of foreclosures.

Just as foreclosures by year-end 2009 were being driven increasingly by the chronic 25 million unemployed and long-term jobless, the fiscal crises of local government were intensified as well by the extreme and chronic high levels of unemployment. Twenty-five million without work represents a massive loss of tax revenue to state and local governments. Contrary to general opinion, the growing fiscal crisis of state and local governments has been due more to the collapse of state revenues than it has to excessive state and local government spending. Thus, for the states alone—not counting cities and other municipalities—in 2009 tax collections fell by $65.4 billion.[10] Including cities and other local governments, tax revenues likely fell by more than $100 billion in 2009. Meanwhile, state and local governments' spending obligations simultaneously rose in tandem with the growing unemployed, with households needing more food stamps (which doubled), and other social services. The Obama 2009 stimulus provided subsidies to the states and local government to offset some—though not all—of their rising costs. But it didn't offset at all state and local government tax and other revenues losses. Moreover, the stimulus subsidies were timed to have a greater offsetting effect in early 2010 than in late 2009 in any event. So 2009 continued to be a very difficult year for states and local governments' finances.

Given the delayed and insufficient subsidies in 2009 and the accelerating fall in tax revenues impacting states and cities, state and local governments undertook major cuts in spending. Spending declined by −1.5% in the third quarter of 2009 and by another −2.9% in the fourth quarter, despite the Obama subsidies to state and local governments.[11]

The chronic 25 million jobless, rising foreclosures and negative equity in housing translated into far-below-average consumption by households after mid 2009, at least for the bottom 90% of households. Total household consumption lagged badly after June 2009. Representing 70% of the U.S. economy, in the second half of 2009 it grew at an average annual rate of barely 1.4%, as average hourly wages adjusted for inflation declined in the first nine months of 2009 by the greatest percentage in 60 years. Falling wages, collapsing home values, rising foreclosures, and 25 million jobless all meant stagnating consumption which left 70% of the economy simply marking time at best. In the earlier recessions in the 1970s and 1980s consumption grew more than 6% in the first six months after the end of those recessions—or four times as fast as during the post-June 2009 comparable period.

The two other major parts of the economy, i.e. business spending and government spending, also remained exceptionally weak after June 2009. Business spending on fixed investment (i.e. structures, buildings, equipment and software) barely grew at all in the third quarter of 2009 (0.7%) and then even fell by –3.8% in the fourth quarter. As previously noted, state and local governments continued to cut spending by –1.5% and –2.9% in the third and fourth quarters of 2009.

What little growth did occur in the economy in the second half of 2009 was due primarily to several temporary factors. Firstly, business spending was mostly restocking of inventories that had collapsed in historic proportions the previous year. Consumption that did occur after June was due to temporary programs like 'cash for clunkers' that boosted auto purchases and the first-time homebuyers' $8,000 tax credit programs added as supplements to Obama's February 2009 first recovery program. Secondly, and of particular concern, the huge services sector of the economy—the projected source of 96% of all new jobs in the coming decade—slipped into negative territory in the last quarter of 2009 after having added jobs throughout the first nine months of the year.

Not surprisingly, employment from July through October fell by 1.8 million with 1.2 million additional full-time workers jobless and another 600,000 leaving the labor force unable to find work. In housing, foreclosures surged to 349,000 in December 2009.[12] By early fall, Congress and the Obama administration became increasingly concerned.

## POLITICIANS' FEEBLE RESPONSE

Throughout the second half of 2009 the Obama administration was reluctant to add more stimulus or programs. It was concerned that to do so would appear as if the original stimulus of $787 billion was not having the impact it promised in February. Secondly, Obama was already beginning to focus on how to cut the deficit.

The administration's concern about deficits began to emerge as early as the development of the original $787 billion stimulus itself, in February–March 2009. The U.S. debt ceiling was projected at $12.1 trillion for 2009 and it was anticipated that another increase of $300 billion in the debt limit would be needed by year-end 2009. Adding more programs and stimulus would thus create more pressure on the deficit and debt, and Republicans were already hammering on this pressure point. Raising the debt ceiling limit was not yet a problem in 2009, given the Democrats' majorities in both Houses of Congress. But that was eventually to break down after the midterm elections in 2010. From the very beginning in early 2009, Obama was consistently to the right of his own party on this issue of deficit cutting and would remain so. The banking sector's 'inside men' in the administration—Treasury Secretary Tim Geithner and top White House economic advisor Larry Summers—were especially vocal early in 2009 about the necessity of tackling the deficit sooner rather than later.

The deficit for 2009 was estimated to come in at about $1.4 trillion. But more than half of that was due to insufficient revenue. The loss of income tax revenue from the 25 million unemployed amounted to no less than $400 billion. The continuation of the Bush tax cuts accounted for another $200–250 billion that year alone. Had the economy promptly recovered lost jobs, and had the administration ended the Bush tax cuts as it had promised during the election, the $1.4 trillion deficit would have been halved. Had other measures promised during the 2008 election also been implemented, there would not have been any deficit issue at all. Those measures included: (1) spending reductions from ending the war in Afghanistan, (2) imposing a bank tax for banks to repay their bailout, (3) recovering taxes from wealthy investors sheltering their income in offshore tax shelters to avoid paying U.S. taxes, (4) stopping multinational corporations moving profits into their offshore subsidiaries to defer paying U.S. taxes, and (5) introducing a 'cap and trade' system for reducing greenhouse gases. Yet none of the above were seriously pushed by the Obama administration in 2009 to cover the cost of the first recovery program. Nor would they be resurrected in 2010–11.

As the original $787 billion stimulus was proving to have little effect on the economy after June 2009, Congress added supplemental programs and extended other programs that were scheduled to expire.

One of the earliest supplemental programs was the 'cash for clunkers' program, or what was officially called the Car Allowance Rebate System (CARS). This was originally a $3.6 billion subsidy paid to car owners who retired their old low-mileage 'junkers' and bought new cars in 2009. The 'cash for clunkers' total stimulus in 2009 was $5–6 billion. The program was designed to accelerate the purchase of an additional 250,000 cars in 2009. An assessment of the program in 2010 by the Council of Economic Advisors estimated it produced an extra 175,000 cars sold in 2009.[13] Nonetheless, its impact in the third quarter of 2009 was not insignificant, contributing 0.4% of that quarter's tepid 1.7% GDP.

A second major contributor to the still anemic 1.7% growth in the third quarter was another subsidy, called the First Time Homebuyers' Credit. Originally passed in 2008, in its earlier version it provided buyers of their first home a credit of $7,500. But the credit was repayable over a 15-year period. The new, 2009, version provided a $8,000 credit for homes purchased up to December 2009 and did not have to be repaid. The program was subsequently extended through April 2010 at a slightly lower $6,500 credit and then—like the 'cash for clunkers' program—was discontinued. Both programs were criticized as simply moving sales 'forward' into 2009 that would have occurred later. This of course was true. But whether 'moved forward' from future sales or not, more stimulus was clearly needed and both programs did help. Nevertheless, they were discontinued.

The overall picture of the economy in the second half of 2009 therefore was one of tentative recovery in some sectors in the third quarter—driven more by factors unrelated to the original $787 billion stimulus—followed by a relapse once again and a clear indication of the inability to establish a sustained recovery.

## THE 'OCTOBER SURPRISE'

With job losses and foreclosures rising, and with sharp reversals once again in housing activity, auto sales and inventories, the administration began internal discussions to consider additional measures. One idea resurrected from the 2008 election campaign was a $3,000 tax credit to businesses for each new job created. The problem was the difficulty of measuring if a net new job was in fact created, or whether the credit was given to a business that would otherwise have created a job anyway. Variations on this same idea were proposed at the time from liberal advisors both within and outside the administration. All these 'tax cut first and maybe jobs later' measures, however, assumed that businesses would actually spend the extra income from the tax credits to create jobs. Proving the business did create a net new job after receiving the credit was an almost impossible administration task.

Another idea resurrected from the campaign was a proposal to allow businesses to deduct net operating losses going back five years instead of two. The original 2009 stimulus permitted a five-year back deduction rule for small businesses only. Both proposals reflect once more the Obama administration's strong preference from the very beginning for tax cut approaches to creating jobs and economic recovery, rather than direct spending on immediate job creation or any kind of direct government job creation programs.

Also back on the policy agenda was the need to extend unemployment benefits once again by year end 2009. Without more subsidy to the states which administered the unemployment benefits, 600,000 workers were due to lose benefits and health insurance subsidies in less than two months. The repeated need to extend unemployment and health benefits—caused by the lack of job creation—in effect drained funds that might have otherwise been used for direct job creation by government. If jobs had been created quickly and broadly, hundreds of billions of dollars in unemployment and health benefits spending could have been saved and in turn used for job creation. As justifiable as extended benefits were for those who were the victims of the recession, not its originators, they nonetheless did not create jobs.

In retrospect, the Obama administration's strategy remained still focused on temporarily offsetting the loss of income from lost jobs, and to a lesser extent on stemming the loss of jobs (i.e. 'saving jobs'), rather than being concerned with how to actually create new jobs. This strategic focus was still dominant in the second half of 2009. Tax cuts were still the central element. The subsidies to 'offset and save jobs' were designed simply to buy time for the central tax cut element to 'kick in' after a year at the most, in the hope that the tax cuts would eventually create jobs and eliminate the need for continuing the original subsidies (i.e. unemployment benefits, health coverage benefits, and payments to the states and local governments to prevent more layoffs) after a year.

To sum up, the administration's jobs program in 2009—if one dare call it that—was a set of temporary measures designed to delay job losses, combined with measures to temporarily subsidize consumption from jobs that were lost, all wrapped in a major package of big tax cuts that created few jobs.

Despite a surprising negative shift in various economic indicators in October 2009, the Obama administration decided nonetheless to stick to its previous policies and do nothing more.[14] To enact a second stimulus was a de facto admission that the first stimulus had failed. A second stimulus, it was feared, would feed the growing crescendo of criticism from Republicans and business groups that government spending did not create jobs, that more tax cuts for business were therefore needed, that more free trade and less business regulation was required, and that the deficit should be cut to restore that ephemeral element called 'business confidence.' In other words, the same Republican chant that was sung by conservative and business interests throughout the Herbert Hoover administration from 1930 to 1933.

The Obama administration was already beginning to drift toward a greater relative concern with deficits than with jobs, housing, or providing further needed stimulus. As the chair of the administration's Council of Economic Advisers, Christine Romer, commented in October, "the growing clamor to address the high unemployment rate had to be balanced against the rising tide of red ink."[15]

By the end of October a strange reversal of roles appeared. Instead of a Democratic administration pressing for more direct job creation measures, certain sectors of business were actually proposing more spending stimulus to create jobs. In particular, construction business CEOs pleaded with the administration to introduce a six-year $500 billion infrastructure program, at the heart of which was rebuilding U.S. highway infrastructure. Concerned about the impact of such a highway transportation bill on the deficit, however, the Obama administration—with the concurrence of Congress—instead opted for more subsidies to extend unemployment and health insurance benefits, to provide more subsidized loans to small businesses through the government Small Business Administration, and to redirect the still unused, remaining TARP funds to help smaller community banks.

## 'JOBS FOR MAIN STREET' VERSUS 'HIRE ACT'

Debate and discussion now shifted to Congress on what additional measures might be needed to get the recovery back on track. With even the conservative U-3 unemployment peaking at 10.2% in October, and six workers looking and competing for every one available job, an extension of unemployment benefits was quickly enacted on November 6 which raised the total potential weeks to collect benefits to 99. Had the extension not been made at the time, more than a million workers would have lost unemployment benefits in the month of January 2010 alone.

Meanwhile, debate on other measures continued in November. The Senate proposed extending the First Time Homebuyers' Credit for another five months and added a measure to allow all businesses to deduct from their taxes losses five years back instead of two. The House debated a financial transaction tax. Although such a tax was estimated at the time to produce $150 billion a year, it was quickly and publicly rejected by Treasury Secretary Geithner and House Finance Committee chairman Barney Frank.[16] It promptly died in the House. The House also proposed instituting a payroll tax holiday for employers equal to 3.1%, or half of the employer's 6.2% share of the payroll tax; creating a six-year infrastructure bank; and introducing a new round of aid to state and local governments to forestall layoffs of more public workers which, despite the earlier $787 billion stimulus, was continuing to occur in the public sector. Apparently not all jobs were 'being saved' by the original stimulus. The House bill's various measures amounted to $154 billion, and was called the Jobs for Main Street Act. About half the total cost was projected to come from remaining, still unused TARP funds.

The final version of the House bill provided $53 billion for unemployment and health insurance benefits continuation. Other measures included another $23 billion in aid to states to cover Medicaid cost increases and another $23 billion to states to prevent schoolteachers' layoffs. The rest included $39 billion for long-term spending for transport, and housing and urban development departments. The Congressional Budget Office (CBO) estimated, however, that only $1.7 billion of the $39 billion highway infrastructures spending would take place in fiscal year 2010 ending the following October, 2010.[17]

From the preceding it is clear the Jobs for Main Street Act was simply more of the same of the ARRA, or initial $787 billion stimulus bill, passed in February 2009. The content was no different: subsidies for states, unemployment and health insurance subsidy extensions, and long-term infrastructure spending—neither of which would have much, if any, immediate impact on reducing the 25 million still unemployed. As one commentator accurately remarked at the time in analyzing the bill, "Much of the money in the House bill goes to programs that may stimulate the economy but don't appear to directly put people to work...Even the investment in 'shovel ready' highway and bridge projects may not immediately translate into a reduction of the nation's 10% unemployment rate."[18] Why more of the same would somehow make a difference for the problem of jobs and the economy in general—when three times the spending earlier in the year did not—is a key question that remained unanswered by the bill. Not only was the magnitude of the House bill insufficient, but once again its target or composition failed as well once more. It did nothing to directly create jobs. Nothing for housing and foreclosures. It only put a little more money in the pot to subsidize the states for a few more months, revealing that the original stimulus bill of February 2009 was even deficient so far as state aid was concerned.

Apart from its deficiencies, the House bill was buried by the Senate. The Senate put off considering the House proposals until the following February 2010. It was effectively 'bumped' off the priority list by the Obama health care proposals that were introduced into the Senate in December 2009, and were given top priority by the administration. Much of Senate debate in December was involved with whether to take up the administration's health care proposals. The Senate voted to do so in late December. The jobs debate was therefore put off until 2010.

Another factor entering the picture in December was the debt limit extension. At the end of December the U.S. government was about to exceed its debt ceiling limit of $12.1 trillion. Extended debate was therefore also undertaken by both the House and Senate on whether to raise the limit by another $300 billion, to $12.4 trillion. It eventually passed. The Defense Appropriations bill of $636 billion for 2010, in contrast, was quickly voted up with little debate, with an expected $100 billion in spending for Afghanistan war costs alone. Thus, raising the debt limit and passing record defense and war spending pre-empted action on the jobs bill in the Senate at the close of 2009.

When the Senate finally did take up the House Jobs for Main Street Act in January–February 2010, it gutted virtually all the provisions. The $154 billion House bill was replaced by a mere $17.5 billion bill called the HIRE (Hiring Incentives to Restore Employment) Act. Nearly all the $17.5 billion was composed of measures that further cut taxes for businesses. $13 billion of the $17.5 billion was absorbed by a proposal to exempt businesses from the payroll tax until the end of 2010 if they hired workers who had been unemployed for at least two months. The Senate version also gave first-year write-offs (a tax cut) to small businesses that purchased office equipment up to $250,000. Municipal bond investors were provided with subsidies as well. No TARP money was allocated to pay for any of this. All the still unused TARP funds were returned to the Treasury for future use for financial institution bailouts, as the banks and Treasury Secretary Geithner had advocated.[19] TARP might be used to bail out GM and Chrysler, but apparently not the unemployed.

The Senate's final HIRE Act provisions were exactly what Obama himself proposed in December before the House final vote on its Jobs for Main Street Act: depreciation write-offs for small business and business tax cuts for hiring. What the Senate didn't include were the president's proposal of still further tax cuts for small business—i.e. eliminating capital gains tax for small business altogether. Obama also did not get from the Senate the agreement he sought to pay for it via TARP funds. As noted, that went back to the Treasury to be used for the banks. President Obama signed the bill into law on March 17, 2010.

The year 2009 ended on a continuing negative economic note. At the end of December the GDP numbers for the third quarter were revised down significantly, from an originally reported 3.5% to 2.2%. They would be revised down further eventually to only 1.7%. In the final quarter of 2009 the construction sector declined at a faster rate compared to the previous third quarter. Consumer spending fell to a nearly stagnant 0.4% annual rate, as retail sales for the holiday season—typically higher than preceding months—was lower in December than in November. Meanwhile, government spending at all levels combined actually declined, as state and local government spending fell faster than federal spending grew. The only relative bright spots were an increase in business spending, as rising exports began to stimulate manufacturing. However, this did not result in jobs recovery. Total private sector jobs declined in the fourth quarter by 367,000.[20] Nor did it reflect any recovery in housing, as foreclosures continued to rise by an additional 795,000 in the fourth quarter. For the entire year, the first of Obama's term in office, total foreclosed properties were a record 3,240,867, almost a million more than in 2008.[21]

Given this scenario, it is not surprising that public opinion shifted sharply. As a major NBC News/*Wall Street Journal* poll conducted in December showed, "for the first time, less than half of Americans approved of the job President Barack Obama was doing, marking a steeper first year fall for this president than his recent predecessors."[22] This did not mean the public thought more of Republican counter-proposals put forward in opposition to the president's economic policies over the course of the year. In fact, a mere 5% indicated a very positive view of Republican alternatives.

## THE FEDERAL RESERVE'S 'FREE MONEY SPIGOT'

During the closing months of 2009 the second source of possible economic stimulus—the Federal Reserve Bank—was more or less 'marking time' after its earlier monetary stimulus measures: lowering short-term interest rates to near zero (0.25%) and its massive direct injection of liquidity into the economy from its first 'quantitative easing' program (QE1). The Fed's QE1 amounted to a total direct purchase of $1.725 trillion in bad assets from the banking system—$1.425 trillion in mortgage purchases and another $300 billion buying up 30-year Treasury bonds. That massive purchase, however, did not result in an equivalent increase in the U.S. budget deficit. The Fed's debt is a totally separate set of 'books' and QE1 was made possible by the printing of money, not by borrowing.

The Fed programs were supposed to have a significant positive impact on the housing sector. The massive injection of $1.425 trillion in purchases of mortgage bonds was theoretically supposed to lower mortgage interest rates and stimulate housing demand and buying, and thereby absorb the excess supply of foreclosed homes coming onto the market. But that didn't happen. At year end the Fed grew concerned that its planned 'exit' from purchasing $1.75 trillion bonds might actually have a negative effect on the housing markets, making them worse. The Fed therefore proposed yet another program at the close of 2009. That was to pay banks interest on the loans they had taken out from the Fed at 0.25% cost to them if the banks, after taking out the free money loans, simply re-deposited the loans back with the Fed.

That arrangement created one of the most amazing government subsidies of the Obama first recovery program. It meant the banks could now borrow from the Fed at the ridiculously low rate of 0.25% and then park the money with the Fed, during which the banks would be paid interest by the Fed on their re-deposit. The subsidy amounted to tens of billions of dollars; in fact, an uncalculated sum that has never been fully reported to this date.

## BANKS' LENDING BY THE 'DRIP'

In the president's 2009 inaugural address he made it clear that the 'key' to economic recovery was "to get credit flowing again." That meant loans by banks to businesses, especially small and medium businesses where most of the job creation occurred. The Fed was the central institution to ensure that credit got going again. Its policies and programs are designed to provide incentives to banks to loan to businesses. But despite a total of $9 trillion of liquidity injected from all programs into the banks by the Fed, that credit did not get 'flowing' as planned in 2009. Nor would it in 2010 either. In fact, total loans outstanding at FDIC-insured banks in 2009 fell by –7.4%, the sharpest decline in 67 years. According to the *Wall Street Journal*, "U.S. banks posted last year their sharpest decline in lending since 1942."[23]

Obama's response to this chronic collapse of bank lending throughout 2009 was to propose in his January 2010 State of the Union address a program to provide $30 billion in TARP funds to small businesses. Earlier in December 2009 he had met with heads of both the largest 22 banks and representatives of the 7,400 smaller banks and asked both to increase their lending to small businesses and consumers, but to no avail. The $30 billion proposed program was thus an alternative to the banks' inaction. But once again little came of the idea of using the unspent TARP funds to jump-start bank lending and stimulate the economy.

The banks hoarded the free money given them by the Fed and collected their safe interest while the rest of the economy—small businesses and consumers in particular—thirsted for credit. A year after President Obama declared a priority of 'getting credit flowing again,' nothing of any significant magnitude in terms of loans by banks had yet occurred.

## A SHORT AND SHALLOW RECOVERY: NOVEMBER 2009–JUNE 2010

After barely growing the third quarter of 2009, some recovery began to appear by late November 2009. It was to last only through the first half of 2010—i.e. barely 9 months. It thereafter began to fade in the summer of 2010.

Near zero interest rates and money injections into the banking system well over $9 trillion did not produce the expected bank lending and business investment by small-medium businesses. Similarly, spending increases and tax cuts of more than $1 additional trillion failed to generate investment and job creation by larger corporations necessary for sustained recovery. The 'recovery' therefore dissipated after only 9 months. There is no precedent in U.S. economic history for so weak and limited a recovery, given such a massive fiscal and monetary stimulus. To this day, professional economists have no explanation.

During the short-shallow recovery from November 2009 through June 2010, GDP grew at a consistent 3.8–3.9% in each of the three quarters. However, it was a recovery that did not include jobs, housing, wages and incomes of 110 million workers, or local governments. This was quite unlike recoveries during even the two worst previous recessions, 1973–75 and 1981–82, when housing, employment, incomes, and state and local governments were able to expand in tandem, after a brief lag, to the fiscal and monetary stimulus policies introduced during those earlier recessions.

Table 4.1 compares the first year of recovery, from the end of the recession in June 2009 to June 2010, to the similar first four quarters of recovery after the recessions of 1973–75 and 1981–82. It compares GDP, as well as the three critical areas of the economy—housing, employment, and spending by state and local governments—that constitute the major failure areas of the Obama recovery.

*Table 4.1*   Recovery in first 12 months following end of recession 2009–10 compared to 1975–76 and 1983
(Real percent change from preceding period)

|  | GDP | Housing | Employment | State-local spending |
|---|---|---|---|---|
| (2007–09 recession) |  |  |  |  |
| 3rd qtr. 2009 | 1.7% | 17.8%* | –8.5% | –1.5% |
| 4th qtr. 2009 | 3.8% | –3.8% | –6.0% | –2.9% |
| 1st qtr. 2010 | 3.9% | 22.8%* | 7.2% | –3.9% |
| 2nd qtr.2010 | 3.8% | –27.7% | 1.0% | 0.4% |
| (1981–82 recession) |  |  |  |  |
| 1st qtr. 1983 | 5.1% | –1.3% | 1.5% | 3.2% |
| 2nd qtr.1983 | 9.3% | 22.2% | 14.6% | –0.2% |
| 3rd qtr.1983 | 8.1% | 25.4% | 13.7% | 4.7% |
| 4th qtr.1983 | 8.5% | 39.1% | 9.6% | 5.3% |
| (1973–75 recession) |  |  |  |  |
| 2nd qtr. 1975 | 3.1% | 8.9% | 2.0% | –2.9% |
| 3rd qtr. 1975 | 6.9% | 30.9% | 10.8% | 5.0% |
| 4th qtr. 1975 | 5.3% | 18.7% | 4.5% | 5.2% |
| 1st qtr. 1976 | 9.4% | 47.6% | 15.2% | 4.4% |

* Reflects the first and second expiration dates of the First Time Homebuyers' Credit.

*Sources*: Bureau of Economic Analysis, National Income and Product Accounts, Table 1.1.1, as updated July 31, 2011, for GDP, housing and state-local government spending; and U.S. Department of Labor, Bureau of Labor Statistics, historical 'A' tables for employment.

From the above data it is clear that the best three quarters of the first twelve months of the Obama recovery, June 2009 to June 2010, were a half to two-thirds weaker than the similar period for the two worst prior recessions. Whether measured in terms of GDP, jobs, housing, or local governments, the first year of recovery after June 2009 was clearly the weakest and the most short-lived.

## WHY 'WEAK' AND 'SHORT-LIVED'

The key question, of course, is why were the best 9 months of recovery from the 2007–09 recession in fact so comparatively weak; and why did the economic recovery begin faltering in the summer of 2010 after only nine months? There are at least three immediate answers to this dual question.

First, business fixed investment (i.e. structures, equipment, software) was exceptionally weak. Despite the trillions of dollars of bailouts, hundreds of billions of dollars in tax cuts, and hundreds of billions in federal government spending, the largest corporations simply hoarded their $2 trillion in accumulated cash from bailouts, tax cuts, and from squeezing labor costs through layoffs, shorter hours of work, and reduced wages and benefits. Large corporations thereafter consistently refused to invest their $2 trillion in the U.S. Smaller businesses dependent upon bank loans were frozen out of credit by the banks, and were thus blocked from investing that would have also boosted recovery. Only in one quarter throughout the entire two years, June 2009–June 2011, following the recession was there any respectable increase in business fixed investment—i.e. the second quarter of 2010. Before that, business fixed investment was either negative or averaging in the low single-digit percentage gains. This contrasted with fixed investment during prior recoveries, in which investment averaged 12–22% quarterly gains on average. The difference then is that business did not hoard cash in the earlier recoveries, but invested in the U.S.

A second reason for the weak and short-lived recovery was the chronic lack of job growth. The failure to create jobs this time around—when combined with falling wages and incomes, collapsing home values and retirement accounts for the same, banks' denial of consumer credit to households, and continuing high levels of household prior debt—resulted in a low level of consumption spending after the recent recession. Consumption barely grew by 2% on average each quarter in 2009–10, whereas the recovery of consumption in the 1970s and 1980s ranged between 6% and 7% on average each quarter. Jobs, falling wages and incomes, decline in asset wealth (homes, stocks, pensions), and denial of credit to households together explain the tepid consumption this time around—and further help to explain why this recovery was so weak and short-lived.

A third reason for the weak and short-lived recovery this time is traceable to the dramatically different role played by state and local government spending in the current recovery. Whereas in prior recoveries such spending averaged 4–5% growth per quarter, in the recovery period from the recent recession state and local government spending actually contracted—not grew—every quarter but one by around –3% per quarter on average. This happened despite the massive federal subsidy injections to States and local government—i.e. more than $260 billion in the initial Obama stimulus bill and more thereafter. It appears, in other words, that either states and cities hoarded that cash, like large corporations hoarded theirs, or else their fiscal condition was far worse than publicly reported. Consequently, the $260 billion provided by Obama's first stimulus was insufficient. It was not enough to prevent state and local government spending reductions.

Areas of the economy that did register modest growth from November 2009 to June 2010 were driven by temporary factors. In the fourth quarter of 2009, for example, about two-thirds of the total GDP was from what is called inventory stocking by businesses. Another contributing factor in the fourth quarter was a modest rise in U.S. exports. The rest of the world was recovering much faster than the U.S. economy at the close of 2009, especially China, India, Brazil, and other emerging markets. Their faster growth increased their demand for U.S. exports. More U.S. exports meant an increase in U.S.-based manufacturing activity. Meanwhile, other sectors of the economy contributed little to the overall GDP growth. Government actually contributed a net reduction to GDP, indicating that the Obama stimulus was being largely offset by state and local government spending declines despite the subsidies of the first economic recovery program; and that long-term infrastructure elements of the Obama stimulus were not having much effect either. Apparently the 'shovel-ready' projects the administration talked about in early 2009 couldn't find their shovels.

GDP in the first quarter of 2010 GDP's was again 3.9%, as in the previous quarter. Growth was once again heavily inventory-accumulation based, but with some growth in consumer spending driven by autos and the 'cash for clunkers' program. But housing was again negative and government was a net negative contributor, while exports played less of a role.

The second quarter of 2010 GDP was 3.8%. For the first and only quarter since 2008, it was driven largely by business investment. This was the kind of spending that potentially could, if continued, lead to a sustained recovery. Inventory accumulation still added to growth, and this time even net government spending was a positive contribution to overall growth. The second quarter of 2010 thus appeared to be for the first time the kind of quarter that might lead to sustained economic recovery—that is, if it was continued into subsequent quarters. But it didn't. Business fixed investment collapsed the following third quarter and consumption also retreated. Instead, the third quarter of 2010—the summer months of 2010—saw the economy retract significantly along a number of fronts.

Referencing economic indicators to explain why the recovery was so weak and short-lived provides an immediate explanation. But it doesn't provide a more fundamental long-term explanation as to why consumption, business spending, bank lending, government spending and tax cuts, net exports, etc., were themselves so weak. To say it was insufficient consumption, weak business spending, declining bank lending, etc., only takes us half way to an answer. For a deeper, fundamental understanding of causes for the weak recovery it is necessary to understand the unique character of the current recession—i.e. an 'epic' recession.[24]

Subsequent chapters will provide further explanation of the nature of Epic Recessions and why 'normal' spending and tax policies, lower interest rates, liquidity injections into the banks, etc., do not succeed in generating sustained recoveries in cases of epic recessions such as the present. For the moment, it is sufficient to point out that Epic Recessions are characterized (in their 'Type I' form) by repeated short and weak recoveries followed by short and shallow 'relapses' and even double dips (i.e. relapses that result in short and shallow negative GDP periods). As a first step to understanding this critical 'epic' character of the recent recession, it is necessary at this point to consider the first economic relapse that occurred in the summer of 2010.

## THE FIRST ECONOMIC RELAPSE: SUMMER 2010

What then is an economic 'relapse'? It is not an official double-dip recession. A relapse represents a significant slowdown, loss of momentum, and even reversal or negative shift in one or more major economic sectors. The sectors could be housing and construction, employment, exports, business investment, manufacturing, government spending, or other. A relapse means a growing momentum toward recovery is decidedly halted. A relapse represents a kind of economic threshold, after which momentum and direction of the economy has clearly shifted—in this case toward a slowing economy rather than an expanding one. Relapses need not lead to double dip or recession, but they may. They may also be reversed. Multiple relapses may also occur before a formal double-dip recession occurs. Relapses are warning indicators on the road to potential double dip recessions that may or may not actually take place. Relapses aren't necessarily reflected in clear GDP shifts. The summer of 2010 represented such a 'relapse'—the first of what would prove to be several on the road to double-dip recession.

To say the economy experienced a 'relapse' in the summer (third quarter) of 2010 is to say one or more of the main four segments of the economy—consumption, business investment, government spending, and net exports—in part significantly slowed or actually declined compared to the preceding second quarter of 2010. As it turned out, all the four segments experienced a degree of relapse during summer 2010. Why this happened has much to do with the failures of fiscal and monetary policies introduced in 2009 by the Obama administration, Congress, and the Federal Reserve. In other words, the failure of the Obama fiscal stimulus of 2009, of the Federal Reserve's monetary policies of 2009, as well as the token attempts to shore up those fiscal-monetary policies in late 2009 and early 2010, explain why the relapse of summer 2010 eventually occurred.

Business spending may account for only around 10% of the total economy but its impact is actually much greater. Firstly, business spending—i.e. investment in its various forms—can potentially create jobs, which in turn provides a continuing income stream for households. In contrast, government subsidies—such as that which composed 38% of the Obama $787 billion 2009 stimulus—have a one-shot effect on income. Subsidies can provide an immediate, short-term boost to the economy but then wear off. That is, the impact of subsidies spending is short term. Only job creation can provide a long term, sustained recovery. Subsidy spending can work providing that, once the short term (subsidy) stimulus wears off, business picks up the slack and invests and creates jobs. However, as has been shown, that did not happen. Obama's 2009 stimulus did buy time, about nine to twelve months. But as subsidy spending wore off business spending did not kick in. The result contributed significantly to relapse.

Table 4.2 shows how the three areas of business spending—i.e. spending on structures and buildings, on equipment and software, and on inventories—peaked in the second quarter of 2010 and then dramatically relapsed in the third quarter of 2010.[25]

*Table 4.2*   Business fixed investment
(2nd qtr. 2010 to 3rd qtr. 2010)

| Spending Type | 2nd qtr. 2010 | 3rd qtr. 2010 |
| --- | --- | --- |
| Commercial structures | 19.5% | 2.3% |
| Equipment & software | 23.2% | 14.1% |
| Residential structures | 22.8% | −27.7% |
| Inventories | 25.7% | −27.3% |

*Source*: Bureau of Economic Analysis, U.S. Department of Commerce, National Income and Product Accounts, Table 1, Gross Domestic Product, percent change from preceding period, seasonally adjusted at annual rates.

Data on inventories from Bloomberg.

Not only did business spending fall off in summer 2010, but consumer and government spending declined sharply as well. All 'cylinders' of the economic engine were thus slowing.

Consumer spending represented 70.4% of the economy (in GDP terms). Consumer spending on services account for about three-fourths of that. Consumer services spending slowed from 2.5% in the second quarter 2010 to only 1.6% in the third quarter. Auto sales fell 21% in August 2010, and new home sales fell from an annual rate of 400,000 to a record low of 280,000 in summer 2010. Excluding home mortgages, consumer credit in June–July fell a significant 15%, explaining a lot of the decline in general consumer spending at the time. Consumer spending in general, when adjusted for inflation, was only 1.6% in June and a still lower 1.25% annual rate in July.[26] That compares after prior recessions to a more normal 3% growth in consumer spending in general after the first year following recession.

Business and consumer spending, about 80% of the economy combined, was thus slowly grinding to a halt. The 2009 stimulus subsidy spending was quickly wearing off by summer 2010. And the early 2009 stimulus tax cuts were not kicking in, were not producing any significant business investment.

To make matters worse by summer 2010, in addition to slowing business investment and consumer spending, the government sector of the economy was now also reducing its spending—both at the Federal and the state and local levels—as Table 4.3 shows.

There are only two possible explanations for the government sector's contribution to the relapse of 2010. Either the Obama 2009 stimulus had run out in terms of its subsidies to the states by mid 2010, or the amount of the subsidy and support in the 2009 stimulus was insufficient. If the latter, it meant that states and local governments were cutting spending even faster than the Obama stimulus was being distributed to them. Especially revealing from Table 4.3 is the sharp drop-off in federal government spending on non-defense items in the summer of 2010. Just as the retraction of federal spending began to occur in the third quarter (summer 2010), state and local governments were also contracting their spending from the previous quarter. And all this as both business and consumer spending were slowing sharply at the same time.

*Table 4.3* Government spending
(2nd qtr. 2010 to 3rd qtr. 2010)

| Spending Source | 2nd qtr. 2010 | 3rd qtr. 2010 |
| --- | --- | --- |
| Federal government | 8.8% | 3.2% |
| Defense | 6.0% | 5.7% |
| Non-defense | 14.7% | −1.8% |
| State and local govts. | 0.4% | −0.5% |

*Source*: Bureau of Economic Analysis, U.S. Department of Commerce, National Income and Product Accounts, Table 1, Gross Domestic Product, percent change from preceding period, seasonally adjusted at annual rates.

There were thus hardly any indicators of the economy that were not slowing down, or even turning negative by early summer 2010. Industrial production growth declined by more than half compared to the preceding quarter, to only 0.3% from 0.7%. Even exports were slowing. But nowhere was the relapse more acute than in the strategic areas of jobs, housing, and the financial condition of the states, as Tables 4.4, 4.5 and 4.6 will later illustrate.

## EXPLAINING THE RELAPSE OF 2010

As was noted previously, the $787 billion stimulus from Obama's 2009 first recovery program did not start to have much effect until late November 2009. Most of the stimulus was designed to impact the economy in 2010. Yet the economy went into relapse after the first six months of 2010, when the stimulus was supposed to have had its greatest impact. The causes for the joint business-consumer-government relapse in summer 2010 therefore must have other multiple explanations aside from the main shortcomings of the first recovery program—i.e. insufficient magnitude, poor compositions, and bad timing.

### Business Spending

There are at least three specific explanations why business spending was as weak and intermittent: first, cash hoarding by large corporations; second, decline of bank lending to small business; and third, business focus in general on cost cutting as a primary strategy for profits recovery instead of expansion and sales.

An important reason why the Obama recovery has failed is that key sectors of business—and large corporations in particular—continued to hoard profits and cash from the very beginning of the recovery in June 2009. That meant historically low investment and job creation. Large corporations accumulated a cash hoard of more than $2 trillion by 2011. They had all the necessary financial means to invest and create jobs, but simply didn't. So why did that hoarding happen is the fundamental question?

The excuse made on their behalf is that they have consistently lacked the necessary 'business confidence' to invest and create jobs. But there are explanations other than poor 'business confidence' that are more convincing. One is that large corporations simply had other plans for that historic cash accumulation. Another is that corporations became addicted to the successes of profit gains from easy labor cost-cutting. A third is that small businesses were consistently starved for credit by the banking sector. A fourth is that stagnant household income restrained sales for their products and they weren't about to invest, expand, and create jobs if there was no clear evidence of recovery in consumer spending.

It is a well documented fact, based on various surveys of corporate CEOs, that large corporations had been planning to commit significant percentage of their $2 trillion cash hoard to buy back their stock, to increase dividend payouts, to raise their investment in emerging markets abroad (e.g. China), to use the cash to finance mergers and acquisitions of other companies, or to increase levels of investment in financial instruments. None of these plans translates into investing in jobs in the U.S.

Large corporations' profits growth 2009–10 was derived from cutting costs, labor costs in particular. By reducing their workforce levels, by lowering wages and benefit costs by hiring part time and temporary employees, and by accruing for themselves all the gains of rising productivity, large corporations were able to boost profits to significant levels without having to invest and expand their sales and revenues. Why invest when profits were obtainable so easily at the time by labor cost-cutting so successfully? Why should businesses invest, expand and create jobs to produce goods and services they might not be able to sell given the uncertain growth of consumer spending? So large corporations continued to hoard their cash and profits, or planned to commit them for the alternative purposes noted above.

A separate set of explanations for the low investment and job creation from business at the time has to do with small business, usually defined as those with fewer than 500 employees but especially those with 50 employees or fewer. Like larger corporations, they too did not increase investment and jobs much in the first year following the end of the recession of 2009 and then sharply reduced jobs in the summer of 2010. The reasons, however, differ from the reasons why larger corporations did not invest and expand jobs.

Unlike larger corporations that raise money by issuing corporate bonds and commercial paper, smaller businesses don't have those options as a rule. They depend much more on bank loans, in particular what are called commercial and industrial (C&I) loans and for commercial real estate (CRE) loans if they are business construction firms. Throughout the first half of 2010 banks continued to tighten their lending standards for C&I loans to small businesses.[27]

Throughout 2009 bank lending had consistently declined by 10.5%, and then another 3.25% in the first half of 2010.[28] That lending contraction continued into the summer of 2010. In fact, domestic bank lending contracted every quarter from the end of 2008 through the summer of 2010.[29] By June 2010, C&I loans were down 25% from their pre-recession highs. That 25% represented an annual retraction of almost $400 billion from the economy—an enormous sum diverted from investment that might have occurred and thus otherwise might have created jobs. The problem was severe enough that by July 2010 Fed chairman Bernanke publicly chided the banks to start lending more to small businesses. By late summer the situation had not improved. "Banks have more than $1 trillion in cash reserves sitting idle, according to the latest Fed data."[30] A year of progressive tightening of bank lending since June 2009 contributed significantly to the relapse by the summer of 2010.

A fourth reason for the largely anemic business spending was the lack of consumption growth and therefore lack of demand to purchase business products that might have led to more business spending. Reasons for that lack of consumption are explained as follows.

## Consumer Spending

Just as there are several identifiable explanations for the sharp slowdown in business spending during summer 2010, there are similarly at least five major explanations for the slowing of consumer spending during the summer 2010 relapse: firstly, a sharp decline in household disposable income in general; secondly, a drop-off in available consumer credit to households; thirdly, a rise in food, gasoline and health care costs; fourthly, a surge in the savings rate by the wealthiest 5% of households as the stock market began a major pull-back starting in the spring of 2010; and fifthly, a general decline in consumer confidence. All translated into a relapse of consumer spending in summer 2010 compared to the second quarter.

Since such consumer spending represents roughly 70% of the U.S. economy, it is not surprising it contributed significantly to the first relapse during the third quarter of 2010. Consumers' disposable income, the main source of spending, fell from 5.9% in the second quarter 2010 to 3.3% in the third quarter. By June–July spending was barely at a 1.25% to 1.5% annual rate, which was about half the normal 3% rate average in the 1990s. Credit extended by banks to households also declined sharply. Credit plummeted by 15% in June–July 2010. As was mentioned in the preceding discussion on business spending slowdown, banks lending to households also continued to tighten in the first half of 2010, with the predictable results by summer 2010. Rising prices for food, gasoline, and health care costs in the first half of 2010 also took a toll on consumer spending by the summer of 2010. Finally, much of consumer spending in the first half of 2010 was driven by increases in spending by the wealthiest 5% of households—i.e. those with annual incomes of more than $207,000 at the time. The top 5% represent about 14% of all consumer spending and their spending patterns are highly influenced by the condition of the stock markets since they are the major holders of common stock. In late 2009 and early 2010 the stock markets surged. But by June 2010 they were in retreat. The Dow Jones stock average declined by 10% in the second quarter of 2010 and the S&P stock index by 11.9%. Nearly all of that decline occurred in May and June. Predictably, spending by the wealthiest households retracted by the summer of 2010 as well.[31]

Together, consumer spending and business spending represented approximately 80% of the U.S. economy. And both were clearly slowing by the summer of 2010.

## Government Spending

The business-consumer spending slowdown was, however, actually a triple conjuncture. Government spending slowed as well by summer 2010. The causes here were several: firstly, the corresponding reductions in spending by the states as the 2009 stimulus subsidies ran out in summer 2010; secondly, the completion of the federal government's 2010 census project and the consequent layoff of hundreds of thousands of government workers; and thirdly, the significant delays encountered in the spending of the infrastructure projects called for in the 2009 stimulus package.

The original 2009 stimulus package contained $787 billion in spending and tax-cut provisions. It was supplemented by several minor additional spending-tax measures passed by Congress between February 2009 and August 2010. Those supplements brought the total dollar value of the stimulus to roughly $862 billion.

By summer 2010 almost all the $296 billion in the federal government subsidy programs part of the $862 billion had been spent. Congress eventually had to add another $26 billion by August to continue support for schools and Medicaid programs by the states. Food stamp subsidies were cut to offset some of the other subsidies at that time. This shift in net decline in federal government spending as much of the stimulus ran out is reflected in Table 4.3. It shows the sharp drop-off in non-defense federal spending from 14.7% in the second quarter 2010 to a negative −1.8% in the third quarter.

Given the discontinuance or reduction of significant federal subsidy spending, the States themselves shifted in turn to additional spending cuts. This reduced total government spending (federal plus state-local) in the summer of 2010 further, and contributed to the summer relapse overall.

The federal government's 2010 national Census Project had also begun to wind down over the summer of 2010, with the consequent result of hundreds of thousands of temporary census workers being laid off during the summer months. The hiring of these temp workers, more than 600,000 in early 2010, had artificially and temporarily improved the jobs picture in the early months of 2010, creating a false impression that the jobs market and economy was briefly improving. Commencing in late spring–early summer 2010, their layoffs amounted to more than 100,000 a month. By August all would be gone.[32] This loss of more than half a million jobs with corresponding income in so short a period contributed not only to the reduction in government spending but also to the slowing of consumer spending over the summer.

A third area of explanation for the relapse in government spending in summer 2010 has to do with the infrastructure spending portion of the original February 2009 stimulus package. In an earlier chapter to this book, it was argued that true infrastructure spending in Obama's original 2009 stimulus package was no more than $100 billion. Other accounts, however, estimate the infrastructure portion of the stimulus as $230 billion. If 'infrastructure' is defined as everything else that is not tax cuts ($336 billion) or subsidy spending ($296 billion), then the remaining $230 billion is considered 'infrastructure'. If all $230 billion remaining programs in the stimulus are defined as infrastructure, then by August 2010—almost 18 months after the initial passage of the 2009 original stimulus in February 2009—only $66 billion had been actually paid by the federal government.[33] That means $164 billion of the original 2009 stimulus had not yet impacted the economy as planned by the summer of 2010. The failure of that $164 billion to enter the economy by the summer of 2010 thus contributed in a negative way to the general economic relapse of 2010.

## THE ROOTS OF RELAPSE: JOBS, HOUSING, AND THE STATES

Describing the dimensions and the causes for the slowdown in business, consumer, and government spending in the summer–third quarter of 2010 shows clearly that a relapse did in fact occur in summer 2010. But that still doesn't explain, at a necessary more fundamental level, why that triple juncture in the form of a relapse in business-consumer-government spending occurred at that time.

Why did business reduce its spending further in the third quarter compared to the second quarter? Why did consumer spending also slow? And why did government spending turn negative at that critical, inopportune juncture as well? The deeper understanding of the summer 2010 relapse lay in the three strategic sectors of the economy—jobs, housing, and state and local government finances. All three of these strategic sectors experienced a sharp deterioration beginning in late second quarter of 2010, continuing through the summer and third quarter of 2010. It was the deterioration of jobs, housing, and local government finances that precipitated the pullback in turn of general spending—business, consumer, local government.

Tables 4.4, 4.5 and 4.6 show categories for jobs, housing, and local government that illustrate how all three strategic sectors of the economy experienced broad-based declines during the summer (third quarter) 2010 period.

The important question that remains is how does the deteriorating condition of the three strategic areas—jobs, housing, state-local government finances, translate in turn into the slowing of business, consumer, and government spending in summer 2010 and thus explain the 'relapse' of that period? To put that question another way, what are the important transmission mechanisms by which the three strategic areas—jobs, housing, state and local government—in turn cause a slowing, a relapse, in business, consumer, and government spending and thus in the economy in general?

*Table 4.4*   Jobs relapse
(3rd qtrs. 2010)

| Employment category | June 2010 | September 2010 | Change |
|---|---|---|---|
| Unemployment Rate (U-6) | 16.5% | 17.1% | +0.6% |
| Total Jobless (U-6) | 25,367,000 | 26,361,000 | +994,000 |
| Involuntary part-time employed | 8,631,000 | 9,506,000 | +875,000 |
| Workers not in labor force but want a job | 5,895,000 | 6,202,000 | +307,000 |
| Full-time employed | 112,646,000 | 111,716,000 | −900,000 |

*Source*: Bureau of Labor Statistics, Department of Labor, Employment Situation Report, September 2010, Tables A-1, A-5, A-9, A-15.

*Table 4.5*   Housing-foreclosure relapse
(2nd and 3rd qtrs. 2010)

| Housing category | 2nd qtr. 2010 | 3rd qtr. 2010 | Change |
|---|---|---|---|
| Foreclosures | 895,525 | 930,427 | +34,902 |
| Mortgages 'under water' | 22.5% | 23.2% | +0.7% |
| Housing starts | 549,000 (June) | 519,000 (Oct.) | −30,000 |
| New home sales | 307,000 (June) | 282,000 (Oct.) | −25,000 |
| Existing home sales | 391,000 (July) | 359,000 (Oct.) | −32,000 |
| Home prices | $269,000 | $263,000 | −$6,000 |

*Sources*: RealtyTrac (foreclosures), Zillow (negative equity), U.S. Census Bureau (housing starts, new home sales, home price averages), National Association of Realtors (existing home sales).

*Table 4.6*   States-local government fiscal relapse
(2nd and 3rd qtrs. 2010)

| Category: Finances | 2nd qtr. 2010 | 3rd qtr. 2010 | Change |
|---|---|---|---|
| Spending % change from preceding period | 0.4% | −0.5% | −0.9% |
| Total revenues (states only) | $204.2 billion | $168.1 billion | −$36.1 billion |
| Government employment | 21,177,000 | 20,855,000 | −322,000 |

*Sources*: Bureau of Economic Analysis, Table 1, Gross Domestic Product; U.S. Census Bureau, and Bureau of Labor Statistics.

## THE 'DEBT-INCOME DYNAMIC' TRANSMISSION MECHANISM

The key mechanisms connecting jobs, housing, and state and local government, on the one hand, and consumption, business spending, and government spending, on the other, are income and debt.

Twenty-five million jobless represents a massive decline in income by households. That depresses household consumption and eventually business spending in turn. To offset in part the decline in income due to joblessness, government spends more, and that raises its deficit and therefore government debt. Lack of employment at the same time reduces government 'income'—i.e. tax revenues and an increase in government debt. Decline in consumption reduces business spending and therefore government tax revenues further— once again raising government debt. Government provides more unemployment insurance to offset household income decline, which raises its debt still further. Slow economic growth also causes consumers and business to take on more debt in order to try to maintain levels of consumption and business investment. These are but a few of the many ways in which income and debt interact and exacerbate each other between the three mini-crises areas of jobs, housing, and local government finances. The interactions result in dampening both household spending (consumption) and business spending (investment) which in turn results in the faltering economic recovery. Government's attempt to intervene to offset the stalling recovery proves inadequate, given the deep contraction character of a financially induced recession. Government action to stem the contraction in effect ends up replicating the debt at the business and household level on its (government's) own balance sheet as a result of deep tax-revenue loss and bailouts. Total debt at all levels—i.e. household, business, and government   consequently rises as income at all levels is not able to recover. The entire system becomes increasingly 'systemically fragile.' These are but a few of the many mechanisms by which income and debt interact to cause relapses, and eventually double-dip recessions as well, following 'epic' recessions. The failure of the Obama administration to address the primary factors of income and debt—as reflected in the three strategic areas of jobs, housing, and local government finances—in effect created the conditions for repeated relapses and recessions in the U.S. economy and its inability to generate a sustained economic recovery.

This dynamic of income-debt and how it undermines economic recoveries is associated with all 'epic' recessions, and will be explained further in Chapters 9 and 10.

# 5
# How More is Less of the Same

'The Second Economic Recovery Program (2010)'

Despite the trillions of dollars spent by Congress and the Federal Reserve on bailouts since 2008, by the summer of 2010 the economy had not turned the corner and was in fact getting worse. Jobs were barely growing, foreclosures and bank seizures of homes were rising while home prices were falling once again, and subsidies to the states and local government were running out. Consumers were in retreat—hammered by escalating commodity and oil prices over the spring—and business investment was slowing while large corporations were accumulating a $2 trillion cash hoard and banks were refusing to lend to all but the largest businesses, speculator-traders, and institutional investors.

At this juncture big business organizations launched a public relations counteroffensive to deflect the growing criticism they weren't creating jobs. The PR counteroffensive was launched on several fronts, led by the U.S. Chamber of Commerce and the Business Roundtable—i.e. the two largest and most powerful business organizations.

Major corporate CEOs, like Jeff Immelt of General Electric and Ivan Seidenberg, CEO of Verizon, openly criticized the president in the press. Their message was intended to directly counter growing complaints that business was bailed out at taxpayers' expense and now it was hoarding cash and refusing to create jobs.[1] Their response was: if hiring and job creation was weak it was because of a general 'lack of business confidence.' A second talking point was that President Obama was 'anti-business' and that too was causing a reluctance to invest. A third theme was business confidence was low due to the rising budget deficits and debt. Still another theme was that Obama's direct advisors had no past business experience. He needed to have more 'insiders' at his elbow from the corporate community.

To improve business confidence a major policy shift was needed by the Obama administration—away from more spending and toward more 'business-friendly' alternatives, according to the Roundtable and Chamber. Translated, this meant the Obama administration needed to reduce costly regulations on business. It needed to more aggressively promote policy pushing U.S. manufacturing exports. It had to conclude the Free Trade deals with Korea, Panama, Colombia and to change the tax code for U.S. multinational companies. The Bush tax cuts, scheduled to expire at year-end 2010, must be extended as well. And the recently passed Health Care reform and Financial Regulation Acts created uncertainty and therefore must be amended and clarified. All that was the solution to restoring 'business confidence' and getting business investment flowing again. Jobs would then follow, foreclosures would slow due to rising employment, and state and local government tax revenues would rise and their finances stabilize.

In early July, in a public address in reply to the criticism, Obama announced that his administration would closely consider further policy based on recommendations by the Roundtable and Chamber of Commerce. Obama quickly set up a new Export Promotion Council, to which he appointed the CEOs of Boeing and Xerox as co-chairs, along with 20 other CEOs as members. Having already announced back in April 2009 that he would not seek to change the NAFTA free trade agreement, he further promised to conclude free trade agreements with Panama, Korea, and Colombia. He promised that his administration would also undertake a review of business regulations. Thus by early July the president's new policy emphasis concentrated on a renewed push of exports and manufacturing. This, he argued, was the best way to create jobs and to boost the now faltering economic recovery. As he put it in reply to his business critics at the time, "exports growth leads to job growth and economic growth."[2]

## MANUFACTURING EXPORTS AS A SURROGATE JOBS PROGRAM

Promoting exports was more a political than an economic solution; more a concession to his business critics than a viable economic plan for recovery. The manufacturing sector in the total U.S. economy at the time was, and remains, a relatively small percentage of the total U.S. economy and U.S. labor force. It accounts only for about 12% of total GDP in the U.S. Manufacturing jobs had been, as continue to be, in steep decline for at least two decades as a consequence of free trade policies, job offshoring, technology, and globalization trends. In December 2000 there were 18.3 million wage and salaried manufacturing jobs in the U.S. By December 2010 there were only 11.6 million—out of a total 154 million workforce, or about 7%. From the trough of the recession in June 2009 through September 2010, only 180,000 manufacturing jobs were created—an average of only 15,000 a month.

How manufacturing and exports would create sufficient jobs to somehow dent even slightly the 25 million unemployed, was something Obama and business failed to explain at the time—and still do not explain today.[3] A manufacturing-driven economic recovery, and a manufacturing-focused solution to the jobs crisis, is simply not possible in the U.S., not in 2010 and still not in 2012. The sector is simply not large enough to make a significant difference. Nor are the big U.S. multinational corporations about to retreat from their global expansion of the last half-century and create jobs here in the U.S. instead of abroad, given that 55% of their global profits are now from offshore.

As the president began his shift in July 2010, from fiscal-spending stimulus to a manufacturing-export centric strategy, on another front the U.S. Senate continued to refuse to pass an extension of unemployment benefits that it had been debating for months. By mid July 3.2 million workers who had been receiving unemployment benefits up to May were now without any benefits. The Senate's main concern was that the benefits would add to the current budget deficit. The deficit issue was thus beginning to loom larger in the debates on how to get the economy to recover. Deficits versus jobs were about to become a central issue. For now, it was deficits versus benefits for those without jobs. The unemployment benefits extension was filibustered by Republican Senator Jim Bunning. It wasn't until July 20 that the Democrats were able to muster the minimum necessary 60 votes to break the filibuster and pass the benefits extension. But to do so, it was necessary to reduce the level of benefits from that which the House bill had previously provided, and to strip out the other House-passed proposals to provide extra aid to the states and a $30 billion direct lending proposal to small businesses that the House had also introduced.[4]

## 'STIMULUS LIGHT': STATE AID, INFRASTRUCTURE, AND TAX CUTS AGAIN

Just prior to the August recess the House voted once again on measures to boost the faltering recovery that summer. The measures involved $26 billion more aid to the states. $16 billion of the $26 billion was additional Medicaid subsidy to the states. It was assumed this aid would then free up the states to 'save' 150,000 police and firefighter jobs. Another $10 billion was designated for schools to enable them to once again 'save' 170,000 teaching jobs. The bill was to be paid for by closing oil and gas corporation tax loopholes. This funding source meant it was guaranteed to be rejected by Republicans in both House and Senate. It passed the House, given the Democrats' majority at the time, but predictably got nowhere in the Senate as Congress recessed for August.

Prior to the Labor Day weekend, the administration leaked to the press that it was considering a series of additional policies to further boost the economy. These were smaller measures in terms of their cost and potential economic impact. Included were the still stalled proposal for a $30 billion program to provide direct government loans to small businesses. Also included were additional small business tax breaks, a possible boost to infrastructure spending, and a rumored payroll tax cut. The measures would be financed by some kind of tax increase, and possibly by discontinuing the Bush tax cuts for those earning above $200,000 a year—i.e. a position held by the president up to that point but which he would eventually drop by the end of the year.

On Labor Day, in a speech delivered in Milwaukee, Obama defined the remainder of his initial proposals for a second new economic recovery program. In addition to the manufacturing, exports, and free trade policies announced in July, he called for a $50 billion long-term transport funding program. This was a five-year program—which meant only about $10 billion a year in spending. The bill called for repair of roads, highways, bridges, and waterways that were much needed as the U.S. transportation infrastructure had been deteriorating for years. In addition to the Transport bill, Obama dusted off his election campaign idea for an Infrastructure bank that would finance additional construction apart from transport facilities. Which construction and how much spending was left undefined. The infrastructure bank, moreover, was not strictly a government bank. It was a joint government-private bank funded by both public and private financing, with profits distributed to private investors.

Obama's second recovery program was slowly rolling out piecemeal from July to September, an eclectic combination of proposals. Apart from the export-manufacturing-trade proposals announced in July and the transport-infrastructure bank ideas in early September, the second program also included once again a heavy dose of tax cuts—business tax cuts in particular. The second-program tax proposals included more generous investment tax credits for business, faster depreciation write-offs for business plant and equipment (from the prior 50% now to 100%), and a proposal both to extend and make permanent the business research and development tax credit, even though 74% of the R&D credit already accrued to multinational corporations.[5] Also included was the still unapproved $30 billion in direct government lending to small business. The total package came to $180 billion, with the business tax cuts and subsidies worth approximately $100 billion.

Even if the total $180 billion was passed by Congress, the projected effect on the economy was minimal. It wasn't a serious package of proposals to address the economic 'relapse' of the summer 2010 period. First, the transport measures were nothing new. In fact, just a continuation of past spending that was now stalled as the election approached. At a mere $10 billion a year, even if passed, it would have little net impact on the economy. The Infrastructure bank was even less likely to pass. It never made the final cut in the past and was unlikely to do so now in late 2010. In contrast, the tax cuts Obama proposed in August–September definitely would reappear again after the November midterm elections.

The Business Roundtable in particular applauded the tax-cut measures, with the exception of the loophole closing on multinationals' offshore subsidiaries. Another tax element they disliked was allowing Bush tax cuts for the 2% wealthiest households to expire at year-end 2010 as scheduled. Obama continued to point out that extending the Bush cuts for the wealthiest 2% would cost $700 billion over the next decade, and he still refused to extend the Bush cuts, at least as of September 2010.

Obama's proposal to allow the Bush tax cuts for the top 2% to expire at year-end 2010 provoked immediate opposition, including from many Democrats. His ex-Director of the Management and Budget, Peter Orszag, who left the administration in July to become a director of Citigroup, came out immediately advocating the extension of all the Bush tax cuts, including for the wealthiest. As Orszag bluntly put it, "There is little reason not to extend the tax cuts...including keeping the high-income tax cuts." Orszag had been and continued to remain a strong voice in the Obama administration up to that point in favor of deficit cutting and cutting of Medicare, Medicaid, and Social Security. Nonetheless, he advocated retaining all the Bush tax cuts even though, as he noted, to do so "would expand the deficit by more than $3 trillion over the next decade."[6]

The generally pro-business, tax-heavy character of Obama's proposed second economic recovery program initially announced in August–September 2010 was summed up by *New York Times* columnist Edward Luce as follows: "Mr. Obama's proposals were taken directly out of the handbook of the main pro-business lobbies in Washington and were designed to appeal to mainstream Republicans."[7] As Luce further remarked, "Mr. Orszag undercut two of Mr. Obama's central objectives: ending tax cuts for the wealthy and making them permanent for the middle class."[8]

## A PROGRAM 'WRIT SMALL'

A 'recovery' package consisting largely of tax cuts and amounting to only $180 billion was generally recognized by most economists as a weak and ultimately doomed attempt to shock the economy out of its 'summer 2010 relapse.'

The proposed second economic recovery program shared all the same shortcomings as Obama's first recovery program. It was insufficient in magnitude, poorly composed and targeted, and its long term (timing) focus on infrastructure would not do much for job creation. The second program at this point was simply '2009 Stimulus Writ Small,' with all the limitations of the 2009 stimulus, only even more so. Why a set of recovery proposals that was smaller, and still improperly composed and timed, should have any effect on economic recovery where the larger first program itself failed to have much effect was never explained.

In so far as the three strategic problem areas of the economy were concerned—i.e. jobs, housing, and the fiscal condition of the states and local government—the second recovery program once again essentially bypassed them. Jobs were supposed to be created by stimulating manufacturing exports and by business tax cuts—neither of which had much of a track record for doing so, as described above. There was very little in terms of state and school aid ($26 billion). Somehow that was supposed to 'save' 320,000 public sector jobs (teachers, and the police and fire departments). Yet there were no guarantees how it would do so and no way to effectively verify if it did so. The only other job-related measure was the unemployment benefits extension, which barely passed in July 2010. But unemployment benefits do not create jobs or even 'save' them. Extending unemployment benefits, as worthwhile as it may be in terms of being morally justified, does not constitute a jobs program.

## THE STILL FORGOTTEN HOUSING FORECLOSURES CRISIS

With jobs and state aid programs essentially on hold in the second recovery program proposals, the third strategic area—i.e. housing foreclosures—received even less attention.

To recall, foreclosures were hitting an all-time high of well over 300,000 properties a month in the summer of 2010, and physical seizures of homes by banks were attaining record levels, approaching 100,000 a month.[9] Most foreclosures at mid-year 2010 were the outcome of job losses and not the result of the prior wave of 2007–09 foreclosures driven by 'subprime' borrowers. As the massive oversupply of foreclosed homes hit the housing market it undermined new home construction and sales, which were down 19% on the preceding year. That in turn meant a further collapse in construction industry employment. With new home sales at their lowest level since data were first collected in 1963, more than 120,000 additional construction-related jobs were lost during the summer of 2010, adding to the already 3 million construction sector jobs lost since the housing sector began its decline in late 2006. By the summer of 2010 a mere 5.1% of all private sector jobs were in construction.

Various industry sources predicted foreclosures at summer's end 2010 were on track for another year of more than 3 million homes. As Rick Sharga, vice-president of the main industry research source, RealtyTrac, commented, "We're on track for a record year for homes in foreclosure and repossessions... There is no improvement in the underlying economic condition."[10]

The second dip already underway in the housing market was testimony to the failure of the Obama administration's 2009 HAMP program to assist homeowners facing foreclosure and with 'under water' mortgages. The administration promised in early 2009 that HAMP, the $30 billion mortgage modification part of HASP, would help between 4 million and 6 million homeowners modify their mortgages. By August 2010 fewer than 400,000 had been modified and half of that number modified only temporarily. Of the $30 billion HAMP program specified for mortgage modification assistance, by August 2010 only $321 million had actually been spent.[11]

Much of the remaining $45 billion of the larger $75 billion HASP program was allocated to subsidize banks and mortgage servicers (also banks) to get them to lower mortgage rates to sell foreclosed properties to new homebuyers. But with the ending of the First Time Homebuyers' $8,000 subsidy on April 30, 2010, the housing market quickly went into a relapse once again and home prices resumed their second decline. The demand for foreclosed homes once again collapsed, just as a record number of foreclosures and seizures were coming on the market in summer 2010. Not surprisingly, home prices and sales plummeted in a second 'dip'.

Elizabeth Warren, chairwoman of the Congressional Oversight Panel, and then candidate for the new Consumer Financial Protection Bureau, remarked in Congressional testimony that summer: "Fifteen months into this program [HAMP], for every one family that appears to have made it to a permanent modification that's likely to stabilize that family in that home, 10 more have been moved out through foreclosure...This is a program that's just...too slow. It's too small." Warren added, "In many cases, the servicers [banks] can continue to make more money if the family goes through foreclosure."[12]

The Obama administration's response at the end of summer 2010 to address the worsening situation in the housing market was to reallocate another $2 billion from the remaining TARP funds to state housing agencies 'hardest hit' to create local aid programs for homeowners. Another $1 billion was authorized from the just-passed financial regulation bill to create interest-free government bridge loans for 50,000 homeowners to continue to pay their mortgages. Other minor projects were also begun, such as giving unemployed homeowners temporary assistance for three months in making their payments, or helping homeowners with home equity loans and short sales. But with consistently more than 300,000 foreclosures taking place every month, such programs amounted to again 'too little too late.' It was all just token measures thrown out to appease public opinion and make it appear the administration was in fact doing something significant.

On August 17 Obama held a Housing Summit. All that came out of the meeting of any consequence was yet another small, incremental proposal to focus on 'strategic defaults'—i.e. homeowners whose mortgages were 'under water,' in negative equity, and were now beginning to walk away from their properties. Strategic defaults amounted to yet a third, new wave of foreclosures beginning to emerge. To stem the development, Obama proposed to let investors in mortgage securities identify loans for refinancing that the government would then guarantee (i.e. subsidize). The refinancing required at least a 10% write-down in principal owed. This too proved to have little impact as few investors bothered to follow up on the administration offer.

By September some Democrats running for office in high foreclosure states like Florida and California called on the Obama administration to initiate a national foreclosure moratorium. The Obama administration publicly refused. As top White House advisor David Axelrod declared in a Sunday TV press interview, *Face the Nation*, in early October, "I'm not sure about a national moratorium because there are in fact valid foreclosures that probably should go forward."[13]

The outright refusal by the administration to call a moratorium occurred in the midst of a rapidly emerging, full-blown mortgage scandal involving the big five mortgage servicing banks (i.e. Bank of America, JP Morgan Chase, Ally-GMAC bank, Wells Fargo, Citigroup) that together process more than $6 trillion of the approximately $7 trillion worth of residential mortgages in the U.S.[14] Throughout September evidence had grown indicating the banks were foreclosing on homeowners in a 'rote' and mechanical manner, and with gross disregard for the law and homeowners' rights. It was dubbed the 'robo-signing' scandal, since untrained and low-paid processors were found to have been processing foreclosure papers (i.e. automatically signing off papers to foreclose) with incomplete documentation and with disregard for appropriate procedures in order to process as many foreclosures as possible quickly. In some cases, falsification of data by processors and outright fraud were involved. Some homeowners received foreclosure notices from banks even when their mortgage had been paid off. Others had their homes broken into on bank orders while they still lived there, as part of the physical seizure of their property—again without any notification of any kind beforehand.

This development offered the Obama administration a one of a kind opportunity to really shift its prior approach and now directly assist homeowners in distress. Not only those homeowners facing accelerated foreclosures and seizures, but also the now roughly one in four mortgages 'under water' in the U.S. Instead, it refused to call even a temporary moratorium on foreclosures and it 'punted' the issue of dealing with the 'robo-signing' scandal off to states' attorney generals to address.

Following initial investigations launched in California, Florida, Iowa and North Carolina, on October 13, 49 states' attorneys general (AGs) announced collectively that they were launching a joint investigation into the mortgage 'robo-signing' scandal. GMAC-Ally Financial—the finance arm of GM that received more than $17 billion in direct loans and grants from the federal government during the banking crisis—in early October halted all of its foreclosures processing. Bank of America and JP Morgan Chase followed after several days in the 23 'judicial' states that required court approval of foreclosures. In contrast, the second-largest mortgage servicer—the California-based Wells Fargo—refused to do so. Wells Fargo's refusal soon stiffened Bank of America which, after a brief week or so, announced it was going ahead with its foreclosures after the Obama administration urged banks "to proceed without delay." Edward Demarco, the acting director of the administration's Housing Finance Agency, gave the go-ahead to restart foreclosures. He justified his recommendation on the basis it was only "fair to servicers, mortgage investors...and in the best interest of taxpayers."[15]

The Obama administration's liberal wing howled at the obvious pro-investor and pro-mortgage (bank) servicer position assumed by the administration. Not only had the administration refused to support a national foreclosure moratorium, after the robo-signing scandal broke, but refused to engage in anything but token programs even after its central program, the HAMP modification, had proven a dismal failure. At the end of 2010 a report was issued by Neil Barofsky, the special inspector general for the TARP program, from which the various homeowner programs described above were drawing their funding. Barofsky's report dismissed the administration's HAMP as largely ineffective. It also noted the more recent programs introduced the preceding September 2010 were "also yielding meager results." For example, the program designed to assist homeowners under water on their mortgages had only refinanced a grand total of 15 mortgages by year-end 2010. Only 5,300 unemployed homeowners were participating in that program; only 3,100 were assisted with home equity loan refinancing; and so on.[16]

What the liberal wing of the Democratic Party failed to realize is that from the very beginning of his election campaign Obama was not in favor of rescuing homeowners from foreclosure. His strategy for housing was always to let the foreclosures run their course, and then work closely with the banks and mortgage servicers to get new buyers into the foreclosed homes. This very private sector, market approach to solving the housing-foreclosure crisis did receive strong applause from an expected quarter. As the arch-conservative editorial page of the *Wall Street Journal* cheered the day after the administration gave the green light to banks to again proceed with foreclosures: "Obama is right to resist the foreclosure wails from the political left."[17]

The first two years of Obama's policies and programs directed at the housing and foreclosure crisis in the U.S. can only be described as ineffective, token-funded, and largely market-based efforts favoring mortgage lenders and servicers. It individually, and collectively, failed to aid homeowners facing foreclosure or home owners in deep negative equity. Given the vast dimensions of the crisis, the paltry funds allocated by the Obama administration to programs addressing the housing crisis were not serious by any measure. Contrast the $75 billion HASP—of which the $30 billion HAMP segment was to assist the 11+ million in foreclosure and 16 million homeowners 'under water' on their mortgages—to the massive multi-trillion dollar bailouts provided by the Obama administration to banks, mortgage servicers, and mortgage investors.

## THE BALL IN THE FED'S COURT: QE2

One of the several programs designed to prop up the banks and housing market investors was the Fed's program, Quantitative Easing, or QE. QE involved Fed direct purchases of several trillions of dollars of mortgage and other long-term loans.

Introduced in March 2009 the initial QE1 enabled the banks and investors to sell their mortgages to the Fed often at, or close to, their full original value instead of at their actual depressed market value after the crisis. It was thus clearly a kind of subsidy to the banks and investors. Fed bond-buying was supposed to lower mortgage interest rates, in theory at least. Lower rates would stimulate home sales and halt the collapse of home prices. That would in turn stimulate home construction and construction jobs. That was the theory. Unfortunately, it didn't work that way in the real world.

QE1, its advocates argued, would also theoretically stimulate the rest of the economy in other ways as well. As the argument went, the Fed's buying up of 'bad mortgages' held by banks and investors would remove those toxic assets clogging up the banking system and preventing banks from lending. Buying the mortgages would inject more money by the Fed into the banks, making it easier for them to lend to business in general, which would stimulate investment in turn and consequently jobs as well.

A second round of Quantitative Easing—QE2—was subsequently reintroduced in early November 2010 as part of the second economic recovery program of the administration. It lasted through June 2011. During the eight months another $600 billion in bonds were purchased from banks and investors by the Fed. QE2, like its predecessor QE1, was again promoted as a solution to the deepening housing crisis as well as a way to stimulate the lagging economy.

However, neither QE1 nor QE2 successfully stimulated the housing sector. And the impact of QE on economic recovery in general—like its impact on housing in particular—was minimal at best. But QE1 did contribute to rising commodity prices, consumer goods inflation, and a weakening of household spending as a result. QE, in both its versions, stimulated speculative investing in stocks in the U.S. and in commodities globally. Instead of lending the money received from the Fed buying their bad mortgages at nearly full value, the banks and investors lent the money in large part to hedge funds and other global speculators and investors. The money thus flowed into stock markets globally and pushed up stock prices in the U.S. and worldwide. It also flowed into global commodity markets, driving up commodity prices of all kinds—from oil to grains and other foods, to metals like gold and silver, as well as currencies of other countries from Brazil to Japan. Of course, not all was loaned to speculators. That which wasn't was simply hoarded as cash by the banks and not lent at all, as has been described previously. The banks thus accumulated a record hoard of cash as a result of both QE programs. Bank cash reserves by mid-year 2011 were approximately $1.6 trillion. Not all that can be attributed to the QE programs, but a good deal can. That means most of QE flowed out of the U.S. into global markets, neither benefiting jobs or housing or economic recovery in general in the U.S. Some observers even argue that most of QE2's $600 billion in bond purchases by the Fed ended up offshore in foreign banks.[18]

The effect of QE may not only not have stimulated the economy. It may have had just the opposite, negative impact on the economy. It is not coincidental that the cost of living rose noticeably following the introduction of both versions of QE and the onset of commodity speculation, especially in food grains and oil and energy. That inflation in turn slowed consumer spending in the U.S. and undermined economic recovery.

If QE resulted mostly in boosting stock and commodity prices a strong correlation should appear between the stock-commodity price surges and the introduction of QE1 and QE2. Stock prices should be declining just prior to the introduction of QE and then rise sharply once QE is introduced. Conversely, once the QE programs had run their course, stock prices should decline once again. This pattern in fact does appear between QE1, introduced in March 2009, and the stock and commodity markets booms quickly followed. Similarly QE2, introduced in November 2010, also produced a strong stock market and commodity recovery in 2011. Table 5.1 shows the clear correlation between the introduction of QE and the stock market—with QE1 and QE2 both driving up the New York Stock Exchange's Dow Jones Industrials' Average for common stock values when introduced, and the Dow Jones average falling once again when both the QE programs had concluded. This raises an interesting and important point: is it possible that the stock market cannot sustain itself during an 'epic' recession without a continuing QE-type massive liquidity injection by the Federal Reserve?

From the forgoing it appears that QE policies not only stimulate speculative investing in stocks and commodities (and other financial instruments as well), but by artificially driving up stock and commodity prices, QE programs also consequently boost profits and incomes of investors as a result. Conversely, however, by driving up commodity prices and thus the cost of living, QE also results in reducing the real incomes of non-investing households. It therefore compressed consumption spending by non-investor households, which preceded the economic relapses in both 2010 and 2011 after both QE programs had ended. The contribution of QE1 and QE2 to the decline of real consumer spending in both mid 2010 and mid 2011 and to the economic relapses in both those periods thus cannot be ignored.

*Table 5.1*   Dow Jones Industrials Average and QE1/QE2 correlation[19]

| QE program | Dow low & date | QE intro date | QE conclusion date | Dow high & date |
|---|---|---|---|---|
| QE 1 | 7,062 (February 27, 2009) | March 3, 2009 | April 4, 2010 | 11,204 (April 23, 2010) |
| QE2 | 9,686 (July 2, 2010) | November 4, 2010 | June 30, 2010 | 12,657 (July 8, 2011) |

*Source*: Dow Jones Industrials Average (DJIA) History, online at www.nyse/tv/dow-jones-industrial-average-history-djia.htm.

Despite these effects, QE was touted widely by September–October 2010 as a key economic stimulus policy option. By October the economic relapse of summer 2010 appeared as if it would continue, given the economic data at the time showing deteriorating jobs, foreclosures, and other economic indicators at that time. On November 4, 2010 QE2 was therefore introduced by the Fed, amounting to buying another $600 billion from banks and investors—only four months after QE1 was concluded. Having declined steadily after April 2010 when the Fed concluded purchases under QE1, the stock market rose strongly with the rumor and introduction of QE2.

However, once QE2 had run its course, the market started falling again in summer 2011. The predictable result was the call for yet another 'QE3' by late summer 2011. But that's a topic for Chapter 9 of this book.

Although QE2 was in place by November 2010 as part of the second recovery program, the fiscal side (tax and spending programs) of the second program were not yet finalized. Two new factors now entered the economic recovery program equation: first, the sweeping victory of the Republicans in the midterm Congressional election in early November, dominated by the ideological wing of the party known as the Tea Party. The other major element injected into the policy equation was the report by the Obama-appointed 'Deficit Commission.' These two new elements proved to have a major impact on the direction and content of the second economic recovery program. Under the influence of both the now Republican-Tea Party (hereafter simply 'Teapublicans')-controlled House of Representatives and the Deficit Commission's report, the fiscal elements of Obama's second economic recovery program assumed a final form by year-end 2010.

## TRADING TAX CUTS FOR UNEMPLOYMENT BENEFITS AGAIN

Following the November elections, the administration's steady drift since July toward policies proposed by the Roundtable, Chamber of Commerce, and other key business interest groups accelerated.

Obama immediately announced he would increase his efforts to close a free trade deal with South Korea and traveled to Korea for a Group of 20 nations conference held in Seoul on November 11–12. Within two weeks of the G20 meeting a deal was cut with Korea, the largest free trade agreement since the passage of NAFTA in 1993.

U.S. multinational corporations, the Chamber and Roundtable all applauded the deal but declared it wasn't enough. The administration needed to similarly accelerate pending free trade deals with Colombia, Panama, and resolve the NAFTA trade dispute with Mexico over use of Mexican trucks in the U.S. Breaking with a long-standing union tradition to oppose free trade due to its effects on job loss and wage reduction, two major U.S. unions—the auto workers and the food and commercial workers—fell in line supporting the Korea deal. The AFL-CIO (the American Federation of Labor and Congress of Industrial Organizations) remained conspicuously silent in turn. Obama declared the deal would create 70,000 U.S. jobs—a highly dubious claim. For autos at least, auto industry jobs in the U.S. from November 2010 to August 2011 grew from only 702,000 to 705,000—a gain of a mere 3,000 jobs.[20]

But the biggest and most dramatic shift by the administration immediately after the midterm elections was toward extending the Bush tax cuts 'as is' for another two years. Prior to the November elections, Obama had held firmly to the position that the Bush tax cuts of 2001–04 should expire, as scheduled, on December 31, 2010. If the Bush cuts were allowed to continue for another decade, *the loss to the U.S. budget was projected at almost $4 trillion over the decade*! Readers should keep that $4 trillion figure in mind. It would reappear in 2011 raised by various quarters and political sources as the amount that was needed to reduce the deficit and debt over the coming decade. Extending the Bush cuts for just another two years was equivalent to a revenue loss of between $420 billion and $470 billion, depending on the calculation assumptions.

According to a bipartisan Congressional study released earlier in August 2010 by Congress's Joint Committee on Taxation, allowing the Bush tax cuts to expire for the wealthiest 2% of households meant the wealthiest 2% top bracket tax rates would rise from 33% and 35% to 35% and 39.6%, respectively. Raising the top rates results in a sizeable tax increase for millionaires among the wealthiest 2%. The Bush tax cuts provided them with an extra $100,000 a year in tax savings. That now would be eliminated. For those in the $500,000 to $1 million a year income range, the tax cut hit would mean a much less $17,500 loss in tax savings.[21] Strategic business organizations like the Roundtable, Chamber of Commerce, etc., launched an intensive campaign in the summer of 2010 to extend the Bush tax cuts. Their now enhanced influence within the Obama administration would soon pay off with regard to the Bush tax cuts extension issue.

Although the issue of the Bush tax extensions continued to grow during the run-up to the midterm elections, Congress did not take action during September and then adjourned in October. Following the election, with the huge majority of Republicans—mostly Tea Party radicals—now running the House of Representatives, the Bush tax cut issue came to the fore with a vengeance. Its ascendance all but crowded out the various piecemeal tax cut measures proposed by Obama and the Democrats in September.

The day after the election Obama indicated he was open to compromise with the Republicans. Another day later, on Thursday, he went further and publicly confirmed he was in favor of extending the Bush tax cuts for everyone—richest 2% included—for another two years, thus "putting to a likely end any debate over whether to extend the breaks for high-income families."[22] Instead of bargaining the issue with the new Republican-controlled House—and eventually later agreeing to the extension in exchange for raising tax revenue by closing tax loopholes—the president essentially conceded on the issue of the Bush cuts beforehand. This left him little bargaining leverage for his other measures. This concede-first-then-bargain-after practice would become characteristic of the Obama policy negotiating style throughout the coming (2011) year.

To expedite the passage of the Bush tax cut extension, Obama called for a special 'lame duck' session of Congress beginning November 15 and a 'tax summit' at the White House on November 18. In the interim, he flew to Korea to conclude essentials on the free trade deal noted previously, after a stop in India to close a multi-billion dollar sale of military hardware on behalf of the big defense contractors.

At the request of Republican and Senate leaders the 'tax summit' at the White House scheduled for November 18 was postponed until November 30. Meanwhile, top Obama administration officials stepped-up their campaign of courting business groups. Meeting with a 'CEO Council' of 100 top CEOs in Washington in mid November, Tim Geithner, Larry Summers, Education Secretary, Arne Duncan, and economic advisor Austan Goolsbee of the administration warmly solicited further business input and suggestion concerning future policy. They were told by the CEOs that 'taxes, trade, and regulations' were their main demands and the precondition for releasing their $2 trillion cash hoard to invest and create jobs in the U.S. 'Taxes' in their view included the Bush tax cut extension as well as concessions by the administration on reducing tax rates for multinational corporations' repatriation of offshore profits.

Multinational corporations' offshore operations were sheltering an estimated $1.2 trillion to $1.4 trillion in business profits and cash, according to some estimates. That brought the total corporate cash hoard being held from the economy and from contributing to economic recovery to $3.2 trillion to $3.4 trillion, counting the $2 trillion cash hoarded 'onshore' by large corporations in general and the $1.2 trillion to $1.4 trillion hoarded offshore. Add to that another $1.0 trillion to $1.7 trillion in excess bank reserves hoarded and not lent by banks. In other words, more than $4 trillion—that magical number to watch once again.

Anticipating the release of the Deficit Commission's report, and a day before meeting with Republican Congressional leaders on November 30, Obama announced another concession before bargaining: canceling the scheduled 1.4% pay raise for 2 million federal workers. Like his November 5 signal that he was now in favor of Bush tax cut extension, on November 29 Obama thus further signaled he was willing to cut wages and benefits of workers as a new priority focus on deficit cutting. Two favorite conservative issues— business and investor tax cuts and deficit cuts—were now being embraced and acknowledged as the administration's key policy issues for the coming year, 2011.

A last-ditch effort to at least allow Bush tax cuts to expire for millionaires was also defeated in the Senate in early December. Had it passed, the 'millionaires-only' tax hike would have saved $300 billion by raising taxes on the approximately 315,000 millionaires in the U.S.

By the end of the first week of December Obama proposed offering to Republicans an extension of the Bush tax cuts for two years in exchange for extending unemployment benefits scheduled to expire at year end for millions of workers. The unemployment benefits, however, were limited to only a one-year extension, while the Bush tax cut extension was for two years.

When news of Obama's deal with the Republicans surfaced, including agreement to extend all the Bush tax cuts for an additional two years, it set off a strong reaction from the president's own base and much of his support in Congress. The shocked sentiment was summarized by one Congressman, Jerrold Nadler of New York, who remarked that "The president has not put up much of a fight" and should be "playing chicken with Republicans, not the other way around."[23] Not only the tax cut extensions but an estate tax even more generous than under Bush was in the Obama offer, as was the surprise of a 2% payroll tax cut for workers. The Progressive Change Committee, a grassroots liberal group with 650,000 members, publicly complained that "he telegraphed his willingness to cave from the start by solely talking about compromise."[24]

Obama's defense was that it was the best deal he could get from Republicans and that it "will make a real difference in the pace of job creation and economic growth" in 2011.[25] But the next six months would register a sharp slowdown in GDP growth as well as employment. Following the deal, the president dispatched his vice-president, Joe Biden, to bring the party back in line, especially Democrat members in the House. Biden had done most of the leg-work negotiating the December deal with the Republicans. That negotiating role would be reprised six months later, when in June 2011 he would negotiate another backdoor deal with Republicans to cut the budget deficit by $3 trillion—87% of which would be cuts in social spending. For now, however, Biden warned reluctant Democrats in the House the president's

December agreement with Republicans was a 'done deal' and not subject to change.[26]

To further calm the still angry House Democrats, Obama invited ex-president Bill Clinton to appear with him at a press conference to defend the deal. Clinton obliged, defending the deal in no uncertain terms, while continuing to chastise disaffected Democrats in the House. Attacking his own members in the House as well, Obama called the Democratic House members who complained about the agreement 'sanctimonious' and 'purist.'[27]

The final version of the tax deal cost a total $857 billion. The unemployment benefits share of the $857 billion was $55 billion. The remainder of the package was all tax cuts. The president had thus come full circle: economic recovery now meant only tax cuts; $800 billion worth of cuts—and virtually all business-investor tax cuts. The main fiscal elements of Obama's final second recovery program are given in Table 5.2.

*Table 5.2*   Fiscal elements of the second recovery program

| Item | Brief description | Cost |
| --- | --- | --- |
| Income tax | Bush tax cuts extended two years | $408 billion |
| AMT tax | Ceiling raised for 21 million taxpayers | $137 billion |
| Payroll tax | Reduced 2% for wage and salary incomes | $112 billion |
| Estate tax | First $5 million exemption; 35% tax rate after | $68 billion |
| Business taxes | Tax loopholes extended | $55 billion |
| Unemployment benefits | One-year extension for long term jobless | $55 billion |
| Business investment tax | Faster depreciation and expensing | $22 billion |
| Total | | $857 billion |

A previous tax cut for middle- and working-class households—the $60 billion Make Work Pay tax credit—introduced in 2009 as part of the first economic recovery program was dropped from the second recovery program in order to help pay for the payroll tax cut. So the net tax cut for middle- and working-class households was really only equal to $52 billion—not $112 billion—since more than half of the payroll tax cut was offset by the loss of the Make Work Pay credit.

What the above December tax for unemployment benefits deal represents is that—apart from the Fed's QE2 monetary policy initiative—Obama's final second economic recovery program was essentially a pure tax program. No jobs program. Nothing for housing and foreclosures. Not even anything new for states and local government. This was tax cuts pure and simple, in exchange for continuing unemployment benefits for another 13 months.

Once again, as in 2009 and 2008, it was sold as a jobs and economic recovery stimulus package. Tax cuts were supposed to create jobs. By June 11 only 126,000 more jobs were created, or about 18,000 a month. Over the same period, economic growth (GDP) would fall to a mere 0.7% average for the next six months. The package was referred to in the business press as the 'stealthy stimulus,' meaning stimulus that didn't antagonize those reluctant to spend more to stimulate economic growth. Perhaps it was 'so stealthy' that it didn't exist at all in the first place.

As other economists have noted, many of the elements of the December proposals were a continuation of already existing measures (e.g. Bush tax cuts, alternative minimum tax adjustments, unemployment benefits extensions), so their impact on the economy provided no net gain. Conversely, the elimination of the Make Work Pay credit was a negative. The final 'net' effect of the proposals on the economy was estimated at no more than $70 billion, or about 0.5% of GDP.[28] Offsetting this minimal positive effect were growing job cuts and tax and fee hikes by state and local governments, which the December proposals did not address at all. Falling home prices that would further dampen consumer spending. And rising job losses by state and local government workers as the last vestiges of 2009 subsidies to the states ran out.

The second economic recovery program was ultimately signed into law on December 16, 2010. The day before, the 15th, Obama held a private meeting with 20 top CEOs. Reportedly in this private session, with no reporters or media, he solicited their further recommendations for 2011 and once again asked they spend some of their $2 trillion in cash on investing and job creation in the U.S. That same week the U.S. Chamber of Commerce praised the president as having "done the right thing" and formally invited him to address the group's general meeting of CEOs in January.

On December 22 the new House Teapublican leaders released new rules for passing even more tax cuts and for cutting social security, Medicare and other 'entitlements' in the coming year. With more than $1.1 trillion in tax cuts having been implemented over the course of Obama's first two years, 2009–10, the stage was now set for another policy shift in 2011: from stimulus and spending to fiscal austerity and budget cuts—to be enabled primarily by historic reductions in Medicare, Medicaid, and other government spending programs.

# 6
# Historical Parallels and the 2010 Midterm Elections

'Obama as Franklin Roosevelt or Jimmy Carter?'

History will show that the missed strategic opportunity for Obama was the summer of 2010. As shown in Chapter 4, it was at that time that the economy underwent its first economic relapse. That relapse was the clear signal to Obama and his administration that a juncture had been reached; that the policies associated with his 2009 first economic recovery program were beginning to fail.

It was clear by late summer that the $787 (later $862) billion stimulus was not sufficient in magnitude, composition or timing to generate a sustained economic recovery. By the summer of 2010 more fiscal stimulus was clearly called for, and with a different composition and timing. Not more tax cuts or long-term capital-intensive infrastructure projects, but more immediate job creation, a real response to stopping foreclosures and stimulating the construction-housing sector, and some kind of permanent resolution to the fiscal crisis of local government. But all that would have required a major, structural approach to the crisis that Obama was particularly adverse to in any situation, let alone a midterm Congressional election one. It was simply not in his character or political will to take a bold step and risk aggravating his corporate campaign contributors or confront the Republican 'deficit cutters' in Congress head-on.

Complicating the situation and adding to his, and Congress's, political hesitancy was the passage of the Dodd-Frank financial regulation bill around mid-year that also gave a false sense that financial instability in the banking system was resolved. But the Dodd-Frank bill's passage did not mean Dodd-Frank implementation. The nature of the financial regulation bill passed at mid-year was that it was designed to take another year or two before implementation even began. During that period Dodd-Frank could be—and eventually was—revised and watered down. In its original form it was even questionable whether it would work long term to fundamentally stabilize the banks and financial system. Regardless of its potential effectiveness or lack thereof, the Obama administration's focus on it in the spring–summer of 2010 served as a major diversion from attending to the general economy's faltering recovery.

Obama's summer 2010 similar focus on passage of the Health Care Reform Act also diverted attention from the growing problems in the economy and the need for quick, aggressive economic policy revisions. The Health Care Act itself did little to help the economy—both in the short and long run. Despite costing hundreds of billions over the coming decade, the Obama health care program left a gaping hole in terms of controlling health care costs—costs which had been seriously undermining the federal budget for years by adding hundreds of billions to annual budget deficits as a result of runaway health care inflation. That inflation seriously impacted the costs of Medicare and Medicaid subsidies by the federal government. More than $100 billion in the 2009 stimulus package, and additions in 2010 to the stimulus, were allocated to help the states cover rising Medicaid costs, supplement Medicare, and provide health insurance subsidies for the unemployed. That amounted, in effect, to a transfer from the taxpayer and federal government to the health insurance and health services industries. The great economic failure of the Obama health care act is not that it mandated individual purchase of health care coverage, but that it did little to control future health care costs.

Focusing on health care and financial regulation legislation at mid-year 2010 as the economy was rapidly deteriorating, while no doubt important, did little for economic recovery. The economy at best took a third seat to the former two objectives circa mid-2010, at a time it was about to emerge as the number one issue once again.

At the same time, in late second quarter of 2010, the stock market began once again to decline as economic stability in Europe began to emerge as an issue with the sovereign-bank debt crisis in Greece moving to front stage. European financial instability had a further depressing effect on U.S. bank lending to small business and households, as well as on business confidence (and thus investment plans) in general.

When the relapse of summer 2010 occurred, the response of the Obama administration was typically slow and incremental, as it had been throughout the previous twelve months. As the relapse became clearer by the end of summer 2010 instead of pushing for major further fiscal spending Obama turned the lion's share of the task of rebooting the economy over to Bernanke and the Federal Reserve. Monetary policy was the primary policy option by fall 2010. But monetary policy in its major form at the time—i.e. QE1 and QE2, zero interest rates, Fed auctions, etc.—had little result in generating real economic recovery. Its primary impact was to boost stock and commodities price inflation. That forced the Obama administration to introduce yet another, even more tax-heavy, fiscal response at the end of 2010.

In the July–October 2010 period, facing the midterm elections in just a few months, Obama began retreating from new spending policy initiatives in deference to Republican criticism about deficits and to his own corporate advisors' recommendations. A good example of Obama's reluctance toward more stimulus spending was his response to the 'robo-signing' scandal that hit the housing sector that summer 2010. Hundreds of thousands of homeowners each month were being foreclosed. Foreclosures and home seizures by banks reached their highest rate since the recession began, at more than 300,000 and 100,000 a month respectively. As described in the preceding chapter, this acceleration of foreclosures and home seizures was done mostly illegally, by clerical processors on the banks' staff who paid little attention to the legalities of processing and homeowners' rights. When the crisis broke and reached its peak in late summer 2010, instead of seizing it and making it a major issue Obama essentially 'punted the ball,' to employ a metaphor, to the states' attorneys general to whom it was left to develop their own approaches to try to stop the robo-signing by the big five banks that dominated the mortgage servicing industry.

It was during summer 2010 and the subsequent election period that Obama also effectively allowed the Republicans to take control of the policy agenda. Deficits and the debt rapidly moved forward during the election period as the prime economic issue—not jobs, housing and foreclosures, or the faltering economic recovery. Obama thus backed off from pursuing further aggressive fiscal stimulus just at the key juncture when a more aggressive second fiscal stimulus was desperately needed. This lack of aggressive response was in keeping with Obama's minimalist policy response to the crisis in general from the very beginning of 2009.

As this writer has pointed out in detail in his book *Epic Recession: Prelude to Global Depression*, bailing out the banks but failing to stimulate the rest of the economy results in an extended period of economic stagnation that may go on for years. Short, weak recoveries from the low point of the recession are followed by economic relapses in the form of similar short, shallow downturns. This 'bumping along the bottom,' a kind of economic stagnation, can go on for some time. This is what has been termed a 'Type I' Epic Recession and that's clearly what the U.S. economy was mired in by the summer of 2010.

By applying small, piecemeal solutions to the crisis after mid-year 2010, the Obama administration fell into the Type I Epic Recession policy trap: failing to initially implement a large enough fiscal stimulus in his first economic recovery program in 2009, it followed that initial inadequate stimulus with an even weaker second economic recovery program in late 2010. Moreover, the second recovery program was more of the same in terms of the composition and timing of the stimulus: i.e. too heavy on tax cuts and infrastructure spending that remained that was too long-term and capital-intensive rather than labor-intensive. The only difference in composition between the two recovery programs, 2009 and late 2010, was that the latter contained virtually no subsidy spending except for some additional unemployment benefits extension. What Obama needed to do in 2010 was not retreat to an even weaker, less effective and more tax centric recovery program, but to move more aggressively toward a set of programs focusing on direct job creation by the government, toward homeowner bailouts, and permanent local government financial stabilization. A fundamental reorientation of policy and restructuring of key segments of the U.S. economy was required to recover from the Type I Epic Recession in which the economy was trapped. The lessons of economic history were there, if he or his advisors had bothered to look.

## FDR 1934 VERSUS OBAMA 2010

Contrast the above policy response of Obama in summer–fall 2010 to that of President Franklin D. Roosevelt during another period of midterm elections in summer–fall 1934.

Upon assuming office in March 1933, FDR's first policy priority was, like Obama's, to stabilize the banking system and financial markets in the U.S. In the first 100 days and through the summer of 1933, various legislative initiatives did just that. Other policies stabilized the U.S. dollar and ended the chronic, destabilizing effect up to that point of the U.S. adherence to the gold standard.

Once he had bailed out the banks, FDR's subsequent objective in 1933 was to introduce a series of measures to support prices and promote business profits. In 1933–34 these policies were subsumed under the multi-program initiative called at the time the National Industrial Recovery Act or NIRA. This was a set of programs focusing on business recovery now that the banks were stabilized. That meant business recovery came first. The NIRA did little for workers, consumers, homeowners, or the growing fiscal crises afflicting states and local government. FDR's initial policies, in other words, were quite conservative—and because of that they failed to address the problems of jobs, housing, income decline and growing debt at all levels—consumers, workers, local government.

The NIRA was not the New Deal, as some confuse it to be. It was not even the 'first' New Deal, as sometimes it is called, followed later by the 'true' second New Deal. The NIRA was a series of programs designed to subsidize prices, for farmers and for business in general. There were some early job creation efforts by the government in 1933–34, like the Civilian Conservation Core (CCC) but not much beyond that.

The CCC was a politically clever move by FDR to get the potentially most dangerous volatile social element—i.e. jobless youth—off the streets of the cities that were about to explode, and into the countryside working on rural redevelopment projects. But other FDR public works jobs programs introduced in 1933–34 were cautious and mostly ineffective in terms of creating jobs. Infrastructure jobs were thus not seriously addressed under the NIRA. Nor were homeowners and the housing sector. Construction employment actually fell in 1933 to a level lower than the 'worst' employment year of 1932, and by the end of 1934 construction job levels were still below 1932.[1] Housing and the homeowner were not yet stabilized at all. Nor was the fiscal crisis of the states and local government, many of which already had or would default.

The NIRA, which dominated policy from 1933 through mid 1934, proved a failure in its primary objective of putting the economy on a sustained economic growth path. While it, together with the bank bailouts, put a floor under the further collapse of the economy in 1933–34, it did not result in a sustained economic recovery.

The NIRA produced a relative short, modest recovery. From March through the summer of 1933 the stock market index rose from 63 to 109. Retail and farm prices rose 16% and 48%, respectively, from recession lows. The index of industrial production rose from a recession low point of 56 in March 1933 to 101 in July, as businesses added inventories in expectation of a full 'Roosevelt recovery' in 1933. But wages, income and purchasing power for the average income household did not rise appreciably, and inflation reduced take-home pay further. A recovery built on inventory accumulation and speculation did not last. Following July 1933 the stock market plummeted once again, from the July high of 101 to 71 by November 1933. To put a floor under the still falling workers' incomes, Roosevelt attempted to establish a minimum wage of 30 cents an hour and limit hours of work in a week to 35. It failed. Hourly earnings continued to decline. The recovery may have benefited some business sectors and stock investors, but it did not include recovery for the typical worker.[2]

The economy in early 1934 struggled to regain the losses of the previous year. But production began to fall once again in May 1934. The industrial production index again declined from 86 to 71 by September, erasing all the modest gains of early 1934. Employment fell over the same period as well, from 86 to 78. A mild 'double dip' was clearly underway, or at least a 'relapse.' After four years of falling wages and incomes popular discontent began to rise, as the number of strikes by workers rose in the summer of 1934 to their highest level since 1922. The economy was slowing and discontent rising just as FDR faced his first midterm Congressional election in November 1934.[3]

Despite having initiated a clear pro-business recovery policy with his NIRA, the business community abandoned continuing to support FDR by the summer of 1934. The banks had been bailed out, business had been stabilized (at least the larger companies), but business's attitude nevertheless shifted from conditional support for FDR, as NIRA policies began to fail to generate a sustained recovery in 1933–34. Would FDR deliver a still more pro-business set of programs in the wake of the NIRA failure, in an attempt to regain their support? Or would he now turn to bailing out Main Street as a follow-up to the NIRA? That was the question of the day in the summer of 1934, with the recovery fading or at least stagnating, midterm Congressional elections just a few months away, and support for the NIRA approach rapidly in decline. It was a similar choice facing Obama in the summer of 2010 as well.

The initial responses of FDR and Obama to the crisis in their first 18 months in office were in a number of ways similar: both bailed out the banks as an initial priority. Both provided some fiscal stimulus to the economy. Both stopped the further collapse of employment and created a token number of jobs. Economic indicators improved modestly for a few months, then fell back, then recovered, and fell back again. An initial surge of the stock market followed in both 1933–34 and 2009–10. Neither FDR nor Obama at first did much for bailing out the homeowner and housing industry during the first 18 months. Both counted heavily on the business sector to pick up the slack in the economy after the initial 12–18 months and become the primary driver of economic recovery. In both cases that too failed to happen. As a result, both FDR and Obama experienced a brief, shallow recovery of the economy following the introduction of their initial programs. But the similarities abruptly stop there.

When the economy began to slow once again in the summer of 1934, unlike Obama, FDR did not wait or hesitate to introduce further, even more aggressive programs. He did not wait for the private sector (e.g. business or 'the markets') to lead the economy once it was clear they had intention of doing so. FDR introduced a new stimulus, and one that focused totally on government spending—not on tax cuts. In fact, taxes would be raised to 78% for the top income brackets. FDR did not rely on business tax cuts to create jobs but on government direct job-creation programs. He did not subsidize the banks to coax them to modify mortgages, but introduced programs to rescue homeowners at investors' expense. He did not stand by while workers were attacked by employers, but he strengthened unions as a way to restore consumption. He did not propose to cut retirement and other benefits, but proposed Social Security to enable retirement and the transfer of income to the retired.

In short, it was in the summer of 1934 that the true New Deal was envisioned and defined, composed of social programs targeting direct government job creation, homeowner and housing rescue, further bank reform, and programs to redistribute income to the middle and working classes after the previous decade of the 1920s witnessed a major tax and income shift to the wealthy These programs were undertaken, moreover, in a context of rising budget deficits and debt, in the face of intense business opposition and almost apoplectic Republican criticism at the time.

The programs were Social Security, minimum wage legislation, unionization rights, tax hikes on the richest, employment and infrastructure programs like the Works Progress Administration (WPA), plus various public works programs. The rescue of homeowners by creating the Federal Housing Administration, the Home Owners Loan Corporation, home loan guarantee programs and agencies, and other measures not only prevented further foreclosures but stabilized home prices.

Still visions of programs to come in the months before the 1934 midterm elections, they became major campaign themes of FDR and the Democrats during the elections of 1934. The outcome was predictable: the Democrats continued and deepened their control of both Houses of Congress—which enabled them in turn to implement the New Deal in 1935. In the midterm elections Republicans lost ten more seats in the Senate and ten more in the House. Historians called the FDR midterm election victory 'thunder on the left,' in contrast to Obama's midterm 2010 election defeat perhaps describable as 'rumble on the right.' Following the election, according to another observer, "the new Congress was expected to demand an end of concessions to business and a whole-hearted farmer-labor program for recovery and reform."[4] The real New Deal was being born.

Contrast that strategic shift—economically and politically—by FDR in mid 1934 as the economy slowed from its initial stimulus, to the lack of a similar shift by Obama at a similar critical economic and juncture in 2010.

Unlike FDR, Obama relied on tax cuts for business to create jobs, not tax hikes on business to fund direct job creation! Obama introduced no rescue of homeowners, and housing and home prices continued to fall. States and cities lurched toward fiscal crisis after the first year once subsidies were exhausted under Obama, whereas state finances were stabilized by FDR. FDR expanded retirement security for the elderly and thereby provided a boost to consumption and reduced income inequality. Obama joined with Republicans and corporate interests to reduce Social Security, Medicare, and Medicaid, and allowed income inequality in the U.S., already sharply deteriorating over the previous three decades, to worsen. Obama hesitated where FDR acted. Obama approached the crisis piecemeal, incrementally, with minor measures that had little subsequent effect on economic recovery. Obama was diverted by Republican calls for a focus on deficits and more business tax cuts, whereas FDR ignored those calls and pushed on with promises of even more, greater deficit spending. Obama turned over the major job of economic recovery to the Federal Reserve in 2010, while FDR sidelined the Fed—a favorite policy institution of the banks—and had his Treasury Department take control of monetary policy and direct its influence on the economy.

The sharp contrasts between the two on the eve of their first midterm elections (1934 and 2010) were dramatic. Their policy responses on the eve of midterm elections were almost diametrically different. The outcome politically was also 180 degrees different: FDR swept his midterm electoral contest despite a faltering recovery, while Obama was virtually 'swept away' politically by it. FDR and the Democrats dominated the political agenda after 1934. Obama and the Democrats were dominated by their political opponents, the Republicans, as the latter assumed control of the political and economic policy agenda and process after the 2010 midterm elections. After 1934 the Republicans were effectively 'sidelined.' As FDR drove toward the rescue of Main Street—i.e. the New Deal—Obama shifted toward a focus on deficit cutting targeting social programs, combined with more and more tax cuts for businesses and investors. Deficit cuts and tax cuts thus became the Obama policy centerpiece in 2011, whereas the New Deal social, job, housing, and income transfer programs became the centerpiece for FDR policy.[5]

## FDR 1937 VERSUS OBAMA 2011

In 1929 federal spending as a percentage of GDP was a mere 1.7%. With the introduction of the New Deal in 1935 that spending had risen to 15.6% by 1936.[6] The New Deal after 1934 succeeded, in part, in generating an economic recovery that appeared to be sustainable by 1937. Employment rose sharply from 34.2 million at year-end 1934 to 39.7 million by the end of 1937 and employee compensation rose by 12%.[7] Homeowners were rescued. States' finances stabilized. Business investment and production rose significantly. So did profits and wealthy households' income, even when taxed at up to 78% at the top income brackets starting in 1936. By early 1937 the economy had surpassed its 1929 level. One of the most robust stock market booms in U.S.

economic history occurred between 1935 and 1937. To many it appeared that the Depression was over, especially to business and investor circles and wealthier households who enjoyed the record returns from the stock market boom of the period.

By 1937 political pressure thereafter quickly intensified, particularly in the U.S. Senate, to retreat from the New Deal social programs and government direct job creation policies. The need to reduce government spending to 'balance the budget' emerged as a growing policy concern. Budget balancing prevailed over continuing fiscal and monetary stimulus by mid 1937, both in Congress and within FDR's own administration. The outcome was an about-face in terms of policy. Monetary policy turned sharply contractionary: the Federal Reserve raised interest rates. Fiscal policy also retreated: federal government spending was cut by 10%.

Predictably, the U.S. economy quickly contracted once again between May 1937 and June 1938 and fell back into the depression. GDP declined by −3.4% in 1938, nearly three times that of 1933.[8] Deflation in prices set in once again. Wages fell by 35%. Employment levels fell by 1.4 million and unemployment rose back to 20%. The decline in jobs was particularly severe in manufacturing, transport and public utilities, as business investment plummeted by 33.9% in just one year.[9]

The sharp retreat of the economy in 1937–38 just as it appeared to be on the way to full, sustainable recovery provided another historical parallel pointed out by a growing number of economists in 2010. Would the Obama administration and Congress make the same mistake of 1937–38 by cutting spending in 2011?

## KEYNESIANS DISCOVER ECONOMIC HISTORY

One of the economists who has frequently raised the historical parallels between 1937–38 and 2010–11 is *New York Times* columnist and economist, Paul Krugman. In op-ed pieces entitled 'That '30s Feeling' and '1938 in 2010,' written during the summer of 2010, as well as in more recent summer 2011 op-eds, 'The Lesser Depression' and 'The Mistake of 2010,' Krugman has consistently raised the warning that the Obama administration is now repeating the mistakes of the earlier period, 1937–38, by not expanding economic stimulus. As he noted in June 2011, "economic conditions today… bear a strong resemblance to those in 1937…in important ways we have already repeated the mistake of 1937…So are modern policy makers going to make the same mistake?"[10] Krugman repeatedly warned in 2010 that somehow for Obama, jobs fell off the policy agenda and became replaced by deficit cutting, and therefore "the mistake of 2010 may yet be followed by an even bigger mistake."

Krugman's fundamental point is that Obama's first recovery program's stimulus was insufficient in magnitude. The consequence of that insufficient spending stimulus is the sluggish and inadequate economic recovery. The failure of the stimulus to generate recovery has made it appear that no stimulus can be successful.[11] True enough. But the problem with Obama's economic recovery programs has not just been inadequate magnitude of spending. The problem has also consistently been Obama programs' poor composition and timing: i.e. their top-heavy concentration on tax cuts and their approach to job creation based on business tax cuts first and, to a lesser extent, their focus on infrastructure projects too long-term and capital-intensive. Krugman's critique is therefore only half right. He is right about magnitude. But his critique fails to adequately stress the broader problems of all Obama's stimulus programs over the past three years. By emphasizing the magnitude of spending primarily, Krugman—like all Keynesians—opens himself to easy criticism from conservatives that 'more' spending is not the answer because spending has thus far not produced results. Their telling rebuttal is: 'if spending did not generate recovery in the first place, why should more of it prove successful now'? How much 'more' spending stimulus is needed? And please explain the details how 'more' will prove better, conservatives reply.

In a more recent commentary, Krugman has continued to explore historical parallels between today's continuing economic crisis and the 1930s. In addition to noting parallels between 1937 and 2010, Krugman has also discovered that other critical year, 1931, concluding that "we could be about to replay 1931" if the growing debt crisis in Europe worsens. 1931 was the junctural year when the U.S. economy fell into a true depression as a second major banking collapse in the U.S. and Europe occurred.

The recognition of 1931 as an important threshold year for the 1930s is what this writer has raised in a previous work, *Epic Recession: Prelude to Global Depression*. Late 1931 was when the Epic Recession of 1929–31 transformed into a bona fide depression, in this writer's analysis. It was a second financial crash in 1931 that drove the U.S. and world economy into a true depression. But today, at year-end 2011, we have not yet had 'our 1931,' while on the other hand we have had our '1934' in the events of the fall and pre-election period of 2010, as described earlier. Our '1934' (2010) has thus historically preceded our '1931.' History's sequence of particular events have thus in a sense been reversed today. In contrast, Krugman has recognized 1937 and has raised vaguely the potential importance of 1931. But he has missed 1934 altogether.

Should Obama and Congress intensify their deficit-cutting austerity policies in 2011–12, which appears quite likely, then 2012 will prove a contemporary repeat of '1937.' The sequencing of historical junctures are thus reshuffled today, with '1934' (2010) having already occurred, with '1937' emerging in 2011–12, and with a '1931' possibly coming in 2013 or even before.

Krugman and others have been referring to a 'potential 1931' as a 'Lesser Depression.' In 2009 he and others called a deep recession at the time a 'Great Recession', a term that subsequently stuck with the media and press. But neither he nor other economists employing the term bother to explain what exactly is meant by a Great Recession, other than it was somehow worse than a normal recession and not as severe as a true depression. But that's not an analysis, just an intuitively obvious term. What was the 'great' recession back in 2009 is now giving way to a 'lesser depression,' apparently according to Krugman. 'Lesser' thus presumably lies somewhere between a Great Recession and a true depression.

Such mere categorization is not particularly useful for understanding the fundamental dynamics as to why the current crisis is not yet over, why recovery is still elusive both in the U.S. and globally, and why it appears that it may be getting worse again. There is, in other words, no analysis appended to the terms used by Krugman and others. 'Great' or 'lesser' are just impressionistic.

What Krugman has called a Great Recession this writer has analyzed elsewhere as a Type I Epic Recession. What Krugman now calls a Lesser Depression this writer has described in detail as a Type II Epic Recession. Both types of Epic Recession have been analyzed in depth, and are not just phrases expressing indeterminant adverbs, 'Great' and 'Lesser'.

What parallels between the current crisis, 2007–13, and that of the 1930s, show is that the earlier decade shares undeniable similarities to the present. But what we are seeing today is a repeat of the 1930s, but repeat in a non-linear, reshuffled and muted form.

The sequencing of the 1930s' key juncture years—1931, 1934, 1937—and related events have been reshuffled in the present period. They have been partly muted and, importantly, telescoped in terms of time frame. Today's 2010 was yesterday's 1934. 1937 is now being repeated in 2011 13. And 1931 will likely find its analogue, this writer predicts, in 2013 or very soon after.

By focusing on 1937 first, Krugman has totally missed the true significant of 2010 as the parallel with FDR's 1934. 2010 was 1934—and not 1937. 1937 is happening second in sequence today. Deficit-cutting austerity programs in 2011–12 in the U.S. will hammer the U.S. economy in 2013 and even more so in 2014, as politicians in the 2012 elections year will likely delay the worse cuts for 2013–14. Thus 1937 is not yet here, but likely will be in 2012–13.

Furthermore, if massive deficit-cutting austerity forthcoming in the trillions of dollars in the U.S. is combined with a major banking implosion in the Eurozone, which is increasingly likely, or even in another part of the global economy in 2012–13, the combination of austerity programs and a second global banking crash will all but ensure a transition to a Type II Epic Recession and thereafter descent into a bona fide global depression. The odds are on for such in 2013–14.

If that scenario proves correct, historically the U.S. economy will have essentially 'jumped over' the experience of a New Deal (1935–37) altogether. It will have leaped from a 1934 experience (2010) directly to a 1937–38 deficit-austerity phase and a second Type II Epic Recession stage. A second banking crash will in turn likely trip the Type II Epic Recession into a true depression, and thus a reversion to a '1931.'

In conclusion on the matter of historical parallels, history does not 'simply repeat itself,' but may skip stages and re-mix possible outcomes in timing and content—much like a game of 'liars' dice, slammed on a bar-room countertop, produces different combinations but the numbers of the die are set and cannot change. Events may become truncated and telescoped, skipped and combined, assuming different forms—but within the same essential content trajectory they remain unchanged.

## OBAMA 2010 AS JIMMY CARTER 1978

The midterm 2010 elections suggest a comparison with a more contemporary period, not just 1934. That is, another set of midterm elections more than three decades ago: 1978. Jimmy Carter was president and another economic crisis was lingering. The economic stagnation of the 1970s. Like Obama, Carter also had a majority of Democrats in Congress. The Republicans under Nixon had thoroughly wrecked the U.S. economy by over-stimulating fiscal and monetary policies from 1970 to 1973. Wars and war spending once again placed excessive stress on the economy. Then it was Vietnam. Global economic instability had produced an oil price shock. Inflation was the greater problem, although it soon led to the deepest recession to date at the time, in 1973–75. That compounded into what was called the 'great stagflation' of the 1970s—excess inflation and excess unemployment at the same time.

Carter came into office in January 1977 with a clear mandate—and then proceeded to waste it. His economic policies were timid and incremental, and solved neither the problem of inflation nor chronic unemployment. Carter thereafter was trounced in his first midterm Congressional elections in November 1978, as Obama would be in 2010. It seems that contemporary Democratic presidents inheriting a crisis, even with both Houses of Congress controlled by their party, are incapable of turning an opportune situation into a success.

Carter's failed midterm election produced a predictable response, what today might be called a 'Carter Effect'—a sharp turn to the right by the sitting Democrat president. A shift toward a set of moderate Republican positions on the economy in a futile attempt to placate Republican opposition and achieve some kind of legislative 'wins,' no matter how disappointing in content, to tout for the subsequent general election two years later. Thus Carter turned into a 'Republican Lite' president after 1978—just as Clinton would shift right after 1994 and champion free trade, ending welfare, promoting supply-side business tax cuts, and opening China for U.S. corporate investment. Similarly Obama in 2011 would shift to embracing deficit cutting, reducing Medicare-Medicaid programs, promoting general corporate tax reform, and reducing Social Security benefits.

In terms strictly of economic policy it thus appears that Obama's recent 2010–11 policy shift is more like Carter in 1978 than any other historical parallel—while simultaneously the opposite of FDR's in 1934. And if the direction of public opinion polls in 2011–12 are any indicator, Obama's political future may also prove similar to Carter's in terms of the forthcoming 2012 general elections.

# 7
# Deficit Cutting on the Road to Double Dip

'Economic Recovery Policy in Reverse'

Prior to his official swearing-in as president, in early January 2009 Obama had made it perfectly clear he was intent on cutting the federal deficit, and that this would include reductions in entitlement (Medicare, Medicaid, Social Security) spending. As the *Wall Street Journal* noted on January 8, 2009, "President elect Barack Obama said Wednesday that overhauling social security and Medicare would be a central part of his administration's efforts to contain federal spending."[1]

## OBAMA'S DEFICIT COMMISSION

On February 18, 2010 Obama issued Executive Order 13531 establishing a National Commission on Fiscal Responsibility and Reform (hereafter called the Deficit Commission).[2] The Commission was composed of 18 members: six appointed by the president, six by the House and six by the Senate. Eight were Republicans and the majority of the eight from the extreme-right Tea Party-leaning wing of the House and like-minded Senators. On the Democratic side, at least five were conservative-leaning Democrats—like Baucus and Conrad in the Senate, Spratt in the House, as well as Erskine Bowles, a former chief of staff for Bill Clinton and now a board director for the investment bank, Morgan Stanley. Completing the Obama appointees was former corporate CEO Ann Fudge.

The administration also appointed ultra-conservative, ex-Senator Alan Simpson as co-chair with co-chair Erskine Bowles. In short, the Deficit Commission from the beginning had a strong conservative-leaning composition, especially with regard to its two co-chairs, Simpson and Bowles. *New York Times* columnist, and Nobel Prize-winner in Economics, Paul Krugman, questioned the appointment of Bowles and Simpson as co-chairs, noting that "Erskine Bowles, the Democratic co-chairman, had a very Republican sounding small-government agenda. Meanwhile, Alan Simpson, the Republican co-chairman… described social security as being 'like a milk cow with 310 million tits'."[3] Why the president would appoint such a pair to chair the Commission has often been queried. But it was no accident or oversight.

The Commission created three internal committees: tax policy, mandatory (entitlements) spending, and discretionary spending. The core battleground within the Commission was clearly going to be entitlement spending. While 9 of the 18 Commission members sat on the tax and discretionary spending subcommittees, 15 of the 18 members ensured they were all on the mandatory-entitlements spending subcommittee. The Commission in general was tasked with recommending tax hikes and spending cuts that would result in a balanced budget by 2015. Both within the Commission and outside it, the battle over the next two years would be over how much deficits might be reduced via raising taxes—especially the Bush tax cuts of 2001–04—and how much reduced as a result of spending cuts—especially entitlements. The composition of spending cuts would become another major contentious issue—whether deficit reduction via cuts in entitlement programs such as Medicare and Social Security or in defense and other discretionary programs' spending.

An early indication of the main focus of the Simpson-Bowles Deficit Commission was revealed in June 2010, six months before the Commission was to complete its work. While the Republican appointees refused to consider any tax hikes whatsoever, the Democrats on the "panel suggested spending cuts would likely have to outweigh tax increases," as one business press source reported. In particular, the Obama appointed co-chair, Erskine Bowles, "also emphasized the need to find significant savings in federal health spending and entitlement programs." In short, the consensus focus of the Commission from the outset was on spending cuts and, in particular, cutting Medicare and Medicaid programs. That consensus on cutting entitlements was perhaps best indicated by the attitude at the time expressed by Republican Tea Party radical on the Commission, Paul Ryan. As Ryan commented, in agreement with Bowles, "I was encouraged by the growing consensus around this obvious reality."[4] That reality was the agreed-upon need to especially target Medicare-Medicaid.

## THE 2010 HEALTH CARE ACT, DEFICITS AND THE DEBT

Not long after the establishment of the Deficit Commission, the president's major health care legislation, called the Patient Protection and Affordability Care Act (PPACA), was passed. The greatest shortcoming of the Obama health Affordability Care Act was its failure to fundamentally check rising health care costs, even after the ACA becomes fully effective in 2014. A national health care system—i.e. Medicare for all—would save the U.S. 7% of GDP, or more than $1 trillion a year. That's $10 trillion over a decade! However, that proposal was not even discussed during the consideration of the 2010 Obama ACA. Nor was its distant cousin, the so-called 'public option' that would have reduced costs within the ACA significantly (though not as much as Medicare for all), seriously considered during the Congressional deliberations. The public option would have enabled at least some degree of health care cost control, but it was prematurely pulled off the bargaining table by Obama personally at the beginning of critical Congressional debate and consideration of the Act. That unilateral removal of the public option was done without any concession in return.

Between 2006 and 2010 the prescription drug program—termed the Medicare Modernization Act of Part D of Medicare, passed during the Bush administration in 2003 (implemented in 2006), added between $385 billion and $552 billion (average estimate of $450 billion) to the federal budget deficit.[5] None of Part D coverage for prescription drugs was paid for by a tax increase. It was all financed out of the general budget of the U.S. by means of borrowing. Its total cost of somewhere between $385 billion and $552 billion from 2006 to 2010 was therefore all added to the growing federal debt.

Budget deficits due to escalating health care costs also increasingly impacted Medicare's Part A and Part B programs, hospital and doctor coverage, respectively. Part A and B Medicare costs surged over the decade 2001–10, well above the normal rate of inflation. Medicare Part A and B costs more than doubled over the past decade, from $244 billion in 2001 to $522 billion, or by 114%.[6] That's a simple average of 11% per year, well above the normal annual consumer inflation rate of about 2% per year for the decade. Assuming just half of that 114% was due to excessive health care price-hikes by health care providers—doctors, hospitals, drug companies, etc.—then at minimum uncontrolled health care cost inflation added $120 billion to overall Medicare costs and in turn to the U.S. budget deficit. Medicaid excessive cost increases added another $80 billion perhaps.

## THE REAL CAUSES OF DEFICITS AND THE DEBT

The total U.S. federal government debt between 2000 and 2010 rose by approximately $9 trillion, from $5.6 trillion to $14.8 trillion, according to the Federal Reserve's 'Flow of Funds' reports.[7]

There are basically eight causes of the $9.2 trillion rise in the U.S. federal debt over the past decade: excess inflationary defense and war spending; the Bush tax cuts from 2001 to 2012; the direct Congressional-funded bailouts of banks and corporations following the banking crash of 2008; Bush and Obama's successive fiscal (tax cuts and spending) stimulus packages of 2008–11; price gouging by health insurance companies and health service providers; and simply interest on the debt from all the above. The amounts and calculations for each are summarized in Table 7.1.

The $2.1 trillion in Pentagon and war spending as a contributing factor to the $9 trillion debt run-up over the decade represents just the excessive inflation in defense and 'Contingency Operations' (CO = direct spending on Iraq and Afghanistan) above the normal average consumer price index (CPI) rise of about 2%. War and defense spending rose annually on average 8.2% over the decade. The $2.1 trillion thus represents just that increase in war and defense spending in excess of the 2% average. The figure is also probably conservative, since it does not include additional long-term indirect war costs associated with military construction, department of energy, veterans' benefits, and the like. It also excludes arguable defense costs in the military and counter-insurgency elements of spending by the CIA, the FBI, NASA, the State Department, Foreign Aid, and Homeland Security. Also excluded is 'black' or 'off budget' secret project military weapons development spending that doesn't show up in public budget data. The latter is estimated at around

$50 billion a year. Homeland Security another $40 billion a year. In total, the U.S. spending was around $900 billion to $1 trillion a year on defense and war. The inflation in these costs over the decade would easily increase the $2.1 trillion allocated to the $9 trillion debt run-up by another $300 billion or so.

*Table 7.1*   Seven major causes of $9.2 trillion U.S. debt increase

| Debt contributing factor | Addition to debt | Percentage of $9 trillion debt |
|---|---|---|
| 1. Defense/war spending | $2,100 billion | 22.9% |
| 2. Bush tax cuts 2001–12 and extensions | $3,150 billion | 34.2% |
| 3. Direct bank and other bailouts (TARP, GSEs*) | $900 billion | 9.8% |
| 4. Bush-Obama stimulus packages, 2008–11 (spending and tax cuts) | $1,896 billion | 20.6% |
| 5. Non-funding of Part D prescription drugs plan | $450 billion | 4.9% |
| 6. Excess inflation costs for Medicare-Medicare | $180 billion | 1.9% |
| 7. Lost tax revenue from 18 million unemployed | $255 billion | 2.7% |
| 8. Interest on the $9 trillion | $270 billion | 2.9% |
| | $9,201 billion ($9.2 *trillion*) | |

\* GSEs = government-sponsored enterprises.

*Sources*: (1) Office of Management & Budget historical tables and Bureau of Labor Statistics for CPI change; (2) Center for Budget and Policy Priorities, June 28, 2010, based on Congressional Budget Office and Joint Tax Committee of Congress data; (3) U.S. Treasury, TARP Report; (4) (5), Medicare Trustees Report for 2011, (6) *Wall Street Journal, New York Times*, Economic Policy Institute, Center for Budget and Policy Priorities articles and analyses; (7) Federal Reserve Bank, 'Flow of Funds' Report, July 2011 and author's calculations.

The Bush tax cuts contribution to the total debt includes a basic $1.7 trillion estimate for the Bush era 2001–03 tax cuts from 2001 to 2008, and the Center for Budget and Policy Priorities' estimate of another more than $1 trillion for 2009–10 plus the two-year extensions of the Bush tax cuts agreed to by Congress for 2011 and 2012 costing about $450 billion. These are also conservative estimates, since they don't include major corporate tax cuts enacted in 2004–05 by the Bush administration. Nor do they account for the $1.2 trillion to $1.4 trillion that multinational corporations are hoarding in cash in offshore subsidiaries today to avoid paying the normal 35% tax rate in the U.S. If the latter were included, the tax cuts for corporations and investors would add another $400 billion or so to the Bush tax cuts.

The $900 billion in bank and corporate bailouts refers only to the $700 billion TARP (Troubled Asset Relief Program) passed by Congress in October. It also includes the roughly $200 billion separately passed by Congress to bail out the government mortgage agencies Fannie Mae and Freddie Mac. They too 'went broke' as a result of the financial collapse of the housing sector in 2007–08 and were bailed out in July 2008. It is important to note that this

$900 billion 'direct' bailout does not include the roughly $9 trillion injected into the banks by the Federal Reserve, which was the true source of the bailout of the banks from 2008. The Federal Reserve has a separate set of books that do not add to the U.S. deficit and total debt of the federal government.

Then there are the three main Bush and Obama fiscal stimulus packages in 2008, 2009 and 2010, which together amount to $1.89 trillion in tax cuts and spending that have failed to date to bring about economic recovery. They include the Bush April 2008 stimulus of $168 billion; Obama's February 2009 stimulus of $787 billion and subsequent $84 billion in supplement spending and tax cuts in 2009–10; and Obama's December 2010 package worth another $857 billion, of which a massive $802 billion was tax cuts.

The escalating health care cost—consisting mainly of unfunded Part D of Medicare and the excessive inflation in health care services well above the average national inflation rate—contributed approximately $630 billion to that $9 trillion U.S. debt run-up from 2000 to 2011. Most of that $630 billion was the $450 billion in Congress's failure to fund the Part D prescription drug program, requiring the program be paid totally out of deficit spending. The remaining cost is attributable to the excess inflation for health insurance and services directly impacting Medicare and Medicaid costs.

Another $255 billion is from lost tax revenue due to chronic unemployment for the past three years. Before the recession began in December 2007, there were 7.1 million unemployed. For the three years 2009 through 2011 that number has consistently remained around 24 million. Assuming a median annual earnings of $47,000 for the 18 million, an unemployment period of six months on average, and an average income tax rate for the group of 20%, the total lost for the past three years in federal income tax revenue is $255 billion. And that does not count lost payroll tax or corporate income tax revenue associated with the layoffs.

The final item, interest on the debt is calculated based on a simple assumption of non-compounded interest over the decade, which comes to $270 billion for the $9.2 trillion.

## WHY SOCIAL SECURITY IS NOT A CAUSE OF DEFICITS

It should be noted that Social Security has not been, nor is it today, a fundamental cause of deficits or the debt. Similarly, the fundamental Medicare-Medicaid program is the smallest of the six contributing factors to deficit and debt and, to the extent that it is a contributing factor, that contribution has been due to the government refusing to fund the prescription drug program by providing a tax base, as well as due to the chronic, excessive health care price inflation of the past decade that still continues.

In fact, contrary to conventional impression by the public, Social Security has been subsidizing the U.S. general budget for more than a quarter of a century, since 1986. The Social Security Trust Fund that pays for old age retirement, disability, and spousal benefits has run a surplus for that quarter-century in excess of $2.4 trillion dollars.[8] However, that surplus has been 'borrowed' by the federal government every year and spent as part of the general budget, replaced by the government in the fund with IOUs in the form of special Treasury bonds that cannot be redeemed. In the last decade alone, the annual surplus—i.e. the amount left after payroll taxes are collected and retirement benefits are paid to all eligible recipients—has averaged more than $150 billion a year. That means that in the past decade $1.4 trillion has been 'borrowed' from the Social Security Trust Fund to cover annual general budget deficits of the U.S. government. Another way to say the same thing, those deficits would have been $1.4 trillion more than they in fact were, had there been no $1.4 trillion Social Security surplus over the decade. Social Security has thus been subsidizing the federal deficits, not in fact causing them—as the general misconception maintains and as certain business press sources are fond of reporting in order to create the false impression that Social Security is somehow a major cause of deficits and the debt.

According to Peter Orszag, ex-director of the Office of Management & Budget, "Social Security is not the key fiscal problem facing the nation. Payments to its beneficiaries amount to 5% of the economy now; by 2050 they're projected to rise to about 6 percent."[9]

## SIMPSON-BOWLES AND FINAL COMMISSION REPORT

The Commission was scheduled to release its final report on December 1, 2010. In an unprecedented move, the co-chairs, Simpson-Bowles, released their own 50-page interim report summarizing the details, on November 10, in an attempt to inject the Commission's proposals early in the deficit-cutting debates that were escalating now that the Tea Party Republicans had taken over the House of Representatives a week earlier.[10]

One might expect such a set of deficit reduction-targeting proposals to include all tax increases in addition to spending cuts. But no such logic prevailed in Simpson and Bowles' interim report or the final Commission report. The Commission report included additional, major new tax cuts in top-income tax rates and top corporate tax rate. It proposed a top rate income tax cut from 35% to 23% and a similar corporate income tax-rate cut from 35% to 26%. In addition, the Alternative Minimum Tax benefiting mostly individuals in the $150,000+ per year income bracket was repealed altogether. These tax cuts for the high-income wealthiest households, investors and corporations were to be offset by corresponding big tax hikes on the middle and working classes. The Commission proposed to cut the mortgage interest deduction, replacing it with a flat 12% tax credit, as well as a 15% gasoline tax and limits on the child tax credit. Workers and their employers would also henceforth have to pay taxes on their employer-provided health insurance. Even the lowest-income segment of the working class would have their taxes raised significantly. The earned-income tax credit for the working poor was reduced and for some even ended.

The tax hikes were projected to raise $995 billion—or about one-fourth of the nearly $4 trillion original deficit reduction goal. $3 trillion was therefore all spending cuts. Moreover, as noted, the 'net' $995 billion included hundreds of billions in tax cuts for the wealthiest and for corporations, so the tax hikes on everyone else were well over the $995 billion. Therefore one way to calculate the total is that middle and working classes would be hit with $3 trillion in spending cuts plus around $1.5 trillion to $2 trillion in tax hikes. The Commission report was a decidedly class-based set of proposals, benefiting the wealthy and corporations while making the middle and working classes pay well over 80% of the total cost of deficit reduction.

Government workers were to take an especially large hit under Simpson-Bowles, their jobs reduced by 10% (more than 200,000 layoffs) and the rest hit with a wage freeze for three years. For Social Security, proposals included raising the minimum age to begin receiving Social Security retirement benefits to 69 and lowering annual cost of living adjustments for benefits. On the other hand, the top 15% of wage earners whose wage income exceeded the $106,800 ceiling on which Social Security payroll taxes were paid, would be reduced only by 5%. That meant the top 10% highest paid salary and wages would continue to get a break and not pay payroll tax on more than the $106,800. Federal and military pensions were also reduced, as was subsidization of student loan interest.

Medicare and Medicaid payments to doctors would also be reduced. The savings from Medicare-Medicaid cuts were estimated at around $400 billion—$110 billion of which came from higher costs paid directly out of pocket by individuals for Medicare-Medicaid services, even though half of all Medicare recipients have annual incomes of less than $28,000.

A reduction of $100 billion in defense spending, which today constitutes more than half of all discretionary government spending, was part of the Commission's recommendations as well. It included health benefits to military families as well as base closings and weapons procurement. Head of the Pentagon, Robert Gates, declared that the Commission-proposed $100 billion cuts would have a 'catastrophic' impact on national security. He instead proposed to redirect all $100 billion cuts in defense toward future, so-called 'force modernization'.

Two other interesting features of the Simpson-Bowles summary of the proposals was the 'mix' of spending cuts versus tax revenue increases. It was not the $2 for $1 mix that Simpson-Bowles had indicated early in the Commission's work. It was 75% to 25%. But even that was a ten-year average. In the first two years spending would bear the brunt of the deficit reduction and tax hikes hardly at all. Between 2012 and 2014, for example, the proposal called for $384 billion in spending cuts and only $60 billion in tax revenue increases.[11] That was a 'mix' of 87% spending cuts to only 13% tax hikes. The spending cuts were thus 'front-loaded,' as they say.

The Deficit Commission plan was never voted on as a document or package of proposals by Congress. However, it served as an important 'template' for future deficit cuts throughout 2011, including its target total of $4 trillion in reduction. That $4 trillion would appear in various proposals, from the Tea Party 'right wing' proposals of Congressman Paul Ryan (April 2011) to

Vice-President Joe Biden (June 2011), to groupings of Senators, like the 'Gang of Six', all of whom were staunch supporters of the Simpson-Bowles report (July 2011), to the later 'Supercommittee' of twelve in Congress, and from Obama himself (July 2011 and after). There was thus general consensus among the ruling elites in the U.S. as to how much to reduce the deficit—$4 trillion. The only difference among them was what would be the 'mix' percentage-wise between tax hikes and spending cuts to get to the $4 trillion.

Public opinion polls released after the Simpson-Bowles preliminary report showed a lack of public opinion concurrence with their proposals in several important areas. For one, 70% of respondents disagreed with cutting Medicare and Social Security. Another 60% opposed raising taxes by means of a gas tax or limiting mortgage deductions or lowering corporate taxes.[12]

Once the co-chairs, Simpson and Bowles, decided to break ranks and issue a report before the final release of the Commission's findings on December 1, that move prompted others to release their own budget-cutting proposals.

Sharply contrasting with Simpson-Bowles, an alternate proposal was announced the next day by Representative Jan Schakowsky, Democrat from Illinois, which called for most reduction in cutting defense spending and raising revenue by means of closing tax loopholes for companies that ship jobs offshore.[13] Another proposal was quickly put forward by the Bipartisan Policy Center, sometimes referred to as the 'Rivlin-Domenici' group. Domenici was an ex-senator while Alice Rivlin was a former budget director under Bill Clinton and also a member of the Commission. Most of the Rivlin-Domenici proposals were ignored by Congress, except for the payroll tax cut that was soon included in the final December 2010 $857 billion stimulus package discussed in Chapter 5. Their idea of the government providing Medicare vouchers would also appear later in 2011 in full form in radical Tea Party Representative Paul Ryan's proposal to convert Medicare to a total voucher system.

Obama met with Simpson and Bowles immediately after the release of the official Commission report in early December. The report garnered only 11 of the 18 members' endorsement, so it was not formally sent on to Congress for legislative consideration or vote. In their meeting, the co-chairs urged Obama to move quickly to adopt their proposals. New Teapublicans in Congress were making it perfectly clear, as early as December 2010, that they would shut down the government if necessary and refuse to approve a debt ceiling increase if Obama and the Democrats did not agree to their proposed deep spending-budget cuts. They also made it clear that the budget agreed to earlier in 2010 was 'fair game' for retroactive cuts. Meanwhile, they opposed any form of tax increase, including closing tax loopholes or letting any prior tax cut lapse from law. The deficit-cutting ball was now in Obama's corner at the year end.

The next confrontation over deficit reduction was anticipated to begin with the president's announcement of his 2012 budget in February 2011. However, the real test of wills would come on March 4, 2011, when a stop-gap special funding law to continue to pay the government's bills was set to expire.

Releasing details of his budget so close to the March 4 date in retrospect was a tactical error. It allowed Teapublicans to use the March 4 date as a means of demanding retroactive cuts in the previous year's budget to offset the future 2012 budget year scheduled to begin in October 2011.

Prior to his January State of the Union speech, Obama publicly announced he was considering major changes in Social Security in his 2012 budget proposal. Insiders noted this meant slowing benefits and cost-of-living increases and/or raising the ceiling on the annual income for the payroll tax. Over the preceding decades, wage and salary incomes for the top 15% of households had risen beyond the $106,800 annual ceiling, so that only 84% of all wage-salary earners were covered by the ceiling. Raising the ceiling to $180,000 would cover 90% of all wage-salary earned income, still leaving 10% of the wealthiest wage-salary earners a de facto partial payroll tax avoidance. A third suggestion from the administration floated to the press was to fold state and local government workers into the Social Security system. The hope was to get Republicans to discuss these options. But the latter did not 'bite' at the suggestion. Meanwhile, Obama's Congressional Democratic base reacted negatively to the idea of throwing these concessions on the negotiating table unilaterally. And a coalition of unions, women's and other groups lobbied the White House aggressively to postpone making these offers. Obama backed off and didn't formally propose the items in his February 2012 budget. But the items were now 'on the table' and well-known by the opposition. They would thus become a starting point for negotiations, a minimum level from which further concessions and Social Security cuts would no doubt be demanded.

## OBAMA'S 2012 BUDGET AND DEFICIT PROPOSALS

Where Obama was going was further indicated by his State of the Union address in January 2011. The two main themes were reducing budgets while increasing spending on 'competitiveness.' The 'competitiveness' theme was a cover phrase for tax cuts for exporting companies, lower tax rates on multinational corporations' offshore earnings, expanding free trade deals, and other pro-big business preferences. In addition, Obama put forth the idea of trading tax loopholes in exchange for a major reduction in the corporate tax rate, as part of a major overhaul of the tax code itself. Another major announcement in his state of the union speech was a freeze on 'non-security, discretionary' federal spending for the next five years. That represented an increase from his 2010 State of the Union address in which he called for a three-year freeze. 'Non-security, discretionary' spending also meant defense spending cuts were not on the table. The five-year freeze would reduce the deficit by $400 billion, according to the White House. Business interests were reported as only 'lukewarm' toward the president's State of the Union address ideas—in contrast to their overwhelming support for his recent December 2010 $857 billion stimulus that provided $802 billion in tax cuts.

Obama's budget released on February 14, 2011, included a deficit reduction proposal of $1.1 trillion over the next decade. The cut in defense spending amounted to only $78 billion of the total, about 7% and less than $8 billion a year over the decade, even though defense spending represented half of all discretionary spending. Spending on nuclear weapons development, contained in the energy department budget instead of the defense department, was in contrast increased by $2 billion, as was other 'off defense budget' defense-related spending for veterans, homeland security, military construction projects, and the like. Oil and energy tax loopholes would be closed, raising $46 billion over the decade, and another $33 billion in cuts in 200 various programs. Modest spending increases were proposed in education, clean energy, R&D, and other 'long term' impact items. However, health service spending—i.e. Medicare and Medicaid—cuts were about $20 billion for the coming year, the first such cuts in 30 years. No cuts in Social Security were proposed in the budget, reflecting the sensitivity of both the Democratic forces in Congress and the grassroots base to such cuts. Indeed, it was more than just the base that was opposed to cutting Social Security and Medicare. According to the latest PEW research poll at the time, only 12% of the public favored cuts in spending on Medicare or Social Security.[14]

Republicans in the House and Senate immediately attacked Obama's 2012 budget, and officially put forth their own $61 billion retroactive cuts for the 2011 current-year budget. Democrats in Congress countered with $10 billion. Despite the public differences between the administration and its Republican opponents, reportedly both sides quietly initiated joint exploratory efforts behind the scenes to find some common ground on how to get to the consensus $4 trillion in cuts. As one prescient press commentator remarked,

The White House has already opened back-channel conversations to test Republicans' willingness to negotiate about the soaring costs of Medicare and Medicaid, Social Security's long-range solvency and an income tax code riddled with more than $1 trillion a year worth of loopholes and tax breaks. The Senate Republican leader, Mitch McConnell, all but invited Mr. Obama on Tuesday to start huddling about the issues, and a bipartisan group of senators held a third meeting to write debt-reduction legislation…[15]

## THE DRESS REHEARSAL: CUTTING $38.5 BILLION FROM 2011

As the March 4 initial showdown date approached, Obama requested and received an extension until March 18. That prevented a federal government shutdown—the first of what would prove in 2011 to be several such shutdown threats by Teapublicans. But to get the House Teapublicans to agree to the extension, the administration had to agree to an immediate $4 billion in spending cuts. That easy concession from the Democrats reportedly surprised and encouraged the Republican opposition. It would not be the last of such concessions extracted in exchange for spending cuts. Obama then assigned Vice-President Joe Biden as his chief negotiator to represent him in discussions with both House and Senate Republicans and Democrats, accompanied by Obama's new ex-corporate chief of staff, William Daley.

March 18 came and went and Obama requested another extension to April 8. House Republican leaders once again extracted another $6 billion in immediate, unilateral spending cuts in exchange for agreeing to the extension. However, they only just managed to do so. This time 54 of the Teapublicans in the House voted against the extension, almost up-ending the deal. In the March 18 first extension vote only six Teapublicans voted against granting the extension. The radical, Tea Party right was clearly growing in influence within the House Republican majority.

The April 8 extension, the seventh such extension since the previous October 2010, also meant that a decision on cutting spending retroactively from the 2011 budget was growing close to a second, separate voting to extend the debt ceiling. The deadline for voting to raise the debt ceiling was April 15, at the earliest, and possibly as late as May 3. The two votes were now close to converging—the vote on the 2011 budget cuts and the vote on a debt ceiling increase. This convergence represented a major strategic error by the Democrats. Failing to pass a final 2011 budget on time by October 1, 2010— when they then still controlled both houses of Congress—was about to come home to haunt them as both the budget extension and debt ceiling voting were about to converge. And the closer the convergence, the more House Republican radicals were willing to engage in brinksmanship.

By the end of March the Democrats had moved closer to the Republican position on the 2011 budget retro cuts, agreeing to $20 billion more in spending cuts. The Democrat offer was now $30 billion, reportedly raised in response to the proposal by Obama chief of staff, ex-corporate CEO, William Daley. Daley would later propose another $3 billion concession.[16]

Realizing their growing political leverage, and the soft response by Obama and Democrats, House leader John Boehner now upped his demand for the spending cuts from his original $35 billion to $40 billion. Democrats were at $33 billion, only $2 billion short of Boehner's original position of $35 billion. The compromise deal at this point likely would have been $34 billion. But Vice-President Biden, lead negotiator for the Democrats, in an interview with the press revealed there were 'confidential discussions' underway between himself and Boehner and a deal was close. Once that fact was publicized, the Tea Party base reacted negatively to Boehner's $35 billion target. They thought it was $61 billion and that was the minimum they'd accept. Boehner went back to Biden and demanded more, increasing his minimal acceptable spending cuts from his prior $35 billion now to $40 billion. Once more, inept negotiations on the Democratic side resulted in having to concede more.

After raising his number to $40 billion, Boehner proposed another extension in exchange for yet another $12 billion in immediate cuts in exchange for the delay. This time, however, Obama refused. By April 7 it appeared as if the government might be shut down over a difference of $2 billion or $7 billion between the parties. But this $2–7 billion didn't count the already $10 billion agreed by Democrats in exchange for the two extensions of time limits. Had the Democrats agreed to another $12 billion offer by Boehner for a third extension, it would have amounted to $22 billion in spending cuts just to get extensions. That $22 billion, plus Boehner's $40 billion position, would have just about added up to the $61 billion total demanded by the House Tea Party-driven Republican camp. Boehner would have been the overwhelming winner in the eyes of his Tea Party caucus, in effect getting all they demanded.

At the final hour of negotiations and at the insistence of the Tea Partyers, Boehner and Republicans had attached further onerous provisions to their $40 billion cuts proposal, including cutting Environmental Protection Agency (EPA) rules preventing the EPA from enforcing the Clean Air Act and virtually ending spending on planned parenthood and abortions. Trying to appear previously not directly involved in the negotiations, now Obama called in Biden and Senator Reid to consider. Less than a day remained before the government shutdown and layoffs of more than 800,000 government workers. Obama blinked. Democrats increased their offer to $34.5 billion on April 7. Boehner reduced his to $39 billion. A final agreement hours before the shutdown was reached at $38.5 billion for the remaining six months of the 2011 fiscal year—a mere $1.5 billion from Boehner's position and $3.5 billion more than he had originally proposed at the start of negotiations. Fifty-nine House Teapublicans nonetheless voted against the compromise. The cuts focused primarily on education grants for poor students, family planning, job training, environment, Medicaid, high-speed rail projects, local transportation spending, and similar Democratic programs.

Having won this round so easily and convincingly, it was not surprising that Boehner and Teapublicans in the House would re-enact the same strategy on an increasingly grander scale throughout the remainder of 2011. There was the debt-ceiling-limit milestone to come, the 2012 budget due on October 1, 2011, and still further opportunities to come with the 'Supercommittee' recommendations by year end.

The even more strategic significance of the April 8 budget cut agreement was that it now essentially changed the agenda. No more stimulus spending to rescue the economy, which was now slowing rapidly. From this point the debates would center around how much to cut, how fast, what would be the 'mix' of tax increases versus spending cuts to reduce the deficit, and how much would tax cuts for wealthy investors, households and corporations offset the tax hikes for the middle class. That shift would in turn have disastrous consequences for the economic recovery, now about to enter a second 'relapse' phase in the summer of 2011.

## THE RYAN-TEAPUBLICAN 2012 BUDGET PLAN

As negotiations intensified in the days immediately leading up to April 8, Republicans led by Tea Partyer Paul Ryan, chair of the Budget Commitee in the House, issued their proposals for draconian cuts in future deficits and budgets over the next decade. The Republican budget proposals, officially entitled 'Path to Prosperity' and referred to thereafter as the 'Ryan budget,' called for $5.8 trillion in budget spending cuts over the next decade. The true 'net' budget reduction figure, however, was $4.4 trillion, since the Ryan budget proposed $1.4 trillion in tax cuts, most of which accrued to the wealthy and corporations.[17]

Those tax cuts included making the Bush tax cuts permanent over the next decade until 2021.[18] The Ryan budget also called for reducing the top marginal tax rates for both wealthy individuals and corporations, from current 35% to 25%, as well as further cuts in the estate tax. It also proposed permanent indexing for inflation for the Alternative Minimum Tax, AMT, benefiting households earning $150,000 a year and above—i.e. about the top 10% of all households in the U.S. The top marginal tax cuts for individuals would raise the budget deficit by $700 billion alone. Millionaires would receive yearly tax cuts of $125,000. The Ryan plan proposed no closing of tax loopholes for big oil companies or Wall Street speculators or hedge fund owners. In this regard it was even more draconian than the Simpson-Bowles Deficit Commission's recommendations (which were to become in the months ahead more congruent in many respects with Obama's counter-proposals to the Ryan plan).[19] To help pay for the new tax breaks for the wealthy and corporations, the Ryan plan proposed to 'broaden the tax base'—a phrase which effectively meant making middle- and working-class taxpayers pay a total like amount. Since the plan was touted as 'revenue neutral,' this in effect meant that tax hikes on the 'broader base' were actually more than $1.4 trillion.

The Ryan plan called for a total $5.8 trillion in spending cuts: $1.4 trillion from the repeal of the 2010 Obama health care law, another $800 billion extracted from Medicaid cuts, and a record $1.8 trillion in cuts in non-defense discretionary programs like food stamps, low-income housing, education, and other social programs. And about $1 trillion more in savings from ending U.S. war operations in the Middle East, but with an offsetting $200 billion increase in all other Pentagon spending from current levels. The remaining $1.1 trillion in cuts would come from other mandatory spending and savings from interest on the debt.[20]

The Ryan plan conspicuously left out reference to Social Security, as did the Obama 2012 budget. Ryan's long-term goal was to reduce all discretionary non-defense spending to a mere 2% of GDP, which was less than it was in 1929. But the plan's main target was health care entitlements, including an eventual total dismantling of the Medicare system. By 2022, Medicare was to transform into a 'voucher program' in which government, according to Ryan's proposals, would replace Medicare with a voucher with which to buy private health insurance. In place of Medicare, it would provide a flat $8,000 a year to each eligible senior. The voucher amount after 2022 would increase at less than half the rate of medical cost insurance inflation. In 2022, seniors would pay at least 25% of insurance premiums and more in co-pays, deductibles and other out-of-pocket expenses. That share of a senior's cost of total health would rise thereafter to 68% of all health care costs.[21]

The Ryan plan was thus a program designed to massively subsidize the health insurance companies even more generously than Obama's ACA subsidized private health insurance companies by providing cash subsidies to the 35 million uninsured to buy health insurance coverage. Another difference between Obama's and Ryan's plans was that the latter aimed also at attacking Medicaid even more aggressively than Obama's plan and at repealing the 2010 health care act, which of course the Obama plan did not. Ryan's plan proposed therefore to cut more than $2.2 trillion out of Medicaid and the Obama ACA and more than $1 trillion out of Medicare. That meant more than half of his goal of $5.8 trillion in spending cuts would come from health care for seniors, the poor, the disabled, and children of the working poor.

Meanwhile, as both Obama and Ryan debated over how to cut health care for seniors (Medicare) and the poor (Medicaid), health insurance companies were heading "into a third year of record profits."[22] Neither focused their concern on the root cause of rising health costs busting the budget: namely, price and profit gouging by the health insurance industry and other health care providers.

By proposing to privatize the Medicare program, the Ryan plan was the descendant of the George W. Bush effort to privatize Social Security in 2004–05. Republicans had learned a lesson not to attack Social Security head-on; the new strategy was to come 'through the back door' by attacking the more vulnerable Medicare program. Medicare was composed of three trust funds. Only the Part A trust, the hospital program, was financed from payroll taxes. It was sound, returning a surplus every year. Part B, the doctors fund, was less sound but still carried a surplus for another decade. On the other hand, Part D which covered the prescription drug plan was financed out of general government revenues and all of its costs were added to the deficit and debt. This was the vulnerable Achilles' heel of the Medicare system. So attacking Medicare through Part D was the anteroom and dress rehearsal to a subsequent broader attack later on Social Security per se. If Medicare could be successfully privatized, a strong example might extend thereafter to try to privatize Social Security retirement benefits once again.

A direct response to the Ryan plan was offered by the Congressional Progressive Caucus, called 'The People's Budget.' Citing numerous public polls showing overwhelming public opinion in favor of raising taxes on corporations and the rich, and corresponding scant support for cutting Medicare and Social Security, the People's Budget proposed a total deficit-reduction package of $5.6 trillion—almost exactly equal to that of the Ryan Republican budget. However, it proposed $3.9 trillion in tax revenue increase and spending cuts of $1.7 trillion. It also called for public investment in the amount of $1.7 trillion to create jobs.[23] The People's Budget was largely ignored by both the administration and Congress, not to mention the public media and press that gave it little if any coverage. None of its alternative approaches or proposals were adopted or integrated into either the Obama budget, the Gang of Six senators' attempts to push the Simpson-Bowles proposals, or the Ryan-Teapublican counter-budget.

With the introduction of the Ryan plan the gauntlet was now thrown down by the Teapublicans. The 2011 budget revision fight may have ended on April 8, 2011. But that event was merely the dress rehearsal for much larger similar confrontations to come: the pending debt-ceiling deadline in August and the final deficit-cutting proposals due out in November. Moreover, a pattern was now emerging: Republicans would take it to the brink so long as Obama and the Democrats continued to back off their positions and unilaterally concede. It was the 'ABCs' of hardball negotiations, a game that Republicans and Teapublicans knew well and Democrats either refused to play or, in the case of Obama, had yet to learn.

## TO THE BRINK: DEBT-CEILING DEAL OF AUGUST 2011

The Ryan budget announced on April 5 flushed out President Obama. Heretofore he attempted to operate behind the scenes, allowing his 'frontmen,' Vice President Biden and Senator majority leader, Harry Reid, to handle negotiations directly with the Republican leaders and their ever-assertive and dominating Teapublican base. Obama invited the opposition leaders to the White House on April 14 to his speech on the matter and to discuss the deficits and 2012 budget. The Teapublicans expected to hear major concessions from an apparent concession-ready president. This time they didn't. Obama concluded, offering Vice-President Biden once again to lead the negotiations. The Republicans, and Teapartyers in particular, left the speech furious, calling the Obama speech 'highly partisan'—a strange phrase given their own even more partisan positions of recent weeks. At first they even refused to meet with Biden. They knew well the strength of their bargaining position given that they were willing to push negotiations to the brink once again, now using the debt ceiling as the lever. As of mid April that debt ceiling was $14.294 trillion and the debt level was $14.216 trillion. It was getting close.

The April 14 speech that infuriated Teapublicans appealed conversely to Obama's party base. Simpson-Bowles thought it was 'unfortunate.' The so-called Gang of Six senators reactivated their discussions as a possible means to stake out a more center-role between Ryan-Boehner and Obama. On the other hand, AFL-CIO leadership loved the rhetoric, declaring "the rhetoric of the speech was fabulous."[24] Obama then toured the country, speaking and attempting to drum up public support for his plan. In early May Biden began his negotiations, with the administration announcing it wanted a $4 trillion minimum deficit-reduction deal with Republicans, including cuts in Medicare and Medicaid.

Pressure on a May 31 debt-ceiling deadline was relieved by an April tax revenue level larger than expected. At the same time, Treasury Secretary Tim Geithner indicated that the Treasury could borrow another $299 billion and extend the debt-ceiling limit to early August. Urgency to come to an agreement was consequently delayed, as the Democrat-controlled Senate put off development of its own budget proposal for 2012, in order to allow the Biden negotiations to continue. So long as those negotiations were not finalized, a Senate version incorporating them was not possible.

The Gang of Six in May intensified their efforts in the interim. Their effort stalled by the month's end, however, as one of its Republican conservatives, Tom Coburn of Oklahoma, withdrew from the group after demanding $130 billion more in Medicare cuts as a condition for his continuing to work with the group. By June the only remaining game in town was Biden's negotiations.

Prior to resuming discussions with Biden, the House budget chair, Paul Ryan, declared it would take $2 trillion in spending cuts to permit the debt-ceiling increase through the November 2012 elections. $2 trillion in spending cuts was now the Republican minimum starting point for negotiations. A symbolic House vote rejecting a debt-limit increase resulted in Obama inviting House Republicans as a group to the White House on June 2. Republican leadership thereafter pressed Obama to get directly involved in the negotiations, but the president still deferred to his vice-president, Biden. An anonymous aide to the Biden negotiating group of six Congressman and Senators noted that the first $1 trillion in cuts was easy, the second $1 trillion hard, and anything beyond that required tax increases and more Medicare cuts—thus confirming the target once again was $4 trillion. By the end of June the Biden negotiations broke down over the issue of including tax increases in the total deficit package. The Republicans—House majority leader Eric Cantor and Republican Senator Jon Kyl—walked out. It would be later reported that Biden had offered $2 trillion in spending cuts in exchange for less than $1 trillion in tax loophole closings. Obama quickly entered negotiations at the end of June, holding private meetings with Boehner and Senate Republic leader Mitch McConnell.

That Obama was clearly prepared if necessary to trade more Medicare-Medicaid cuts for some tax loophole closings was indicated by his public statement at the end of June, in which he said: "Before we ask seniors to pay more for healthcare...I think it is only fair to ask an oil company or a private jet owner that has done so well to give up that tax break."[25] He then indicated that July 22 was the de facto deadline to avoid a risk of defaulting if the debt ceiling were not raised by August 2.

With the July 22 deadline to avoid default less than two weeks away, on July 10–11 Obama engaged in direct negotiations with House Speaker John Boehner; first, just the two on the golf course, and later at the White House. Although the talks between the two were considered confidential, reports nevertheless leaked out that Obama offered $200 billion in cuts to Medicare and Medicaid as an initial incentive to get Republicans to agree to $130 billion in tax increases, and then he further indicated there could be even higher cuts he might agree to in exchange for tax hikes. Not only Medicare-Medicaid but now Social Security retirement were all put on the table by the president.[26] However, in addition Obama wanted a 'grand deal' of $4 trillion total cuts in exchange for the big entitlement cuts, plus an agreement of no more debt-ceiling brinksmanship up to the November 2012 elections.

With bigger Medicare-Medicaid, and now Social Security, cuts on the table, House Speaker Boehner was reportedly amenable to considering a 'grand deal' of $4 trillion. But word leaked of the president's eagerness to trade Medicare and now Social Security for a 'grand deal' plus an agreement to get the debt ceiling issue off the table until after the 2012 elections. This set off a firestorm of protest by both the president's Congressional base as well as traditional Democrat interest groups outside Washington.

The administration quickly back-tracked. Presidential Press Secretary Jay Carney publicly announced that the president would not agree to any benefit cuts in Social Security. But he added further that this didn't mean the president "would not place the subject off limits in negotiations to reduce the deficit."[27] Former Democratic Senate staffer Larry O'Donnell, now an MSNBC-TV political talk show host, offered the official administration 'spin' on his July 12 show on the leak about the president's offer to cut Social Security as well as Medicare. O'Donnell argued that "Nothing was ever agreed to by Obama... Nothing's agreed to unless everything is agreed to." And since Boehner did not agree to the $4 trillion, there wasn't really an offer by the administration to cut Social Security and Medicare. It was a clever tactical move by the president, O'Donnell argued, to draw out the Republicans to see if they would ever agree to a 'grand deal' of any kind.

Following the collapse of the 'grand deal' proposal over the weekend of July 9–10, Senate Republican minority leader McConnell proposed a new solution—i.e. an 'escape window' out of which Obama and Republicans might scramble to avoid a debt-ceiling default. McConnell proposed that Congress authorize Obama to raise the debt ceiling and then take responsibility unilaterally for doing so. According to the McConnell proposal, if Obama raised the debt ceiling unilaterally himself, the Republicans would vote against it knowing they could not override a veto by Obama to sustain the ceiling increase. The debt ceiling would be raised and the Republicans could claim they opposed it. Both sides jockeyed back and forth for the remainder of the second week of July over this proposal. The 'escape window' idea was soon pre-empted by other initiatives.

By mid July the respective positions were: the Republicans would agree to $2 trillion in spending cuts but no tax-loophole closing; the Democrats preferred $4 trillion with $1 trillion in loophole closing—for which they were prepared to up the amount of Medicare-Medicaid cuts and even agree to Social Security cuts—but only so long as Republicans agreed to no more brinksmanship on debt-ceiling issues until after November 2012. Between $2 trillion and $2.4 trillion in spending cuts was conveniently about what was needed to get through 2012 without further debt-ceiling extension votes. It's just that the Republicans had to agree if the $2 trillion in spending cuts was agreed to, they in turn would agree not to raise the debt ceiling issue again. The $2 trillion was also approximately what Biden had offered back in June, but with $1 trillion in tax-loophole closings—the latter over which, to recall, Republicans had broken off negotiations at that time. The final issues were thus coming down to $2 trillion in cuts in exchange for loophole closings and/ or no more debt-ceiling brinksmanship up to the 2012 elections.

Over the weekend of July 16–17, McConnell and Democratic Senate leader Harry Reid held intensive negotiations between themselves. On Sunday, July 17, the Reuters news agency announced that "Reid wants up to $1.5 trillion in mandatory spending cuts." This signaled that Obama and the administration were about to agree to a spending cuts-only deal worth between $1.5 trillion and the $2 trillion minimum demanded by the Republican side. There was no mention of accompanying tax increases or loophole closings. The Democrats had caved in once again to the Republican position. The only unknown elements at this point were whether the Republicans would agree to not re-raising the debt-ceiling extension issue until after 2012, and whether defense would be included in the spending cuts.

## MORE RADICAL PROPOSALS EMERGE

While Reid and McConnell were slouching reluctantly toward some kind of $2 trillion spending-cut deal, other forces were in motion and increasing the pressure to cut some kind of deal. The July 22 date passed and only one weekend remained to come to an agreement before the August 2 true debt-ceiling deadline. As McConnell and Reid were working out their deal, two sets of deficit-cutting proposals even more draconian than the Ryan plan emerged in the public view: one from the House and another from the Senate.

Both made the pending $2 trillion spending-cut deal appear benign and even generous.

The independent Senate package announced on July 20 was the brainchild of the Gang of Six senators (i.e. Simpson-Bowles retread advocates), who had been quietly restructuring their proposals since June. It called for reducing deficits by $3.7 trillion over ten years. In terms of spending cuts, however, it was really $4.2 trillion, since it included $1.5 trillion in tax cuts and $1 trillion in offsetting additional middle-class tax increases. The $1.5 trillion in tax cuts was composed of reductions in both the top tax rate for individuals and for corporations, from the current 35% to 23–29%. It also abolished the Alternative Minimum Tax for upper-households altogether. The additional tax revenue derived mostly from reducing homeowners' mortgage deductions, health insurance tax credits, and other consumer tax credits—i.e. mostly middle-class tax measures. Another $500 billion over the decade would be taken out of Medicare and health care spending. Particularly serious was a proposal for the immediate reduction of $500 billion in spending—a major 'front-loaded' spending reduction.[28] This was the Simpson-Bowles plan with a kick. In fact, the two co-chairs, a day before the Gang of Six's release of the proposal, in a public statement urged "Pray for the Gang of Six."

A second, far more draconian proposal announced on July 20 was offered by the House Teapublicans. It was a legislative proposal that was passed by the House and was called the 'Cut, Cap and Balance Act.' It proposed to cut federal budget back to the level it was in 1966. That amounted to a 25% across-the-board cut in everything in the federal budget—including defense, Social Security, Medicare, and all the rest. Now 24% of GDP, federal spending would be 'capped' thereafter at 18% of GDP and the budget balanced. That was an immediate 35% spending cut of about $1.2 trillion. Moreover, any future tax increases required a two-thirds vote in both the House and the Senate.

If the Gang of Six proposal meant returning the economy to the deep recession level of 2008–09, then the House Teapublican 'Cut, Cap and Balance' ensured the economy would be thrust far deeper into a depression. A 6% cut with capping at 18% of GDP represented a –$1.8 trillion reduction in GDP, or in percentage terms an equivalent –12% drop in GDP. That was twice as severe as the Gang of Six proposals and equal to depression-level GDP declines not seen since the 1930s.

At this point business interests both in the U.S. and abroad intensified their pressure on the parties to settle, in particular on the recalcitrant House radicals. Now that there were no proposed tax hikes, the latter's position was decidedly weakened. The normally ultra-conservative U.S. Chamber of Commerce pushed for a settlement. The Federal Reserve chairman, Bernanke, warned of the consequences of no settlement. The rating agencies Standard & Poor's and Moody's Inc. warned of consequences of default and a downgrade on government securities. Global capitalist institutions like the International Monetary Fund issued warnings, as did European central banks. On July 28 the stock markets gyrated globally; the U.S. market experiencing its worst day in two months, its worst weekly run in a year, falling to a level not seen since 2008.

By July 27, less than a week before the August 2 deadline, Boehner and Reid had closed the gap. Both called for non-defense, discretionary spending cuts of between $740 billion and $751 billion, and additional mandatory spending cuts of $20–41 billion. Both were willing to increase the debt ceiling by $2–2.7 trillion—thus putting off subsequent debt-ceiling fights until after the November 2012 elections. A major difference remaining was that Reid wanted to include cutting defense and war spending by another $1 trillion, whereas Boehner wanted an additional $1.2 trillion in spending cuts decided in a second vote and no cuts in defense whatsoever. Reid rejected another vote.

In the final compromise reached on July 31, Reid dropped all cuts in defense spending, as both agreed to approximately $840 billion in guaranteed spending cuts, with no cuts in defense. Boehner in turn dropped his prior demand for a second vote by both the House and Senate for an additional immediate $1.2 trillion deficit reduction. The additional $1.2 trillion was delayed until year end 2011. Thus, at minimum, a guaranteed $2 trillion in spending cuts only was agreed by the parties. And no tax increases included in the $2 trillion deficit reduction.[29]

In addition, both Reid and Boehner agreed to set up a separate Congressional group (thereafter called the 'Supercommittee' of twelve) to decide on possibly as much as $1.5 trillion more in deficit reduction by November 2011. That $1.5 trillion could potentially supercede the $1.2 trillion. So total deficit reduction could be as high as $2.3 trillion—or even more if the Supercommittee wanted to raise its target beyond $1.5 trillion, which was a minimum. On the other hand, if the Supercommittee could not agree on the additional $1.5 trillion, or if it did but Congress rejected it, then the additional $1.2 trillion in spending cuts agreed on August 2 would automatically take effect. If the automatic $1.2 trillion option occurred, the spending cuts were to be divided roughly equally between defense and non-defense spending and any tax hikes were prohibited. However, if the Supercommittee option prevailed and was passed by Congress—thus superceding the $1.2 trillion—then any percentage mix of defense versus non-defense was possible. Furthermore, also possible were tax hikes as well as cuts in Social Security, Medicare, and Medicaid.

The Supercommittee was scheduled to report out its recommendations to Congress on November 23 on how to reduce the deficit by the additional $1.5 trillion. Congress would have until December 23 to vote on the Supercommittee's recommendations. Boehner and Reid agreed in the August 2 deal that there would be no amendments after the November 23 recommendations. It was 'an up or down vote' of the Supercommittee's recommendations. Democracy was thus to be reduced from 535 to twelve individuals in Congress. Both Houses of Congress passed the bill on August 1, 2011, one day before the default deadline. Obama signed it into law on August 2.

## ASSESSING THE DEBT-CEILING DEAL

Summarizing the final deal of August 2 clearly Boehner and the Teapublicans had 'won' more from the deal than Obama and the Democrats had. Firstly, there was the guaranteed approximate $2 trillion in all spending cuts, that had been the House radicals' main demand for months. Secondly, their equally priority demand of no tax hikes, including tax-loophole closings, was also obtained. Obama and the Democrats caved in on both their positions to include tax-loophole closings. What the Democrats did trade in return for these concessions was the agreement to raise the debt ceiling by at least $2 trillion through the election period. Apparently, one way to prevent getting beaten up by bullies is to pay them off in order that they not punch you for another year!

There was still, moreover, the open-ended possibility of $1.5 trillion—or more—in further deficit reduction if Congress agreed in December to vote to replace the $1.2 trillion automatic spending cuts with the Supercommittee's recommendations offered on November 23, 2011. But for Congress to 'vote up or down' the Supercommittee recommendations meant the possibility of 'tax hikes' in the mix of recommendations, less in terms of defense spending cuts, and the very likely possibility of including cuts in Social Security and Medicare that were not included in the automatic $1.2 trillion. Clearly, if Teapublicans wanted more cuts, no defense cuts, and the cuts in Social Security and Medicare that they also demanded, they might have to accept tax hikes in some proportion of the $1.5 trillion. This reopened the door once more to proposals put forth in the original Simpson-Bowles Deficit Commission report.

It also opened the door to new proposals by Obama as well, in which he resurrected once again his preference to trade tax-loophole closings in exchange for cuts in Medicare-Medicaid and even Social Security. That trade-off would soon emerge when Obama revealed yet another, third economic recovery plan within weeks of closing the debt-ceiling deal—as will be discussed in Chapter 9. Before considering that third, and most recent, recovery program of the administration, it is first necessary to address the economic relapse of 2011 itself, which ultimately forced the administration to develop yet another recovery program in an attempt to prevent an economy faltering badly once again two years after the recession had officially ended in June 2009.

# 8
# Sliding Toward Global Depression?

'The Second Economic Relapse of 2011'

Obama's second economic recovery program introduced in late 2010 was far more weighted toward tax cuts than the first recovery program—in fact, more than $800 billion in tax cuts compared to about $300 billion in the first program. Not surprisingly, it's impact on recovery was even less. There were no subsidies to states and local government and no additional infrastructure spending to speak of included in the second recovery program. It was essentially all tax cuts with some unemployment subsidy extensions. The tax cuts were largely business tax cuts, the largest being the $408 billion cost of the two-year extension of the Bush tax cuts. The second largest tax element was the 'fix' for the 21 million upper middle class and above taxpayers in the Alternative Minimum Tax, AMT. It cost $137 billion for two years. The estate tax was also liberalized further by Obama, costing $68 billion. Tax-loophole continuation and faster depreciation cost another $77 billion. The remaining tax cut was the payroll tax cut of 2% for workers. That cost about $112 billion. The only spending provision was a one-year extension of long-term jobless unemployment benefits, costing $55 billion—a subsidy.

On the monetary policy side, the second recovery program included the further injection of $600 billion into the financial markets by the Federal Reserve, called Quantitative Easing 2 (QE2). The $600 billion QE2 was barely a third of the prior 'QE1' in 2009. QE2 was supposed to give another boost to the housing market by lowering mortgage rates. It had an impact, but not on mortgage rates or the housing sector.

QE2 resulted in a decline in the value of the dollar in international markets. That provided a small boost to U.S. exports in the first half of 2011 and to the export sector of manufacturing. But QE2 also contributed to speculation in global commodities of all kinds. That had two effects, both of which resulted in a drag on the U.S. domestic economy in the first half of 2011.

Firstly, the $600 billion QE2 helped provoke a commodities price bubble that subsequently in 2011 drove up oil, gasoline, food, clothing and other prices for U.S. consumers. Commodity-related companies, however, saw their profits spike. Higher profits meant a second brief boomlet in U.S. stock markets as demand for the stocks of commodities and other manufacturing companies drove up their stock prices. On the other hand, there was no evidence that it stimulated the housing market, which continued to decline in the first half of 2011. So the net effect of QE2, much like that of QE1 before although now on a smaller scale, was to drive stock and commodity markets and produce nice profits for stock and commodities speculators and their companies. Banks' profits rose as they, in turn, lent money to the speculators. But in terms of the domestic economy in the U.S., the Fed's QE2 policy had little impact. Not only did the housing sector not respond, but the rising prices for gas, food and other essentials reduced real consumption for most households in the first half of 2011, as described in Chapter 6.

The oil and other commodities inflation of the first half of 2011 had a negative impact on households' incomes, which in turn contributed to the slowdown in consumer spending. Escalating gasoline prices absorbed as much as 60% of the $112 billion in payroll tax reduction, according to some reports. The payroll tax cut was supposed to put dollars in the hands of the average household to spend and thus boost consumption. Instead, as a consequence of accelerating oil prices, about $70 billion of the $112 billion payroll tax cut was diverted mostly to the oil companies, whose profits surged once again in the first half of 2011. Another way to look at it is that $70 billion was diverted from the Social Security Trust Fund, where the payroll tax otherwise would ordinarily have been deposited, and transferred instead to the oil companies.

## THE SLOWING U.S. ECONOMY: JANUARY–JUNE 2011

The more than $850 billion cost of Obama's December 2010 second economic recovery program could therefore hardly be called a 'recovery' program in any sense. This is evident by the trend for GDP from the fourth quarter of 2010 through the second quarter of 2011. During that period GDP continued to trend downward despite the $800 billion additional tax cutting, as Table 8.1 clearly shows.

*Table 8.1*   GDP declining trend 2010–11
(percent change from preceding period)

| | |
|---|---|
| 3rd qtr. 2010 | 2.5% |
| 4th qtr. 2010 | 2.3% |
| 1st qtr. 2011 | 0.4% |
| 2nd qtr 2011 | 1.3% |

Source: Bureau of Economic Analysis, National Income and Product Accounts, Table 1.1.1, as updated July 29, 2011.

The causes of the emerging relapse in the economy were obvious. Consumption, which is 71% of the total economy, was quickly stagnating— while government spending on all levels was already contracting. The 2009 stimulus was over and nothing new in terms of spending stimulus was forthcoming. There was little 'net new' in the 2010 second recovery program. Continuing Bush tax cuts and the AMT fix, and even the unemployment benefits extension, did not constitute additional stimulus. And by early 2011 the deficit battles were about to reduce spending at the federal level, just as state and local government spending was declining after the 2009 stimulus subsidies had been spent.

The economy demanded more spending, but all it was given was more tax cuts that were either continuing to be hoarded or not invested.

As the economy entered 2011 and a new relapse, Obama and Congress were not only moving away from a necessary second spending stimulus, but were shifting the composition of fiscal policy rapidly in the wrong direction—i.e. toward more useless and ineffective tax cuts. Not only were they not providing programs to generate jobs in the short term, they were even discontinuing infrastructure job creation in the longer term. In other words, the errors of the first economic recovery program of 2009 were being repeated in an even more exacerbated form. Not surprisingly, the economy in the first half of 2011 began deteriorating even more rapidly.

The breakdown of this general drift of the economy toward relapse in the first half of 2011 becomes clearer when the three major elements—consumption, government spending, and business investment—are each considered in further detail.

## CONSUMPTION DECLINE 2011

In the first quarter of 2011 consumer spending fell by half from previous-quarter levels, a harbinger of things to come. With the escalating oil, food, health care, clothing and other commodity-driven prices, combined with the retreat of the stock market, by the second quarter consumer spending collapsed to essentially zero: 0.1%.

It is generally not acknowledged how big an impact commodity price inflation—that drives up prices for gasoline, food, and other consumer essentials—has on consumption. But strong evidence of just this impact of commodity price inflation occurred both in 2011 and in 2008.

What consumption that did occur in the first half of 2011 was driven largely by stock market gains and spending by the top 10% wealthiest households—at least until April. After April, even consumption by the top 10% began to slow as well, but for different reasons than for the bottom 80% middle- and working-class households. During the rise of the stock market from 2010 to April 2011, the top 10% group accounted for more than half of all consumer spending, according to Moody's Analytics and other market research sources.[1] In contrast, spending by the bottom 80% of households accounted for less than 40% total consumption. As stock values surged for the top 10% following the introduction of QE2 by the Fed in November 2010, the wealthy 10% group's spending accelerated with it. This wealthy 10% stock market-driven consumption was reflected in retail sales at luxury goods stores. It was no coincidence that luxury stores like Tiffany's (jewelry) did quite well up until the second quarter of 2011 as the stock market continued to rise, whereas sales at stores like Walmart continued to struggle.[2]

This significant slowdown in consumption in the first half of 2011 is also evidence that Obama's payroll tax cut, introduced as part of his second economic recovery program the preceding December, had little effect in stimulating consumer spending in 2011. Most of it was absorbed by the sharp rise in commodity price inflation in the first half of the year. Some estimates are that as much as 60% of the payroll tax was thus absorbed, especially in higher gas prices, essentially negating the stimulus effect of the payroll tax cut.

The simultaneous effects of the escalation in commodity price inflation on the bottom 80% of households and the re-decline of the stock market on the top 10% of households in the first half of 2011 is illustrated in Table 8.2 and the rapid slowing of consumption during that period.

*Table 8.2*   Decline in consumer spending

|                      | 4th qtr. 2010 | 1st qtr. 2011 | 2nd qtr. 2011 |
| -------------------- | ------------- | ------------- | ------------- |
| Total consumption    | 3.6%          | 2.1%          | 0.1%          |
| Goods consumption    | 8.3%          | 4.7%          | −1.3%         |
| Services consumption | 1.3%          | 0.8%          | 0.8%          |

*Source*: Bureau of Economic Analysis, National Income and Product Accounts, Table 1, July 31, 2011.

While the shifting consumption patterns of the wealthy may be largely determined by the values of their stocks and other financial assets, consumer spending by the bottom 80% of households that represent the middle and working class is determined by what is called their 'real disposable income'—i.e. what they actually have to spend after taxes.

Real disposable income has been stagnating for many of that 80% for several decades now, even before the economic crisis emerged in 2008. Both jobs and wages growth have lagged the rest of the economy for decades. Much of the job growth since the 1980s has been low-paid service, part time and/or temporary jobs, with few or no benefits. These lower-income jobs have replaced higher-paying manufacturing and construction jobs that have been disappearing by the tens of millions in the U.S. due to offshoring and technology substitution. The decline of unions and union wage differentials, slowing minimum-wage adjustments, and jobs destroyed by imports have added to the slowing and decline in wage income in general. Added to these trends, double-digit inflation for decades in health care, education, food and other 'core' items has further reduced the 'real' value of the weekly earnings of the bottom 80% as a group, especially the 50% and below within the group.

The bottom 80%, and median and below wage-earners in particular, have made up the real income loss by putting other family members to work, typically female spouses; by reducing their savings; by refinancing their homes if they had one; and otherwise by increasing their use of other forms of consumer credit. With the economic crisis and recession, however, all such means for offsetting declining real disposable income have been constricted or even eliminated. Then came the massive job losses after October 2008. Real disposable income took a further major hit. For those still with jobs, wages and benefits were often reduced. Another hit. Then the two commodity inflation events of 2008 and 2011 drove up basic goods and services prices further, reducing real income still more. It has all resulted not only in a notable decline in real disposable income for the bottom 80%, but also a consequent weak and tentative recovery for consumption overall. As Stephen Roach, chairman of Morgan Stanley Asia, noted at mid-year,

> The 13 quarters since the beginning of 2008, inflation-adjusted annualized growth in consumption has averaged 0.5%. Never before in the post-second world war era have U.S. consumers been this weak for this long...there is no quick end in sight to the chronic weakness of U.S. consumers.[3]

The primary cause of the consumption problem to which Roach refers has been the weakening of disposable income, primarily for the bottom 80% of households and especially for the bottom 50%. In a normal economy, consumption grows 3–3.5% per year, but it fell by more than –4% in 2009, turned positive only briefly for six months in 2010, and since late 2010 has been on a steady downward trajectory.

What the consumption trend in Table 8.2 and the real disposable income trend in Figure 8.1 together strongly suggest is that the U.S. economy has an underlying long-run structural problem in its distribution of income between the top 10% and bottom 80% of households—a problem preventing the economy from achieving a sustained recovery. That problem has become significantly worse since 2009. Nor has it been addressed by any of the Obama recovery programs to date. Until it is, the U.S. economy will continue to not fully recover, instead experiencing only short, weak recoveries followed by relapses and even double dips—a condition this writer has described as a Type I Epic Recession.

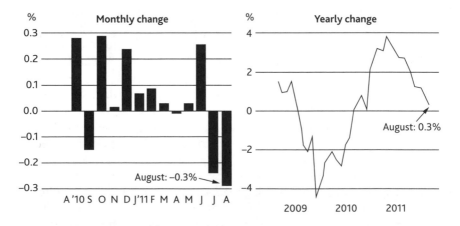

*Figure 8.1*    Real disposable income 2009–11, monthly and annual change

*Source*: Investors' Business Daily, www.Investors.com.

What happened to consumption in the first half of 2011 explains a good part of the slowing of the economy at that time. The collapse of consumption in the first half of 2011 set the stage for the subsequent second economic relapse. But stagnating consumption alone cannot explain the eventual relapse. Government and business spending were equally critical. For unless government and/or business spending rises to offset the combined 10%/80% of households' consumption decline, the outcome is a strong tendency toward economic relapse. And the government in 2011 not only did not offset the consumption decline, it too reduced its total spending and thus contributed in turn to the forthcoming second economic relapse of 2011. Eventually thereafter, business spending would do the same in response to a combination of growing global financial instability and the slowing of global manufacturing and trade.

## BUSINESS SPENDING SLOWDOWN

Although not as large in an absolute sense as consumption, business spending is especially important for job creation. While it did not slow as much as consumption, the key area of business spending—i.e. spending on equipment and software—slowed sharply in the first half of 2011 from an average of 20.5% in 2010 to only 5.7% in the second quarter of 2011, as shown in Table 8.3.

*Table 8.3*   Slowdown in business spending

| Spending type | Average 2010 | 1st qtr. 2011 | 2nd qtr. 2011 |
|---|---|---|---|
| Equipment & software | 20.5% | 8.7% | 5.7% |
| Commercial structures | −0.6% | −14.3% | 8.1% |
| Residential structures | −4.4% | −2.4% | 3.8% |

*Source*: Bureau of Economic Analysis, U.S. Department of Commerce, National Income and Product Accounts, Table 1, gross domestic product, percent change from preceding period, seasonally adjusted at annual rates.

It is important to note that the slowdown in business spending in 2011 occurred despite the continued accumulation of record profits and cash on hand by corporations. It is not as if corporations lacked necessary funds for investing. Rather there was a glut of funds available for investing and consequently for job creation in the U.S. Corporations simply refused to commit the money to investing in the U.S. in any significant sense.

At the end of summer 2011 the Federal Reserve released figures on how much cash was being hoarded as of June 2011. As the business press reported,

Corporations have a higher share of cash on their balance sheets than at any time in nearly half a century, as businesses build up buffers rather than invest in new plants or hiring. Nonfinancial companies held more than $2 trillion in cash and other liquid assets at the end of June, the Federal Reserve reported Friday, up more than $88 billion from the end of March.[4]

Estimates of the amount held offshore in corporate subsidiaries in order to avoid paying U.S. corporate taxes ranges from $500 billion to $700 billion, according to Moody's Inc. Other sources cite the total as high as $1.4 trillion.[5] The biggest cash hoarders offshore were large pharmaceutical and tech companies. The large pharmaceutical corporations alone have stashed $113 billion in cash offshore. Instead of investing in jobs in the U.S., much of the $2 trillion has been earmarked for stock buybacks, dividend payouts to shareholders and acquisitions of other companies. By early May 2011 more than $215 billion for share buybacks alone had been authorized.[6]

The offshore cash hoard produced calls, and then legislative proposals, in Congress for an offshore profits tax-holiday to allow drug, tech, and banking giants to bring back their cash to the U.S. and pay a corporate tax rate much reduced from the normal 35%. This was not new. In 2004 a similar tax holiday was proposed and passed. It was argued by proponents that it was better to get some tax revenue rather than nothing. The rate was lowered to 5.25%. Corporations brought back about $300 billion of the then estimated $700 billion held offshore. The legislation required that they use the cash brought back to invest in jobs in the U.S. That didn't happen. The cash was used to buy back stocks, pay out more dividends and acquire other companies. Despite this past record, Congress introduced a bill once again in May 2011. Once again the rate proposed was 5.25%. Corporations pushing the bill include three dozen major companies, mostly in tech, energy, and pharmaceuticals. Drug giant Pfizer alone had accumulated offshore foreign profits of $48.2 billion in 2010. The Joint Committee of Congress estimated, however, the tax revenues collected would amount to only $25 billion, while the loss to taxpayers would exceed $80 billion.

## OBAMA'S DEEPER CORPORATE TURN

Immediately following announcement of his second recovery program in December 2010 with its $800 billion in continuing and new business tax cuts, Obama received widespread praise from the business community. He was then invited by the U.S. Chamber of Commerce to address its general meeting on February 7, 2011.

Having already appointed a new corporate chief advisor, William Daley, prior to attending the Chamber meeting, the president further deepened his ties with corporate America on his inner team by appointing General Electric CEO Jeff Immelt, a major advisor on economic matters, just a few days before his January 2011 State of the Union address. Immelt assumed a new role as head of a new Council on Jobs and Competitiveness. General Electric is a manufacturing-export giant corporation, one of the largest in the U.S., and a multinational corporation with more than half of its sales and profits offshore, in particular in China. Immelt was given responsibility by Obama to develop a new 'jobs program' as the head of the new Council on Jobs and Competitiveness.

Two days prior to appointing Immelt, Obama ordered a 'government-wide review' of federal regulations "that stifle job creation and make our economy less competitive."[7] Thus, the new logic was that corporate cost-reduction equaled competitiveness equaled job creation. That, in short, was the new Immelt plan parading as a jobs program. Emphasizing his new commitment to reducing business regulations, pushing free trade, and manufacturing exports, Obama wrote a lengthy editorial for the *Wall Street Journal* entitled 'Toward a 21st Century Regulatory System.' In it he signaled a new emphasis on balancing "benefits and costs," a phrase typically meaning that more consideration would henceforth be given to business costs than to the benefits of safety and health of the public.[8] In his editorial piece the president made several specific references to the Environmental Protection Agency, EPA—i.e. another signal that it would likely be a target for rules elimination. And in fact it was, as announcements reversing EPA policy would soon follow from the presidential office.

The Chamber of Commerce quickly praised Obama's appointment of Immelt, as the president prepared to address their meeting. At the Chamber meeting on February 7, 2011, the president inquired of his audience why, after corporate profits had more than recovered to their pre-recession highs, business wasn't using more of its record cash and liquid assets on hand to invest and create jobs in the U.S. He added that business failing to invest after accumulating so much cash and apparently fully recovering "breaks the social compact" and "makes people feel as if the game is fixed." The response of the attending CEOs at the Chamber event was not particularly warm. Attending CEOs responded in press interviews following the meeting that merely hiring more workers won't necessarily stimulate consumption, they noted. Others responded that Obama's promises of deregulation were not enough; that more tax cuts, more reductions in Medicare costs and in other entitlements were necessary before their 'confidence' was restored and they would invest in jobs. In short, more incentives and still more concessions from the administration were necessary before they would "get in the game." Six months later, by summer 2011, they still were not "in the game." As Table 8.3 shows, business spending on equipment and software continued to decline.

## GOVERNMENT SPENDING CONTRACTION

As significant was the slowdown both in consumer and business spending in the first half of 2011, an equally serious contribution to the emerging economic relapse was the contraction in government spending. Both federal, and state and local-level growth was 'negative' for the entire nine-month period from October 2010 through June 2011, as Table 8.4 indicates.

With consumer spending flat and business spending rapidly slowing, it was a remarkable development that government spending at all levels by mid 2011 was in even more rapid retreat. That had never happened in any of the ten previous recessions and recoveries in the U.S. since 1945. On the other hand, never before was the federal government called on to bail out banks and corporate America on so massive a scale—and in the process take on massive debt on its own federal government balance sheet. It is as if corporate America dumped all its losses onto the government and the taxpayer, recovered all its profits, accumulated record cash on hand, and then just sat on it whining about 'business confidence,' a business-unfriendly president, and the lack of consumer demand for its products.

*Table 8.4*   Government spending contraction

|  | 4th qtr. 2010 | 1st qtr. 2011 | 2nd qtr. 2011 |
| --- | --- | --- | --- |
| Federal spending | −3.0% | −9.4% | 2.2% |
| State-local spending | −2.7% | −3.4% | −3.4% |
| Total government | −2.8% | −5.9% | −1.1% |

*Source*: Bureau of Economic Analysis, U.S. Department of Commerce, National Income and Product Accounts, Table 1, gross domestic product, percent change from preceding period, seasonally adjusted at annual rates.

It should be noted that Table 8.4's data indicating retrenchment of government spending through the first half of 2011 will also likely prove to be an underestimate for the year. The data do not reflect the growing federal deficit cutting that began in March 2011 in the form of a $38 billion cut from the previous year's budget and the continuing slashing of government spending with the August 2011 'debt-ceiling deal' of $1 trillion. Once all such spending cuts are considered, and added to the figures for the first half of 2011 in Table 8.4, federal government spending reduction will almost certainly register an even greater spending decline in the second half of 2011.

Nor does Table 8.4 indicate the likely continued decline in state and local government spending for the remainder of 2011 either. For as the federal deficit cutting began to ramp up by March 2011, more than 30 states launched new state and local government budget-cutting initiatives of their own. Those mid-stream budget cuts are also not reflected in Table 8.4 and will likely prove to be significant. In addition, future cuts at the federal level, as they occur, will accelerate state and local government spending cuts even further.

## THE SECOND 'RELAPSE': JOBS, HOUSING, THE STATES

The preceding data show that the slowing of the economy—the prelude to the relapse—had in fact begun early in 2011. That slowing in the first half of 2011 spread and deepened in the summer of 2011. The three critical areas of jobs, housing, and state and local government reveal a relapse in the summer of 2011 most clearly.

### Jobs

Measured by a host of multiple indicators, the job market over the summer of 2011 seriously deteriorated further from the first half of 2011. When factoring in growth of part-time jobs, discouraged and marginal workforce trends, and hundreds of thousands leaving the labor force unable to find jobs (and thus not considered unemployed by U.S. definitions), the picture is one of actual net job loss.[9] Employment levels fell for the private sector in general, for government workers, and even for the self-employed. Jobs that were created were to a great extent involuntary part-time and temp work, and hundreds of thousands wanting work left the labor force. The plight of the long-term unemployed also worsened. The broad-based deteriorating jobs condition is indicated in Table 8.5.

*Table 8.5*   Jobs second economic relapse, May–August 2011

| Employment category | May 2011 | August 2011 | Change |
|---|---|---|---|
| Unemployment rate (U-6) | 15.8% | 16.2% | +0.4% |
| Total jobless (U-6) | 24,283,000 | 24,882,000 | +599,000 |
| Private wage & salary jobs | 128,803,000 | 128,552,000 | −251,000 |
| Government jobs | 20,309,000 | 20,286,000 | −25,000 |
| Self-employed jobs | 8,655,000 | 8,551,000 | −114,000 |
| Involuntary part-time employed | 8,400,000 | 8,670,000 | +270,000 |
| Workers not in labor force but want a job | 6,227,000 | 6,493,000 | +266,000 |
| Long-term unemployed | 39.7 weeks | 40.3 weeks | +0.6 |

*Source*: Bureau of Labor Statistics, Department of Labor, Employment Situation Report, September 2, 2011, Tables A 1, A 8, A 9, A 12, A 15, A 16.

In an early indicator of much worse to come on the jobs front in the last quarter of 2011, the business consulting firm, Challenger & Gray, reported in early October that businesses were planning 115,730 additional layoffs— twice the number of planned layoffs in the previous month. The 115,730 also represents the highest number of planned layoffs by business since April 2009 when monthly job losses were still in freefall and the recession had not yet reached its low point in June 2009.[10]

## Housing

On the housing front, after having slowed in late 2010 due to the 'robo-signing' scandal and banks' temporary retreat, foreclosures and bank seizures of homes were rising once again over the summer, June through August 2011, well over the 200,000 a month mark.[11]

At the rising rate, total foreclosures for 2011 were on track to register another 2.45 million for the year—bringing the total foreclosures since Obama took office in 2009 to 8.1 million. When added to foreclosures in 2006–08, the total foreclosures amount to 12.4 million, about 1 in 4.5 of the roughly total 54 million residential mortgages in the U.S.

In all likelihood the number of foreclosures will significantly exceed the 2.4 million mark in 2011, since the slowing of foreclosure processing by banks since late 2010 by the summer 2011 appears once again to be picking up. As James Saccacio, CEO of RealtyTrac, noted in August 2011, "Unfortunately the falloff in foreclosures is not based on a robust recovery in the housing market but on short term interventions and delays that will extend the current housing market woes into 2012 and beyond."[12] Saccaccio further noted that "lenders are starting to push through some of the foreclosures delayed by robo-signing...It also foreshadows more bank repossessions in the coming months."[13]

The temporary slowing of foreclosures in late 2010 was due to the robo-signing scandal. The Obama administration, as noted previously, initially washed its hands of the matter and turned it over to states' attorneys general to confront. After a year of no collective progress at the states level, the Obama administration jumped in and proposed a settlement between the banks and the millions of illegally foreclosed homeowners: a fine of a mere $25 billion levied against mortgage lenders and the banks which essentially let them off the hook. The money would go to the states, moreover, not the homeowners. The settlement would absolve the banks from future legal action and prevent homeowners from filing future claims against the banks for processing up to 4 million foreclosures improperly and illegally. Although quickly agreed to by the banks, New York and California AGs balked and refused the deal.

The breakdown of the settlement meant as of late summer 2011 there remained essentially no vehicle for assisting homeowners facing foreclosure— i.e. more than a year after the robo-signing scandal became public and after three years into the Obama administration's first term. Given the failure of the administration to force state AGs to accept its pro-bank $25 billion settlement, and with evidence of growing divisions between AGs themselves over what to do next, banks not only started increasing their foreclosures and seizures as of late summer 2011 but also began reducing the number of loan modifications by late summer 2011 even as the rate of mortgage delinquencies began to rise again for the first time since 2009.[14]

The other major indicator of the deep plight of homeowners is negative equity. It indicates homeowners whose mortgages are 'under water'—that is, whose homes are worth less on the market than the original mortgage. According to Zillow Inc., the major source for home value determination, homeowners with negative equity mortgages rose from 22.5% in the third quarter of 2010 to 26.8% by June 2011.[15] Furthermore, as in the case of foreclosures, the predicted trend for negative equity is that it too will worsen. According once again to the primary source of such data, Zillow Inc., "we continue to expect a true bottom in 2012, at the earliest."[16]

Table 8.6   Housing-foreclosure second economic relapse, June–August 2011

| Housing category | June 2011 | August 2011 | Change |
|---|---|---|---|
| Foreclosures | 222,740 | 228,098 | +5,358 |
| Mortgages 'under water' | 22.5% (3Q10) | 26.8% (2Q11) | +4.3% |
| Housing starts | 629,000 | 571,000 | −58,000 |
| New home sales | 312,000 | 295,000 | −17,000 |

Sources: RealtyTrac (foreclosures), Zillow (negative equity), U.S. Census Bureau (housing starts, new home sales, home price averages).

Other important indicators of the state of the housing sector include housing starts, sales of new and existing homes, and home prices. All also show a further deterioration in the summer 2011 period and thus further confirmation of a relapse underway for housing, along with the rest of the economy, as shown in Table 8.6.

## Government Spending

The most significant developments in government spending during the summer relapse of 2011 was the decision by Congress to cut federal government spending by $1 trillion as part of the debt ceiling-deficit deal of August 2, 2011. Those cuts will not take effect until the next fiscal year beginning October 2011–12 and thereafter. Nor will the $1 trillion be the ceiling, but rather the floor for what will be at least another at minimum $1.2 trillion in further, additional spending cuts at the federal level that will be determined before year-end 2011 by Congress. Government spending cuts at the federal level therefore promises to be of historic magnitude. It is also quite possible that the additional spending cuts will exceed $1.2 trillion. Whatever the amount, the combined cuts of August and December 2011 will have a significant negative impact on the U.S. economy in 2013 and beyond. The cuts will ensure at a minimum the deepening of the relapse and more likely the descent into a bona fide double-dip recession no later than 2013.

A second major development in the third quarter 2011 is the deepening of state and local government spending reductions. Those budget cuts were initially estimated at $103 billion earlier in 2011 but will more likely exceed that estimate if the economy continues to weaken and if current trends at the state level to consistently cut business taxes continue as well.

Most states' budgets took effect on July 1, 2011. On that date, all but $6 billion of the original 2009 Obama first recovery program's $263 billion in aid to states will have been spent. The cuts projected in the states' 2012 new budgets are no less historic than the federal level spending cuts. The states' budget cuts will start impacting the economy much sooner, however, than the federal spending reductions. Together, they will amount to a one-two punch to the economy.

The vast majority of the state cuts are targeted for education and health care services—just as the August 2, 2011, debt ceiling $1 trillion cuts at the federal level targeted the same. As just a few data points of some interest:[17]

- No fewer than 38 states plan cuts in education spending to levels lower than in 2008
- 25 states plan to include cuts in higher education colleges and universities support
- 20 states plan deep cuts in health care
- 16 states plan major public worker layoffs and wage and benefit cuts.

The scenario is no less dismal in terms of spending at the city and local government level. According to a study by the National League of Cities at the end of September 2011, "nearly a third of the nation's cities are laying off workers this year." Tax revenues will fall in 2012 for the fifth straight year. It is at the city and local government level in particular that the bulk of layoffs of public workers have been occurring in 2011, and where future layoffs will continue to be concentrated. Layoffs of K-12 teachers have been the target.

Cities and local government employ nearly five times the number of federal government workers, and three times the number of state government workers. Over the period just from June to July 2011, no fewer than 106,000 city, schools, and local government workers have lost their jobs.[18] Figure 8.2 shows the precipitous fall in state and local government employment since Obama took office in 2009. As of the end of the third quarter 2011, a total of approximately 600,000 state and local government workers had lost their jobs.

State and local government employment in millions

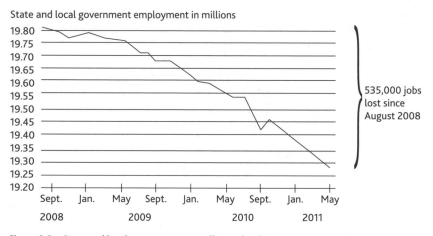

*Figure 8.2*    State and local government payrolls are shrinking

*Source:* Center on Budget and Policy Priorities website, cbpp.org.

The brunt of spending reductions at the city and local government level has fallen not only on employment, but also on basic services of all types. Unlike the states and federal government, local government does not typically have tax revenue sources from sales taxes or income taxes. It relies on property taxes and various fees. With the collapse of the housing sector, property taxes have plummeted as home sales and home values have collapsed in turn. The cities' only recourse is therefore to cut services, lay off workers, and raise fees. And all three have been increasing at the local government level throughout 2011 and after July 2011 in particular. That means even less stimulus for the economy and represents a further contributing source to continuing economic relapse through 2011 and into 2012.

What the various data for government show, therefore, is government spending at all levels—federal, state and local—is producing a growing drag on economic recovery going into 2012 and beyond.

## MANUFACTURING BEGINS TO RETRACT

A major theme of this book is that the three Obama recovery programs to date have failed because they did not seriously address three key areas of the economic crisis—i.e. jobs, housing-foreclosures, and fiscal crisis of state and local governments. Obama's consistent idea of a 'jobs program' was tax cuts. But tax cuts do not equal a jobs program, as has been repeatedly shown in preceding chapters. Nor do subsidies and incentives to banks and mortgage companies. Nor token investment in very long-term infrastructure projects. Nor would Obama's turn in late 2010 to a manufacturing sector-driven strategy and policies providing even more benefits to multinational companies and exports.

The modest recovery of U.S. manufacturing in 2010—driven by manufacturing exports that were in turn driven by what is called 'emerging markets' demand (i.e China, Asia, Brazil, etc.)—was one of the few positive signs of recovery following Obama's first economic recovery plan. But that modest recovery was grossly over-hyped by the administration, and then leveraged by manufacturing corporations to squeeze additional benefits and incentives from the administration and Congress. Obama in mid 2010 'doubled down' his bet on manufacturing and export stimulation. This bet dovetailed nicely with his bringing onto staff more corporate advisors just before and after the 2010 midterm elections. The appointments of William Daley and Jeff Immelt were a reflection of this 'bet on manufacturing and exports' as the source of job creation after mid-year 2011. So too were the president's new emphasis on pushing free trade agreements with Panama, Korea, and Colombia; his retreat from reforming the offshore foreign profits tax; the new initiative to reform patent legislation benefiting multinational tech companies; and the exempting of non-finance corporations from financial derivatives trading rules under the Dodd-Frank regulation act of 2010—a shortlist of measures and new initiatives introduced by the administration favoring U.S. multinational corporations.

But promoting manufacturing and exports as the new strategy to create jobs and lead the economy out of recession was fundamentally wrong. There was, and remains, no way that stimulating manufacturing could lead the economy out of recession.

To begin with, U.S. manufacturing is not a sector that can have much of an effect on reducing the 25 million jobless in the U.S. Its current 11.7 million workers represents a small percentage of the 154 million U.S. labor force. Secondly, the long-term trend in manufacturing, well before the beginning of the current recession, has been massive job-cutting by companies due to foreign direct investment, offshoring of jobs, free trade effects, and substitution of labor by technology-related capital equipment. Manufacturing is only a relatively small part of the total U.S. labor force today. Even with job increases, it would hardly dent the 25 million total jobless. Thirdly, manufacturing has been driven by U.S. exports until recently. But the global economy by the second half of 2011 was rapidly slowing and with it total world trade as well.

That promised even fewer U.S. manufacturing exports and, in turn, less growth in U.S. manufacturing and jobs in the near term. Problems with manufacturing as the lead sector of the U.S. economy were both short and long term.

Concerning the long term, in 1980 there were 18.6 million manufacturing jobs in the U.S. representing about 17.3% of the total U.S. workforce. By 2000, manufacturing jobs had fallen to 17.3 million or 12.1% and from 17.3 million to only 11.7 million by 2011. That's 5.7 million lost manufacturing jobs in just the last decade.[19] That manufacturing job loss can be directly attributed to the acceleration of free trade, explosion in trade with China, massive offshoring of jobs by U.S. multinational companies over the last decade, and the equally serious displacing of U.S. manufacturing workers by new technology and equipment due to expanding business tax incentives. If Obama were serious about manufacturing job creation, he would address the real sources of that job loss—i.e. free trade, offshoring, and massive tax incentives given to business to replace workers with capital. Instead, his proposals were to expand those same causes of manufacturing job loss—and then call the proposals a jobs program.

More recent short-term trends further show that programs to create manufacturing jobs based on more tax incentives, more free trade, and more concessions to multinational and other U.S. export companies will not grow manufacturing jobs. At the bottom of the recession in June 2009, for example, there were a total of 11,728,000 manufacturing jobs in the U.S. As of August 2011 there were 11,757,000 jobs—i.e. virtually no change after more than two years.[20] Manufacturing companies like GE may be creating jobs, but not in the U.S. And there's no reason to believe that expanding the policies that have been largely responsible for manufacturing job loss over the past three years, and decade, will now have a positive effect in terms of job creation. Especially as the global economy has now begun slowing, dampening world exports and thus manufacturing in turn.

The short-term trends in U.S. manufacturing after GE's CEO, Jeff Immelt, was put in charge of Obama's manufacturing-centric jobs initiative clearly show that that approach is already a failure. The primary indicator of manufacturing activity in the U.S. is called the purchasing managers index. That index during the summer 2011 showed a slowdown, especially in new orders for manufactured goods and in manufacturing exports, as Table 8.7 shows.

*Table 8.7*   Purchasing managers U.S. manufacturing index, June–August 2011

|  | *June* | *July* | *August* |
|---|---|---|---|
| Overall activity index | 55.3 | 50.9 | 50.6 |
| New goods orders | 51.6 | 49.2 | 49.6 |
| Manufacturing exports | 53.5 | 54.0 | 49.6 |

*Note*: Numbers over 50 represent a continuing growth; under 50 a contraction or recession conditions. A lower number for 'orders' represents a future decline in the overall index. A 49.2 number for 'orders' in July was the lowest since June 2009.

*Source*: August 2011 ISM Manufacturing Report on Business, released September 1, 2011.

## FALTERING BUSINESS AND CONSUMER SPENDING

Consumption and business spending comprise 71% and 10% of the U.S. economy, respectively. A brief look at the two in the longer term, beyond 2011, supports the view that the U.S. economy will continue to undergo a relapse or even enter a double dip after 2012. This is due to several reasons.

Firstly, business spending on inventories is likely to prove weak in the months ahead. It reached its peak in early 2010. It is now past its peak and inventories are now overstocked, with declining demand for those stockpiles on the immediate horizon. As one business source remarked in late September 2011, "Businesses continued to build stockpiles, with inventories rising 0.9% to $365.3 billion, *the highest level since tracking began in 1992.*"[21]

Secondly, according to the quarterly survey for the third quarter by the Business Roundtable—the premier U.S. business lobbying organization whose member companies generate more than $6 trillion in sales and employ 14 million—CEO plans to increase business spending are being reduced dramatically. Plans to increase business spending on plant and equipment fell by half, from 61% to 32%.[22]

Still another explanation why business spending was likely to decline is that business in general continues to sit on more than $2 trillion in cash. As the Federal Reserve reported, non-financial companies alone (i.e. not including banks) are hoarding "$2.5 trillion in cash and other liquid assets as of the end of June, the most since 1963."[23] And as various sources reported, there appeared no plans to commit any significant percentage of the $2 trillion to investment, and jobs, in the U.S. anytime soon.

Similarly, bank lending to small-medium businesses appears also to continue to be minimal in the longer term, into 2012 and beyond. Like the large non-financial corporations, banks too continued to hoard cash and not lend, up to $1.7 trillion according to some estimates. That will translate into yet another drag on business spending, as smaller businesses continue to be denied the loans to expand.

As the summer 2011 came to an end, bank lending it appeared would likely tighten still further in the coming months. More U.S. banks are becoming increasingly fragile once again—in particular well-known players like Bank of America, Citigroup, Morgan Stanley, and hundreds of the 7,600 remaining local-regional community banks. The number of regional-community banks on the Federal Deposit Insurance Corporation's (FDIC's) 'banks in trouble' list has risen to 888 at latest count. Simultaneously, government programs targeting increased lending by community banks to small businesses have been stalled.[24] Then there's the European banking instability problem, which is causing U.S. banks to conserve cash even more in concern of future losses associated with the Euro banks. Apart from the European bank crisis, banks worldwide "owed nearly $5 trillion to bondholders and other creditors that will be due through 2012, according to the Bank for International Settlements."[25]

Together the cash hoarding and bank lending trends, the slowing of new orders, top CEO plans to cut capital spending, record excess inventories, and the slowing new orders for capital equipment all suggested at summer's end 2011 that business spending could soon slow significantly, and join other indicators showing that the second economic relapse that emerged in the summer 2011 had perhaps some distance yet to go.

A similarly poor long-term scenario exists for consumer spending beyond 2011. As data presented earlier in this chapter showed, consumer spending had turned flat and had essentially stagnated by the end of June 2011. A longer-term trend showed consumption rising only 2.2% from July to July 2010–11 and consumer confidence in the U.S. has been falling rapidly, portending possible even weaker consumer spending on the horizon.

To the extent that there is still consumer spending, it appears to be driven by the wealthiest households, on the one hand, and by consumers spending out of their savings instead of from any real income gains, on the other—an unsustainable trend in the longer term. As the chief economist for Wells Fargo bank, Mark Vitner, remarked, "Consumers are having to pull out all the stops in order to maintain their standard of living."[26]

The key determinant of consumer spending over the longer run is income growth—or the lack thereof.

At the end of summer 2010, the U.S. Census Bureau reported that between 1999 and 2009 median household income had declined by –4.8%, or about –0.6% per year. It declined for three consecutive years, 2007–09. In 2010 alone, a year during which recovery was supposedly occurring, that same median income fell another –2.3%.[27] Figure 8.1 showed clearly that behind the first half of 2011 collapse of consumer spending, to only 0.1%, lay the single most important cause of that spending collapse—i.e. the corresponding fall in disposable income between January and June 2011. In August 2011 the income decline was another –0.3%, representing an even faster –3.6% annual rate of decline.[28] Clearly, both longer- and shorter-run trends show a significant decline in median incomes, the most important predictor of consumer spending. At some point in the not too distant future, consumers spending out of their dwindling savings will most certainly give way to consumers contracting spending significantly due to declining disposable income growth.

## THE RAPIDLY SLOWING GLOBAL ECONOMY

The U.S. economy represents approximately one-fourth of global GDP. The Eurozone and U.K. economies about the same. The U.S., Eurozone and U.K. economies are tightly integrated, not just financially but in a host of other economic ways. Together they constitute over half the world's output. What happens on either side of the Atlantic soon produces a similar reaction on the other. The collapse of the U.S. investment bank, Lehman Brothers, in September 2008 precipitated a banking crash in the U.S. that was soon echoed in Europe. Conditions for a second crisis, both financial and real, are building inexorably in the Eurozone. Should it erupt there in 2012 or soon after, it will certainly drag an already again seriously weakening U.S. economy and

U.S. banking system with it. Can the world economy resist such a second crisis event?

Defenders of the economic status quo in business and government circles insist that businesses and banks are better prepared to resist another crisis event. They have more liquid assets and are better capitalized, it is argued. But their debt levels have not been appreciably reduced. In fact, much of business on both sides of the Atlantic has loaded up on more 'junk' bond debt and are therefore more fragile today than in the past. Consumer households are certainly more debt-fragile and stressed after four years of no recovery, massive stagnant job creation, loss of financial assets, and declining real incomes for the past four years. On top of it all they now face years of ever-deepening 'austerity' programs. They are certainly not prepared to weather another economic storm.

Similarly for government at all levels in the U.S. They loaded up on deficits and debt as well. The states and most cities are still financially in trouble, after hundreds of billions of dollars of federal subsidies, but subsidies that have now run out. The government bailouts of Wall Street and corporate America in the past three years were of the worst possible kind. They did not eliminate the bad debt that remains as an anchor on recovery and on bank balance sheets. They only 'offset' it with government and central bank free money. It remains to be seen if, in the event of another global financial crisis, governments are able to provide yet a second round of fiscal and monetary liquidity injection. It certainly does not appear possible politically. Nor perhaps even economically.

In this writer's previously published work, *Epic Recession: Prelude to Global Depression*, it was argued that bona fide depressions are just a series of banking crashes strung together, each driving the real economy down a deeper level in terms of economic decline in an interdependent, linked, sequence of financial-real cyclical contractions. The global economy may be on the verge of just that occurring again. This time the epicenter is in Europe, not the U.S. But the one cannot resist the other's trajectory today any more than it could in 2008. If Europe followed the U.S. in 2008, the U.S. will soon follow Europe in 2012–14.

It was argued three years ago that China et al. were not only decoupled from the U.S.-European crisis but that they, along with other second-tier economies, would 'lead' the U.S. and the world economy out of recession. But it didn't happen. China et al. were able to fend off the contagion and prevent their economies from similarly contracting. But they weren't large enough to pull the rest of the world economy out of its hole. They still aren't. And what's different today from 2008 is that China et al. are not booming, but are actually slowing their economies as well.

A proxy indicator of the current state of the global economy, and the unlikelihood that economies like China's and others outside the U.S. and Europe can offset another crisis in the U.S. or Europe, is global manufacturing. As Table 8.7 showed, manufacturing in the U.S. has slowed over the summer 2011 and appears to be headed for an even faster slowdown. The Eurozone's recent trends and prospects are much worse. Even China, a manufacturing powerhouse, has dipped into negative territory—as have global indicators for manufacturing as well. Table 8.8 compares the global manufacturing slowdown across the several major areas of the world economy. The picture is ominous.

*Table 8.8*   Global manufacturing indexes, June–September 2011

|  | *June* | *July* | *August* | *September* |
|---|---|---|---|---|
| Eurozone | 52.1 | 50.4 | 49.0 | 48.5 |
| China | 50.9 | 50.7 | 49.9 | 49.4 |
| United States | 55.3 | 50.9 | 50.6 | 51.6 |
| JP Morgan Chase Global index | 52.3 | 50.7 | 50.1 | 49.9 |

*Source*: *Wall Street Journal*, October 4, 2011 p. 14, and August 2, 2011, p. 6.

The global slowing trends are not limited to manufacturing. The following summarizes various key economies and their current condition and economic direction, as of the start of the fourth quarter of 2011, in terms of economic growth.

### Eurozone

Within the global economy, the Eurozone and the United Kingdom are currently the weakest and are slowing the fastest. The odds are also greatest that a second banking crash and panic will emerge in 2012 in the Eurozone, spreading subsequently to North America and elsewhere. The Eurozone is particularly weak in its 'periphery' economies of its southern 'tier'—Greece, Italy, Spain, and Portugal. By late summer 2011 those economies had already entered a double-dip recession or worse. Should a major bank in any of the southern tier become insolvent and require fundamental restructuring, that will spread to the northern tier banks relatively quickly. The subsequent impact on the rest of the Eurozone's non-financial economy will cause an even more serious slowdown and almost certainly push the Eurozone main economic engines of France and Germany, already in a no-growth situation, over the economic edge and into a double dip. Early indications are that France and Germany before year-end 2011 may have already entered a second recession. The key transmission mechanism for a possible second financial crisis centered in Europe is not Greece or Portugal. It is the Italian banks and the heavy exposure of the French banks in turn to Italy, Spain and Greece.

A survey of the Eurozone economies at the start of the fourth quarter of 2011 is as follows. In France, the national statistics agency in September 2011 lowered its estimate of the country's economic growth in the third quarter to only 0.3%, and lowered its fourth quarter 2011 estimate to 0%. Italy and Spain both entered recession in the third and fourth quarters. Greece has been in a near-depression contraction of more than 8%. In short, the general picture in Europe is one of stagnant growth at best, with the main economies of the Eurozone hovering on the edge of a general double-dip recession more precariously than even the U.S.

The key to the Eurozone economy is Germany. It grew at a fast rate in the first quarter of 2011, then slowed sharply to a 0.5% rate in the second quarter of 2011 and thereafter to an even slower 0.2% in the third. It is projected to enter recession territory in the final quarter of 2011, according to Organization for Economic Cooperation and Development (OECD) forecasts.[29] Should French and other banks experience more severe problems, as is likely in the year to come, that will almost certainly impact Germany's economic growth negatively as well.

In the United Kingdom the scenario is also a slowing of economic growth, to a mere 0.2% in the latest reported quarter as austerity spending program cuts begin to reverse what was a very modest recovery before. The U.K. is an excellent test case showing why austerity budgets and spending cuts result in a slowing real economy. Greece is a similar, more extreme, example of the same. What Greece, the U.K., and other economies following a similar 'austerity' solution to economic recovery show conclusively is that it is simply impossible to generate sustained economic growth as a consequence of introducing austerity programs.[30] As even the International Monetary Fund (IMF) has concluded, "The idea that fiscal austerity triggers faster growth in the short term finds little support in the data."[31]

## China and Emerging Markets

In 2009 the debate among economists was whether China and other emerging markets like Brazil, India, and elsewhere were 'decoupled' from the economic crisis in the advanced economies. Some argued that this decoupling was in fact the case, and that continued growth in these economies would pull the advanced economies of U.S., Europe, and Japan out of the recession. The growth in the emerging markets, in retrospect, did dampen the recession in the U.S. and Europe. But it did not 'lead' the rest of the global economy onto a sustained global recovery path. So long as the emerging economies, China in particular, were able to continue robust growth, it meant global trade recovered, and that stimulated the advanced economies' exports and manufacturing to a modest extent. But China cannot pull the rest of the global economy out of recession, nor can it prevent another global double dip from occurring. China and the other economies themselves began to slow their economies by early 2011. As it did, the cushion of global manufacturing and trade began to dissipate. In turn, so did manufacturing in the U.S. and Europe. As Table 8.8 shows clearly, that global manufacturing—driven largely by global trade recovery—has recently begun to slow noticeably. Estimates are that China's growth rate could slow to 5–6% in the period ahead, about half of what it has been for several years. Even the 5–6% growth rate assumes China will be able to get its household consumption, now only 35% of its total economy, to increase by 10–11% per year.[32] That is not likely to happen. China's growth may therefore slow even more in the months ahead. That slowdown will in turn slow global trade, already declining, even further and also the rest of the world's major economies in turn. In other words, China will no longer play even its past role of dampening the economic decline in the rest of the major economies as it once did in 2009–11. Rather, it's slowing rather will accelerate that decline elsewhere.

India's economy also began to slow in the summer of 2011. It's economic growth rate declined to 7.7% from 9–10% in recent years, and the slowest in the past two years.[33] Like China, it has been attempting to engineer a slowing of its economy by sharp increases in interest rates, and it appears that that policy had begun to take effect by summer 2011.

Like China and India—so Brazil also began by late 2010 taking measures to slow its economy to address accelerating inflation. Brazil raised its interest rates to double-digit levels (12%) by early 2011, which succeeded by summer 2011 in beginning to slow its economy.[34]

## Japan

The world's third largest economy, Japan, has experienced an Epic Recession for nearly two decades, with short and weak recoveries followed by shallow, relatively brief declines in a repeated fashion since the mid 1990s. The March earthquake and tsunami added a further negative. But the Japanese economy had already begun declining before the tragic events of March. It had already entered recession in the first quarter of 2011 with a GDP decline of –3.6% on an annualized rate, which followed a prior October–December GDP decline of –3.0%. The impact of the earthquake and tsunami in the second quarter of 2011 saw another –1.3% decline.[35] Japan's decline will continue in 2011–12.

What the combined scenarios for the global economy illustrate is that several critical sectors have already entered a double-dip recession, others are precariously close and on the edge, and the strongest economies are slowing rapidly. This general scenario translates into a slowdown of global manufacturing, exports, and trade.

The U.S. economy shows early signs of joining the global manufacturing slowdown, which means that Obama's manufacturing-exports driven strategy for jobs and economic recovery cannot succeed. Promoting U.S. exports via more free trade will prove a failure. It will not generate jobs and will not result in the U.S. manufacturing sector leading the rest of the U.S. economy to a sustained recovery. It will not even prevent the U.S. economy from falling into a double-dip recession in 2013.

So why has the Obama administration been so vigorously pursuing such an economic recovery strategy? The answer has more to do with politics than sound economics. It's about the deep influence of multinational corporations in determining the policies of the current administration, in particular after mid-year 2010 and the November elections. It's also about Obama's own strategy for re-election in 2012, which will depend upon gathering huge contributions from corporate America. The perverted form of American electoral democracy today is an environment where money now plays a greater role in election campaigns than ever before in U.S. history. No doubt Obama's advisors are telling him that campaign contributions are one of the two or three keys to winning an election. Another is orienting toward the 'independent' voter instead of the traditional Democratic Party base of unions, workers, ethnic minorities, urban voters, etc. But these aren't normal economic times, nor normal political times. The equations are changing—just as they had in 1979–80. Obama does not yet understand the nature of the changes, and the economic (and political) structural policies that are necessary to generate a sustained economic recovery in today's economy mired in an Epic Recession.

# 9
# From Failed Recovery to Austerity Recession

'The Third Economic Recovery Program (2011)'

A week after the signing of the debt-ceiling deal of August 2 to cut $1 trillion in spending from the budget, Obama hastily called a meeting of CEOs to the White House. The purpose of the meeting was to solicit business's proposals for economic policies. A list was offered by the CEOs to the administration, including proposals for more business deregulation, more tax cuts, and fast-tracking free trade.

Immediately following the meeting Obama embarked on a three-day bus tour of the Midwest. At various stops he spoke about his forthcoming new economic plan to create jobs, to be announced around Labor Day, September 5. Among measures he floated to his audiences were proposals to extend the 2% payroll tax cut for workers, previously passed in December 2010, for another year. The first year, 2011, had cost the deficit $112 billion. It was supposed to stimulate consumption by wage and salary earners. At least half the 2010 payroll tax cut's effects were negated and offset, however, by gasoline, food, and other commodity price increases during the first half of 2011. The rest of the $112 was offset by the discontinuing in December 2010 of the 'Make Work Pay' $800 tax credit that median working families received as part of the 2009 stimulus. So the 2% payroll tax cut had virtually no effect on the economy or jobs.

Obama also tested the waters on his tour by advocating fast passage of pending free trade deals with Korea, Panama, and Colombia, and raising the idea of still further tax cuts for business for R&D and equipment investment. He also dusted off his dormant 2008 campaign proposal for an Infrastructure Bank to fund transportation-related public works. The I-bank was not a true government bank, though. The proposal was for a jointly funded government-private investors initiative. It would make loans only to projects that produced an income stream, like toll bridges and highways. In addition, its proposed funding was a paltry $30 billion over six years. At $5 billion a year it was therefore not a serious public infrastructure initiative so far as job creation was concerned.

Upon returning from his bus tour, Obama promised he would soon announce specific recommendations to the newly appointed Congressional 'Supercommittee' of twelve on how much and where to cut the budget deficit. They were tasked, as part of the August 2 debt-ceiling deal, to come up with a minimum $1.5 trillion in further deficit reduction measures by November 23— in addition to the $1 trillion spending cuts passed on August 2. In a clear message to the Supercommittee, on August 18 Obama announced, "I'm going to make a presentation that has more deficit reduction than the $1.5 trillion they've been assigned."[1] He further added, "we'll have more spending cuts than we have revenue." The direction was now clear: cut more than $1.5 trillion and focus on social spending programs and health care entitlements, especially Medicare and Medicaid.

Obama next released rules announcing $10 billion in business deregulations. Public rumors abounded about what the president's Labor Day speech would actually include in terms of stimulus, tax cuts, housing, job creation, and other measures. Would he come out 'bold' and propose fundamental measures to get jobs, housing, and the economy finally turned around? Or would he repeat his prior emphases on tax cuts and cautious partial measures to try to obtain Republican support, despite the continuing refusal by the opposition to cooperate or compromise on any measures except their own?

Speculation rose that the president might finally get the government mortgage agencies, Fannie Mae and Freddie Mac, to finally do something to help homeowners. With the government—Fannie and Freddie—holding trillions of dollars in mortgage notes there was no reason why the government couldn't simply renegotiate principal and interest for homeowners facing foreclosure or in negative equity. That would greatly lower their monthly payments, and free up $70 billion a year in income to homeowners to stimulate recovery.

The September 2 jobs report from the Bureau of Labor Statistics showed there were no jobs whatsoever created in August, even by the Labor Department's conservative U-3 statistic measure. The Democratic Party's union and liberal base optimistically conjectured that the president must now surely do something about the further deteriorating job situation.[2] The jobs crisis was also showing a deeper integration with the deepening fiscal crisis at state and local government levels. Job cuts for teachers and public workers were leading the collapse in employment.

Concern was growing within the Democratic party over Obama's ratings with the public, which were now falling to dangerous low levels—a serious concern given the 2012 elections only a little more than a year away. A *Washington Post*-ABC News poll taken about the time showed, for example, that among those surveyed a huge 77% thought the country was on the wrong track. Of even greater concern, "60% disapprove of his handling of the economy".[3] Something bold indeed was needed.

## OBAMA'S INITIAL THIRD RECOVERY PROGRAM

Obama addressed the joint session of Congress on September 8. The main thrust of his proposal for a third new economic recovery program was the extension and expansion of the payroll tax cut now to business as well as workers. The president offered to cut the business share of the payroll tax, from 6.2% to 3.1%, for small businesses. With the prior 2% payroll tax cut for workers extended as well, the combined payroll tax cut was projected to cost $240 billion, or more than half of the total economic recovery package of $447 billion. But that was only the tip of the business tax-cut iceberg. The payroll tax-cut proposal included a further measure, to cut the entire 6.2% payroll tax share paid by employers if they hired a new worker—or even if they simply gave their workers a raise. That, of course, would mean almost all small businesses would give their workers a token wage hike—perhaps one they were already planning—and make sure they then claimed the full 6.2% payroll tax cut in turn. Administration accountants later assured that the full 6.2% tax cut for business would not exceed $65 billion. But administering and verifying this fact for more than 7 million small businesses was an impossible task. Small businesses would almost certainly 'game the system' for a total tab well beyond the $65 billion.

The impact of the now much greater payroll tax cut for the social security trust fund was not discussed. A $112 billion reduction in the trust fund from a 2% payroll tax cut for workers the preceding year, another $240 billion in 2012 by raising and extending it to 3.1%, and the most likely additional amount from the open-ended feature of the payroll tax cut—all could result easily in double the estimated $240 billion. A payroll tax cut over the two years 2011–12 approaching $500 billion would devastate what remained of the Social Security projected $1 trillion surplus for the next decade and create a real issue of Social Security solvency when there wasn't any such issue before the payroll tax slashing.

For those wishing to render Social Security insolvent in order to break it up or privatize it, the Obama-proposed payroll tax cuts of September 8 were most welcomed. If Social Security benefits could not successfully be reduced directly, as was the attempt under Bush in 2005, perhaps a destruction of its funding base would provide sufficient argument for eventual deep cuts in the program in subsequent years.

Other tax cuts were also proposed by Obama on September 8, including another $8 billion in business tax credits and $5 billion in credits for investing in new plant and equipment, plus another $5 billion in miscellaneous measures. Thus the total package of recovery programs proposed by Obama on September 8 amounted to $447 billion, of which $258 billion and almost 60% was composed of tax cuts.

Apart from more tax cuts, on September 8 Obama yet again put forward his idea of an Infrastructure Bank. But instead of the previously rumored $30 billion funding to start it, now only $10 billion was offered—i.e. a mere $2 billion a year for infrastructure loans. The I-bank proposal was therefore not serious and its paltry funding no doubt sent a signal to Congress that it was an expendable measure. He also proposed a $50 billion new transportation bill for highways, rail and other transit. In addition to the I-bank and transport proposals, Obama called for $25 billion for school modernization and $5 billion for community colleges. Conspicuously absent from his September 8 list of economic recovery measures was the previously rumored assistance to homeowners to refinance mortgages held by Fannie Mae and Freddie Mac. For the still bleeding homeowners and housing sector, the only measure offered by the president on September 8 was called 'Project Rebuild', allocating to local government $15 billion to fix vacant and foreclosed properties. Another $49 billion was earmarked for unemployment insurance extensions for the long-term jobless. Plus a further $35 billion to help keep teachers, police, and firefighters employed instead of laid off. All the preceding proposals—tax cuts, infrastructure, housing, unemployment, public sector jobs—comprised approximately the $447 billion package.

Obama additionally recommended that the $447 billion should be added to the Supercommittee's deficit target of a minimum $1.5 trillion. That meant the forthcoming December 2011 additional deficit cuts mandated to Congress by the August 2 debt-ceiling deal would now amount at least to $2 trillion. That $2 trillion was in addition to the August $1 trillion, for a total of at least $3 trillion.

Obama promised to announce details of his own deficit-cutting recommendations on September 19 directly and publicly to the Supercommittee, hinting that his recommendations would include cuts to Medicare and Medicaid as well as a tax reform plan. In an extremely important 'signal' to the opposition, Obama made it clear that he would consider even more cuts to Medicare and Medicaid than he might announce on September 19, so long as Teapublicans in the House and the Senate agreed to raise some tax revenues as part of any budget reduction deal in December.

## THE SEPTEMBER 19 ADDENDUM

On September 19 Obama offered $320 billion as a 'free down-payment' concession in Medicare-Medicaid cuts. In other words, that was the floor from which to start bargaining on such cuts, and he was willing to go higher in terms of health care spending cuts. He then laid out the possibility of even more than $320 billion, if the Supercommittee agreed to raise taxes in its revenues as well. As the mainstream press reported, "Mr. Obama did not just propose but insisted that any long-term debt reduction plan must not shave future Medicare benefits without also raising taxes on wealthiest taxpayers and corporations."[4] But the wording of his comments was careful not to indicate that he might veto Medicare cuts without a tax increase. That too was still possible.

That the $320 billion was only a starting point for cutting Medicare-Medicaid was evident from his previous offer in July to cut $425 billion from Medicare and Medicaid as part of a proposed 'grand bargain' at the time to resolve the debt-ceiling standoff with the House and Teapublicans.[5] And if $425 billion was Obama's true bottom-line offer, no doubt Teapublicans and the House would up that ante further. That the amount the president was willing to cut was in fact much higher was also corroborated in late October, when his close supporters in the Senate indicated the Congressional Democrats' recommendations to the Supercommittee. Those recommendations now called for $500 billion in cuts in Medicare-Medicaid. The Republicans in Congress thereafter quickly upped the ante and recommended $768 billion in Medicare-Medicaid-only cuts to the Supercommittee.[6] Obama's July 'grand bargain' offer to Boehner and the Republicans was a minimum $725 billion in entitlement program spending cuts. No doubt the Republicans recalled that prior position and offer of the president in their reply in late October.

On the other hand, Obama's July grand bargain offer to cut $300 billion in Social Security retirement benefits was specifically excluded from his September proposals. The total focus of entitlement cuts was thus now on Medicare-Medicaid. But, of course, as was evident throughout the year-long deficit-cutting debates, nothing is really 'off the table' once it is offered. No doubt the president's strategy was to allow the Supercommittee to recommend cuts in Social Security retirement, specifically raising the retirement age to 69, and not have to take the political heat himself for the recommendation.

In the week before September 19, Obama and billionaire Warren Buffet, a supporter of the administration, announced their mutual proposal for a 'millionaires tax'. Millionaires should not pay a lower tax rate than their secretaries, as Buffet put it. This became popularized by the press as the 'Buffet Rule.' In his September 19 address Obama adopted the Buffet Rule/ millionaires surtax as his own proposal. As the administration argued at the time, the average tax rate for the top 400 wealthiest taxpayers—mostly billionaires—was only 16.62% in 2007. It rose in 2008 to only 18.11% and no doubt fell again in 2009.[7] Other tax increase measures were also proposed on the 19th, including ending the Bush tax cuts for those earning $250,000 a year incomes, raising $1.276 billion over the coming decade.[8]

The total package of measures proposed on September 8 and 19 was called a 'jobs bill.' Republicans in the Senate dared the president and Senate Democratic leadership to bring it to a vote. They did. And it was defeated. The president thereafter vowed to bring each major element of the September proposals up for individual votes. Several were, and were defeated in turn as well. First the proposal to fund jobs for 35,000 teachers, police, firefighters and other 'first responders.' Then other measures. In sharp contrast, however, proposals to approve free trade legislation for Korea, Panama, and Colombia were quickly passed on an almost unanimous vote, showing that Democrats would vote with Republicans on measures the latter wanted, but Republicans would not vote with Democrats in turn.

## A PRELIMINARY ASSESSMENT OF SEPTEMBER 8 AND 19

The September 8 payroll tax cuts amounted to $240 billion. But $112 billion of this was a continuation of the previous year's 2% tax cut for workers. So only a 1.1% net additional, or about $60 billion, was potentially new stimulus to boost the economy and jobs. Moreover, the track record for the first worker 2% payroll tax cut was clear: it didn't create jobs. It was absorbed by other inflation factors in early 2011, and consumption fell to 0.1% while the payroll tax cut was implementation. Why then should another 1.1% fare any differently? Similarly, so far as the employers' 3.1% payroll tax cut was concerned, why would it not simply result in an increase in further cash hoarding? After all, more than $2 trillion was being hoarded by bigger businesses after receiving the trillions in tax cuts from 2008 to 2010. Why should smaller businesses not also hoard the cash? Or, why hire an unemployed worker to get the first half 3.1% payroll tax cut, when all a business had to do was claim the second 3.1% by giving employees a token raise? Better yet, why not hire a new worker the employer was planning to hire anyway, claim the new hire was given a 'raise,' and claim the full 6.2%? The employer 3.1% and 6.2% payroll tax cut was a Swiss cheese of loopholes, opening new ways for business to 'game' the payroll tax system to a long list of existing manipulations.[9]

The $35 billion for re-hiring of teachers and other public workers, the $30 billion in school modernization, the $49 billion in unemployment benefits, and the $15 billion in property restoration, was once again just another $129 billion in subsidies to state and local government by another name.[10] In the first economic recovery program of 2009, to recall, the total in state subsidies was about $264 billion. In many cases the states and cities held the money and laid off teachers and public employees anyway. Subsidies might temporarily prevent some layoffs, but they do not create net new jobs. Similarly for unemployment insurance subsidies. As essential and justified as such subsidies may be, they are not job creation programs.

The $50 billion transportation measure and the $10 billion I-bank also compare in part to the 2009 stimulus, or first recovery program. In the first recovery program its cost was approximately $100 billion. Now it was about half, or $60 billion. Whether $100 billion in 2009 or $60 billion in 2011, however, these are mostly very long-term spending programs. And whether spending $100 or $60 billion, when divided over ten years, in a specific year the spending is much too small to make a dent in the current 26 million jobless.

In summary with regard to jobs in Obama's third recovery program, while the $35 billion to save teachers' jobs might slow the loss of jobs at the state and local level, it would not create jobs. Secondly, the additional business tax cuts would not have much impact on job creation, for reasons discussed repeatedly in preceding chapters. Third, once again Obama's infrastructure spending measures were much too long-term to have an immediate impact on jobs. In short, Obama's September 8–19 proposals and third economic recovery program did not constitute a realistic jobs program in any sense.

So far as addressing the second great 'mini-crisis'—the homeowner foreclosure and growing negative equity problems—the third economic recovery program's $15 billion housing rescue provision did nothing whatsoever to resolve the homeowner crisis. Critics have often wondered why the administration in all three versions of its economic recovery programs has provided only token measures to rescue homeowners. The answer is not difficult. Banks and other financial corporations continue to retain a strong presence among inner 'advisors' in the Obama administration. A brief look at who attends the Obama-CEO planned and ad hoc meetings from time to time, at which policy is determined and revised, shows a continuing heavy direct influence by the banks and real estate corporate interests within the political boardrooms of the administration.

Unlike jobs and housing , states fared a little better in Obama's September 8 proposals, receiving $129 billion to play with and move around from project to project. But the infrastructure projects would be blocked, including the transportation project spending proposals of the third recovery program, and the teacher hiring provisions were rejected outright by the Teapublicans in Congress. Meanwhile, states' and especially cities' finances continued to deteriorate.

Tax revenues continued to lag as job recovery and incomes remained stagnant and business spending remained low. Housing's depression-level activity further depressed capital gains tax revenue as a source of funds. Further exacerbating state tax revenue collections was the continuing intensification of efforts by states to steal corporate headquarters from each other by lowering business taxes to lure companies from each other. There can be no solution to the state and local government fiscal crisis without a major resurgence in job creation, without an end to the business tax cut 'race to the bottom,' and without a fundamental restructuring of the tax system for states and cities. But there was never anything remotely resembling these kind of proposals in any of the three Obama economic recovery programs.

With regard to how to pay for it all—i.e. the September 19 addendum to September 8 programs—Obama on September 19 reiterated his original 'grand' goal of $4 trillion in deficit cuts, now raised to $4.4 trillion to cover the cost of the $447 billion third recovery programs.[11] The third recovery program would thus be financed by deficit reductions, to be determined by the Supercommittee and Congress by December 23, 2011.

## THE FEDERAL RESERVE'S 'OPERATION TWIST'

As in previous recovery programs of 2009 and 2010, the Obama programs were accompanied by shifts in Federal Reserve monetary policy as well. In 2009 it was QE1. Other Fed policies provided zero-interest loans to banks while paying banks interest just to borrow at 0.1% and then leave it with the Fed. Other special auctions and swaps injected still more. The Fed was also directly involved in the government financing of partial nationalizations of companies like AIG and others. With the second economic recovery program in late 2010, once again the Federal Reserve introduced a second quantitative easing program, or QE2. It was a 'mere' $600 billion mortgage-bond-buying effort. It produced an even smaller impact on the economy and recovery. However, it did succeed, like its prior QE1 cousin, in generating a stock market and commodities bubble, as banks took the free money and instead of lending and investing to small business, loaned it to hedge funds and other 'trader-speculators' that bought stocks and commodities worldwide.

Once QE2 bond-buying ended in April 2010, the stock market began its steady decline immediately thereafter. The commodities boomlet also peaked around that time, and began its subsequent descent. By the summer of 2011 another stock market falloff was in progress. S&P 500 stocks declined by about 20% by October 2011. Calls from investors rose once again by August for yet more Fed QE to stimulate stock and commodity buying. With Congress and the president grappling with the debt-ceiling deal in August 2011 and the appearance of fiscal policy gridlock for the long term, and with European banks and sovereign debt becoming a growing issue, the Federal Reserve found itself under great pressure to 'do something,' if for no other reason than to appear that 'something was being done.'

In this environment the Fed chairman, Ben Bernanke, introduced on September 21—just two days after Obama's September 19 speech—what was called 'QE2.5.'[12] QE2.5 was something of a misnomer, however. The new policy was not a true new bond-buying 'QE' effort by the Fed. Rather it was called 'Operation Twist.' The 'twist' simply meant the Fed would sell $400 billion of its short-term securities in the market—i.e. Treasury bills and such—and with the money from those sales turn around and buy long-term bonds from the market. The selling of short-term notes would theoretically raise short-term interest rates. That would potentially have the positive effect of attracting foreign capital into the U.S. to buy short-term Treasuries from the Fed now that the interest rate from those short-term Treasury securities was now higher. Conversely, the Fed's buying in turn of longer-term bonds from the market would theoretically have an opposite effect of lowering long-term interest rates, including mortgage rates. Lower mortgage rates thus might stimulate homebuying and help the housing sector. Higher short-term rates, conversely, might not also dampen stock and commodities speculative borrowing. In a nutshell, that was the theory behind QE2.5 and Operation Twist.

But the stock market was not impressed with Bernanke's Operation Twist. It had wanted another convenient drug fix, shot in the arm, of free money from the Fed. It wanted another QE3. All the Fed did was move the money around. The New York stock market responded by falling 283 points the same day.

If the purpose of the additional $400 billion in mortgage bond-buying was to lower mortgage rates and stimulate housing sales to absorb the continuing record supply of foreclosed homes coming on the market, that purpose failed. Even record low mortgage rates cannot stimulate the housing market. The administration's goal should have been to get home prices to rise and to keep foreclosures coming onto the market and causing a glut of supply of homes that kept depressing home prices. But the Obama administration's policy toward housing had always been to subsidize mortgage lenders and servicers first—in both cases largely the big five banks—to help builders work off their new unsold inventory of homes second, and only after to undertake some token mortgage loan modifications for homeowners facing foreclosure or being 'under water'.

Banks were intent on hoarding their cash, and not lending to homebuyers any more than they were interested in lending to small businesses. Thus, bank practices were stifling a recovery of the housing sector as well as investment and job creation by the small business sector. The Obama administration should have addressed that real core of the problem, which it could easily have done. Of all mortgages issued in the previous three years, 90% were now held by government agencies—Fannie Mae, Freddie Mac, and the FHA.

If those mortgage loans were now held by the government, it could easily have restructured the principal and interest and lowered payments to prevent foreclosure. That would have restored home prices, now experiencing a third dip by late 2011. Restored prices would have stimulated demand and resolved the negative equity problem. But to do all that would have required the administration to go head to head with the banks and other investors who invested in the mortgages originally. The problem, in other words, to solving the housing crisis was not economic; it was political. The Obama administration was not about to take on the big banks who were the lenders and mortgage servicers.

Few economists or industry experts publicly or privately expressed the view the Fed's Operation Twist would have much effect on the economy. After 33 months of zero interest rates and $2.3 trillion in Fed direct mortgage bond purchases, another $400 billion shifted from one area to another over the next nine months promised to have even less impact. A growing number of economists and businesses began raising the idea that perhaps the Fed had run out of policy ammunition and was now a spent force as far as generating economic recovery was concerned.

## 'WHY RECOVERY FAILED' REVISITED

Obama's initial proposals for a third economic recovery program announced on September 8 and 19, 2011, once again repeated the fundamental failures of his 2009 and 2010 first and second recovery programs. The third recovery program once again was top heavy in tax cuts that most likely would end up hoarded or not invested to create real jobs. The roughly $189 billion in non-tax-cut spending measures in the third program amounted to a spending stimulus that was token given the emerging second relapse of the economy in the summer 2011. Like the two previous 2009 and 2010 recovery programs, the third provided subsidies that did not create jobs and infrastructure spending that mostly would create jobs only in the longer term.

As argued elsewhere in this book, three fundamental reasons underlay the failure of all the Obama recovery programs: firstly, all had an 'insufficient magnitude' of spending stimulus; secondly, all were poorly composed, both in terms of disproportionate emphasis on tax cuts as well as disproportionate emphasis on spending subsidies rather than spending on direct job creation and housing bailout; thirdly, all were inadequate in terms of 'poor timing.' They were short term, for one year, relying thereafter on the market and business to take up the slack, with no intermediate program solutions if it didn't. In addition, the timing was bad in the sense that the infrastructure spending was much too long-term in character and far too capital intensive rather than labor intensive. The third program tried to address this latter shortcoming, but by then it was politically too late as well as continuingly too little.

A comparison of these common errors in all the three recovery programs is represented in Table 9.1, which summarizes the distribution of program costs between tax cuts, subsidies spending, and long-term infrastructure spending.

*Table 9.1*   Economic recovery programs, tax cuts versus spending and subsidy versus infrastructure, 2009–11
(billions, current $)

| Program | Total cost | Tax | Spending | Subsidy spending | Infrastructure spending (long) |
|---|---|---|---|---|---|
| Bush I: (3/08) | $168 | $90 | $78 | | |
| Bush II: (10/08) | $700* | $700 | $700 | | |
| Obama I (2/09 + supplements) | $862 | $417 | $445 | $314 | $130 est. |
| Obama II (12/10) | $857 | $802 | $55 | $55 | |
| Obama III (9/11) | $447 | $253 | $194 | $89 | $105 |
| Totals | $3,034 | $1,562 | $1,472 | $1,158 | $235 |

*Notes*: * = TARP subsidies to banks. Obama I includes additional miscellaneous spending (neither subsidy nor infrastructure) in the amount of $79 billion.

*Source*: Author's calculations from public sources.

## SECOND RELAPSE, DOUBLE DIP...OR WORSE?

All indicators strongly suggest the U.S. economy by late summer 2011 was experiencing what is called a relapse—i.e. a sharp deterioration in several key indicators and a drift toward negative growth and possible recurrence of recession (i.e. double dip).

Concerning the timing of a possible double dip, Congress, with the president agreeably in tow, appears intent on cutting deficits. That may negate any typical election year 'political business cycle' temporary stimulus in 2012. Should Congress and Obama deeply cut spending in 2012, it will virtually ensure a trajectory from 2011's second economic relapse to an austerity recession and double dip in 2012. But the deficit cuts of August and December 2011 may be backloaded, i.e. that take effect only in 'out years' commencing after the 2012 election. In that case the odds are that the double dip will be delayed another year to 2013. Whichever occurs, it is likely that the U.S. economy will transition from a relapse condition to a double-dip recession no later than 2013.

2013 is also the most likely year for the double dip since that is when trillions of dollars of corporate junk bonds start to come due for rollover and refinancing. Over the past three years of the present crisis and failed recovery, many companies that were financially fragile avoided default and bankruptcy by issuing a record level of high yield (called 'junk') bond debt to raise cash and buy time to put off default. Trillions of dollars of these bonds will come due for refinancing starting in 2013–14. Many will not survive another financing round. The result will be a further contraction on the business side of the economy and a new loss of business confidence across wide swaths of the

U.S. economy. That will come at a time when the government deficit cutting begins in earnest. Households at that juncture will also be in worse shape, given the continuing downward drift of their real disposable income (pointed out in Chapter 8) and little change in the continuing deterioration of jobs and housing foreclosures-home values.

With the prospect of the U.S. economy continuing slow growth through 2012—and simultaneously facing deep government spending cuts, business defaults, another year of poor job growth, more foreclosures, and a further decline in disposable incomes—the possibility of double dip no later than 2013 is real.

There are two 'wild cards' that may precipitate a double dip even before 2013. One was just mentioned—i.e. Congress and Obama cutting spending in earnest in 2012 instead of backloading the cuts to later years. The second wild card is the growing instability in the world banking system, driven by growing troubles in the Eurozone. The crisis there is not simply one of sovereign debt. It is not Greece or Italy or Spain. It is the banks throughout Europe that loaned to those peripheral economies. The borrowers in the peripheral economies—i.e. their banks, their businesses, as well as their governments— face increasing difficulty repaying both principal or interest due on their loans to the banks elsewhere in the European 'core' that lent them the money. It is therefore not a government-to-government sovereign debt crisis; it is primarily a bank-to-bank and bank-to-government financial crisis.

By late 2011 the crisis began spreading toward its core economy bank roots—the banks in the northern economies of France, Belgium, Germany, etc. The deepening recession and in some cases depression (Greece) in the peripheral economies meant their increasing inability to repay the core banks. As a result, they have been loaned further funds by other governments, the IMF, and the special Financial Stability Fund put together by those governments, so they can continue to make payments on their loans to the northern banks. The institutions insist they introduce austerity to get the bridge loans. But austerity ensures the peripheral economies cannot raise their own funds to repay the northern banks. Thus they must borrow even more. The peripheral economies have thus become stuck in a vicious cycle. At some point they will not be able to repay their loans and they will not be given additional institutional loans to make the payments. At some point the cost of default by Greece or some other peripheral economy will become less than the cost of continuing bailouts. Defaults will then occur and the northern banks will have to write down the losses. Where and how this impacts the U.S. economy has to do with the connections and interdependencies between the banks in the core economies—i.e. France, Germany, and the United Kingdom—and the U.S. core banks (Chase, Citigroup, Bank of America, Wells Fargo, Goldman Sachs, Morgan Stanley, and the larger regional banks). The U.S. core banks are deeply exposed in terms of lending to the Euro core banks. When the Euro core banks record losses from the inevitable defaults coming, it will reverberate in turn in losses for the U.S. core banks.

Several of the largest U.S. banks never fully recovered from the 2008–09 crisis. Their profits recovery was artificially dependent on speculative trading profits and government liquidity injections, neither of which are likely to be repeated again. The U.S. banks' bad debts were never removed from their balance sheets; they were only 'offset' by Federal Reserve massive liquidity injections. The banks remain fragile, therefore, which becomes increasingly apparent as their own revenues and profits decline once again in late 2011 and 2012. In short, sovereign defaults in Europe could precipitate a deeper crisis in the Euro core banks that in turn might push the worst-case U.S. banks over the edge in 2012. Should that wild card scenario unfold in 2012, then all bets are off that a U.S. double-dip recession would be delayed until 2013. It will happen earlier.

In other words, the key to the timing of a double-dip recession in the U.S. depends upon the magnitude and timing of deficit cutting by Congress and on financial instability in the European banking system.

Some of the best economic minds with the ability to see the long trends going forward have been predicting an inevitable double-dip recession, and even a growing possibility of still worse—i.e. a new global depression. These are serious commentators who, like this writer, successfully predicted the coming problems in 2007, the banking crash in 2008, and the faltering recovery of 2009–11.

One of this small group has been economist Nouriel Roubini, of New York University, who predicted the coming crisis in 2007 and now forecasts the coming double dip. At the close of the third quarter of 2011, Roubini observed that there was "60% chance of U.S. Recession."[13] He added,

we're running out of policy bullets...Until last year, policymakers could always produce a new rabbit from their hat...But now we have run out of rabbits to pull out of hats...So can we avoid another severe recession? It might simply be mission impossible.[14]

As evidence for his view, Roubini pointed out that a number of key global economies were either already in recession, nearing stagnant growth, or else rapidly slowing. He noted that global manufacturing and exports were falling and could set off currency wars between the advanced economies, which would prove a no-win game for all. He even suggested that failure to act soon to stimulate the Eurozone economies and stabilize the Euro banks might very well lead to a global depression.

Other respectable sources in the U.S. raised a similar scenario of inevitable double dip. A *Wall Street Journal* poll of economists was more optimistic, but nonetheless reported that those economists surveyed "saw a one in three chance of recession within the next 12 months."[15] More ominously, the Economic Cycle Research Institute (ECRI), a highly respected economic forecasting source in the U.S., declared on September 30, 2011, that the double dip had in effect already arrived. The ECRI had correctly predicted the beginning and the end of the recent recession in December 2007 and June

2009, respectively, while the vast majority of other academic and business economists were predicting continued economic growth of 2.2% for 2008. Using proprietary information and models, the ECRI also correctly predicted all the beginnings of recessions over the past 15 years, and never predicted a recession in error. Its track record of recession predictions is thus impressive. Therefore its prediction of a double dip already in progress was significant when it reported at the end of September 2011 that "Early last week, ECRI notified clients that the U.S. economy is indeed tipping into a new recession. And there's nothing that policy makers can do to head it off."[16] As ECRI's chief operations officer, Lakshman Achuthan, added in a *New York Times* interview in early October, "If the United States isn't already in a recession now it's about to enter one."[17]

Even more sobering scenarios of something worse than double dip began to appear as well. Some sources began describing the current faltering global recovery as a 'Lesser Depression.' What was generally referred to over the past three years as a 'Great Recession' but is now called Lesser Depression suggests something worse is now underway. Somehow the severity has worsened, from a Great Recession to a Lesser Depression, and not just in the U.S. but globally.

What others choose to carefully call a Lesser Depression, global financier and economic commentator George Soros has addressed more directly by raising the specter of a possible depression. In a recent article, 'How to Stave Off a Second Great Depression,' Soros directly warns that "financial markets are driving the world toward another Great Depression. The authorities, particularly in Europe, have lost control of the situation."[18] Soros correctly adds that there is no way out of the European sovereign and bank debt crises without economic growth. Austerity programs cannot succeed and will make things worse. Concentrated deleveraging "is one of the main causes of the crisis" in the Eurozone and must be stopped. He goes on to describe how the fiscal and monetary systems of Europe must be radically restructured, and further notes that "only public pressure can make it happen."

The truth of the likelihood of double-dip recession in the U.S. lies somewhere between Roubini and the ECRI, while the growing possibility of something much worse in the not-too-distant future is correctly recognized by Soros. The U.S. economy is mired, in late summer 2011, in yet another second economic relapse. A future, more severe double dip is just a matter of timing—both in Europe and the U.S. and elsewhere abroad.

When it does arrive, it will confirm this writer's previous 2009 predictions that the U.S. economy had entered an 'Epic Recession.' Unlike Great Recession or Lesser Depression, Epic Recession is not just a general descriptive term for a contraction that is not typically normal, but is a theory of why the current recession is fundamentally different. Epic Recessions come in two forms: 'Type I' and 'Type II.' In their Type I form they are essentially a series of double dips (or more than two) strung together, interrupted by brief, weak recoveries followed by short, shallow downturns—i.e. relapses. Relapses are thus an aspect (and indicator) of Epic Recessions as well as double dips. This scenario is precisely what happened, this writer argued in a previous work, in 1907–14 in the U.S. It is also what has happened in Japan for the past two decades. But Type I Epic Recessions may also, under certain conditions and policy responses, transition into a Type II, which is a precondition for descent into global depression as well.[19]

## WHY HAS FISCAL-MONETARY POLICY FAILED?

In the Introduction to this book it was noted that one of the main themes of the book was to better understand why traditional fiscal-monetary policies have failed to generate a sustained recovery. We can now comment on that theme. Our commentary will lead in turn to our final chapter and another primary theme of the book: what different policies are necessary, given that recent policies in the form of the three Obama economic recovery programs have failed to generate a sustained economic recovery.

The first reason why traditional fiscal and monetary policies have not 'worked' these past three years is the huge debt load still overhanging the three major sectors of the economy: households, banks, government, and certain subsectors of business as well. Some say the problem of faltering recovery is due to the drag on the economy of slow debt deleveraging. Deleveraging means the paying down of debt. But it is not that deleveraging has been too slow; the problem is that deleveraging has hardly occurred at all – at least not for the vast majority of consumer households, small businesses, and local governments.

Except for the wealthiest 10%, households have not been able to pay down their record level of debt accumulated in the run-up to the crisis in 2007. Mortgage debt, credit card debt, consumer debt, health care services debt, and student debt remain at near peak levels. To the extent that any debt has been reduced in the past three years, it has not been because households have paid off that debt; it is because credit card companies have written-off bad debt and more than 11 million foreclosures have similarly resulted in mortgage debt write-down. The remaining household debt has not been paid off and recently has begun rising again.

The primary reason for the inability of the majority of households to truly deleverage is the lack of income growth. It is impossible to discuss debt as a drag on recovery without recognizing stagnant incomes for the bottom 80% of households. The persistence of 25 million jobless explains a good part of the income stagnation problem today, but not all of it. Nominal wages and earnings have also persistently declined since 2000, and that decline has accelerated since 2008.

Two major bouts of commodity inflation (gas, food, etc.) in 2008 and 2011 have reduced real incomes of the bottom 80%, and thus contributed to the income stagnation problem. So has the continuing escalation of health care services prices, prescription drugs, and higher education costs—all rising in double digits in recent years. Nearly zero interest investment earnings for tens of millions of households, especially seniors, has further contributed to income stagnation. Rising local government taxes and fees of all kinds and stagnant transfer payments (Social Security cost of living increases) has added to the problem. Wealth in the form of 401k pension balances,[20] home values, and what other few fixed investments the bottom 80% have also exacerbates the problem. In other words, to pay down debt—i.e. to deleverage—there must be income growth. But there hasn't. In fact, income growth has been negative and declining in recent years, following decades of prior slowing and stagnating incomes for the tens of millions of families constituting the bottom 80% of households.

The lack of any real deleveraging of debt means that households must continue to pay past high debt-interest and principal when their income and ability to make those payments have been declining. Take, for example, the 17 million households with mortgages 'under water' today. Their debt payment obligations haven't declined, but their income in the majority of cases has either stagnated or declined. In addition they have had to pay more for the costs of basics like food, gas, clothing, and especially health care and education and local taxes as their income has declined. That means there hasn't been much left to spend on increasing their consumption of other goods and services. Only the wealthiest households have increased their consumption. Seeing no return of consumption, business spending also fails to continue to expand. After an initial adding of inventories in expectation of future consumption increases by households, business spending flattens out and waits. Businesses hoard their cash. In short, the serious mal-distribution of income in the U.S. over the last three decades, exacerbated by the recent crisis, functions as a major drag on recovery. The high household debt that still remains makes the matter worse.

The two poles of the problem in fact exacerbate each other: stagnating income makes it difficult to pay off old debt and pushes households to take on new additional debt in order to make up for the stagnating income. Consumption 'fragility' thus deteriorates further.

Traditional government policies have been inadequate, poorly targeted, and badly timed to address the consumption fragility of most households today. Tax cuts to consumers are simply used to make up for lost income, not to pay down debt. Unemployment insurance and subsidies to states simply prevents an even worse consumption collapse, but does not result in a consumption net increase. Government fiscal policy in the three successive Obama recovery programs has insufficiently offset income decline, let alone provide sufficient income to pay down debt and to deleverage. The result is that households and consumers are unable to lead an economic recovery.

Instead of partially and temporarily offsetting income decline, policies should have been adopted by the Obama administration both to redistribute and restore income growth for the bottom 80% of households, on the one hand, and to expunge the debt overhang for same households, on the other. The targets of policy should have been debt retirement and sustained income generation. But for that the Obama programs would have had to focus on job creation and foreclosure prevention-home value restoration as a start. Solving the health care inflation problem now—not in 2014—and relieving students of ever-growing education debt should have been directly addressed. So should directly providing low-cost 0.25% money loans to small businesses and restoring retirement income security for seniors. Instead, small businesses were all but ignored for the first two years and seniors were given token, temporary subsidies. But Obama's biggest policy failure was not to pay adequate attention to immediate income restoration by creating jobs quickly and by not attending to immediate debt reduction for homeowners by requiring banks to reduce the principal and debt of homeowners in foreclosure and 'under water.' Once again, policies targeting real income generation and debt reduction were the key to recovery—not tax cuts, government spending on subsidies, or even token long-term infrastructure spending job creation. But Obama chose the latter and ignored the former.

A parallel 'fragility' problem (excess debt, onerous debt terms, and falling income) has existed for state and local governments since the crisis began. That same problem has been increasingly replicated at the federal government level as well, as deficits have risen due to bailouts, wars, and corporate-wealthy tax cuts and as revenues have fallen due to lack of economic recovery. Government at all levels is experiencing what might be called 'balance sheet fragility,' an analogue to households' 'consumption fragility.' The income of government is its tax revenue. That has fallen with the recession, while government debt has risen as a consequence of more tax cuts that were theoretically supposed to generate more tax revenue but didn't. The loss of tax revenue has been the primary cause of both federal and local government budget deficits. Spending increases are significant but secondary. At the federal level alone, tax revenue decline is responsible for 58% of the budget deficits, driven by failed recovery and ever-continuing tax cuts.

Obama administration policies have failed to address this tax revenue collapse at the state and local government level. Its solution has been to periodically provide direct subsidy payments to the states, which then dribbled out some of the subsidies to the cities.

Instead of pumping temporary subsidies into states and cities to offset their declining revenues and growing deficits, the administration should have targeted local government income, or tax revenues, as a solution. The state and local tax system in the U.S. needs fundamental restructuring. To start, states should be relieved from competing with each other by lowering state taxes to lure businesses from each other. Secondly, a business-to-business value added tax is needed, not just sales taxes on final purchases. Business property should also be taxed at the same rate as residences, which it is not. Like homeowners, local governments are also faced with escalating health care costs. Those costs, in the form of Medicaid, are the number one cause of spending increases that are driving state deficits. Here the problem is once again the failure by the Obama administration to control health care costs, which then translate into escalating Medicaid payments by the states. Then there are retirement costs in the form of local government employees' pensions. A restructuring of the entire national retirement system is necessary to relieve local governments of this debt burden. Another measure to reduce state and local government debt is a fundamental reworking of the municipal bond market by the government to reduce the cost of borrowing by local governments and thus their debt burden. New ways to finance local government besides accessing the municipal bond markets are needed. Debt elimination and write-offs are another unused policy option. During the run-up to the recent crisis banks lied and took advantage of cities and local governments by selling them derivatives and interest rate swaps. That led to an epidemic of indebtedness by cities and school districts to the banks, and in many cases to subsequent local government defaults. That debt should be overturned and the banks should repay the cities and districts, starting with debt write-offs and including penalty payments back to the cities and school districts affected.

As in the case of households and consumers, the Obama administration recovery programs and policies toward state and local government during the recent crisis relied on subsidy spending. That simply offset the debt and revenue decline problems temporarily and bought some time. That brief time bought was then wasted. When the general economic recovery did not happen, and the subsidies were spent, the bottom once again dropped out of state and local government finances. Instead of temporary subsidies, the administration should have focused on restoring state and local governments' tax base (i.e. their incomes) on a more permanent basis. It should have focused additionally on reducing their debt load and liberalizing debt servicing terms.

Tax revenues for local government are the analogue for disposable income for households. Spending on services is the analogue for consumption spending. The Obama administration has made the same error with regard to trying to resurrect the important economic sector of state and local government, just as it has with consumer households: token, temporary, and ill-timed tax and spending policies cannot overcome the bigger problems of debt overhang and falling income levels. The administration's policy targets should have been income restoration and debt elimination.

Unlike the majority of households and state and local governments, large non-financial businesses are not 'fragile.' The same cannot be said for an important segment of business: the small business sector, defined as those businesses with 50 or fewer employees. Like households and local government, their debt levels also remain high, their debt terms increasingly stringent, and their incomes stagnant. This segment is not the large Fortune 500 or even 5,000 companies and multinational corporations. Those do not have a financial fragility problem. Their income has accelerated to record levels. Nor do they historically depend on raising debt so they do not have a particularly serious debt overhang problem. If they do issue debt it is generally in the form of high-grade corporate bonds, which carry low interest costs and favorable terms. This group or segment has also in recent years accumulated record amounts of cash from bond issuance, from deep reductions in their labor costs and from rising productivity that have produced record profit margins.

Medium-sized businesses have also added debt, not reduced it. But unlike their big corporate cousins, that debt has not been the low cost-generous terms of payment debt. They have added debt in the form of junk bonds, at high costs and on less favorable terms. In fact, junk bond issues reached record levels in 2009–10. But that record issuance of junk is due for rollover—i.e. to be refinanced—in the next few years. Their debt costs may thus soon rise much more. Whether these medium-sized companies' income (sales revenue and profits) can service these higher costs remains to be seen. If not, defaults will escalate once again after 2013.

The federal government, like state and local governments, has also become decidedly more 'balance sheet fragile' in recent years. Its debt has accelerated from $9 trillion to more than $15 trillion since 2008. The reasons behind the federal debt run-up have been explained in Chapter 7 of this book. But the federal government also has an 'inadequate income' problem. Its tax base has also been eroded seriously. Thus a fundamental restructuring of the tax system in the U.S. at the federal level is also required in order to reduce its balance sheet fragility. On the spending side, significant contributions to reducing its fragility are also possible, in the areas of health care services costs and retirement systems restructuring as well.

But the federal government instead has chosen to address its growing balance sheet fragility by focusing on cutting spending instead of raising revenue. Those spending cuts will only serve as a further drag on economic recovery. And that will result in even less tax revenue and thus even more fragility. The federal government must therefore find new ways to raise tax revenue (i.e. income) from new forms of taxation and from new forms of government direct investment.

Lastly, there is the matter of banks' financial fragility. Contrary to official administration assurances, the banking system in the U.S. did not fully recover after the banking panic and crash of 2008. Many banks still remain financially fragile, just as do the majority of households, local government, and a good part of the small business sector. Together, the entire economic system might in turn be called 'systemically fragile.'

Most U.S. banks never eliminated the mountain of bad debt on their balance sheets. Debt levels today still remain inordinately high. As pointed out repeatedly in this book, the Federal Reserve's policy was to offset the massive bad debt with huge liquidity injections (i.e. money, cash, 'income') into the banks. That liquidity is still there, but so too is much of the original bad debt. Furthermore, previous levels of 'income' from stock price appreciation and speculative trading revenues have now fallen. As their stock prices and trading income have fallen, banks' fragility has deteriorated given that their bad debt on their balance sheets has remained. Big banks' turning to massive layoffs of thousands of their employees in the fall of 2011, in order to cut costs, is an indication of their growing fragility.

The Obama administration has employed the wrong policies with respect to the banking sector over the past three years—just as it has with respect to households, local government, and small businesses. Back in early 2009 when it introduced its 'bank rescue policies' it had a clear choice. It chose not to rid the banks of their 'bad assets' and debt, but to simply offset those bad assets, allowing them to remain on banks' balance sheets, with massive liquidity (free money) injections by the Federal Reserve. Instead of the Federal Reserve offsetting the banks' bad debts with liquidity injections, it should have taken action to remove the debt by establishing what is called a 'bad bank,' transferring the bad assets and debts held by the banks to a fully nationalized bank run by the federal government. Forms of consumer credit should also have been taken from the banks and financed going forward in a utility banking system. In exchange for eliminating their bad debt, the Obama administration should have required that the banks immediately reduce by an equivalent amount of their write-offs the principal and interest of homeowners having mortgages with them. Furthermore, the mortgages held directly by the federal government in the hands of the FHA and Fannie Mae and Freddie Mac, could also have been immediately 'restructured' in similar fashion by the federal government. A similar process of required write-downs by banks for outstanding small business loans should have taken place.

This approach has a double positive result: it reduces the debt overhang in the banks, theoretically allowing them to lend more, and it reduces the debt overhang for homeowners and small businesses, theoretically permitting them to consume and invest more. In other words, the way to increase consumption is to eliminate debt permanently by government policy direct action—not to subsidize consumption temporarily.

The major problems of continuing massive debt overhang and stagnating and falling incomes by the majority of consumer households, by state and local governments, and by small businesses negates normal fiscal (tax and spending) and monetary (QE, zero rates) policy approaches. These traditional policies have, after three years, clearly proven inadequate. They cannot get the economy on a sustained growth path. That is because their impact is reduced by the debt and income effects described above. A fundamental restructuring of the U.S. economy is necessary, beginning with the banking, tax, and retirement systems. Only that can successfully address the deeper, long-run problems of income maldistribution and debt overhang that prevent traditional fiscal and monetary policies from having any success in the shorter run.

In economists' parlance, the problem of the ineffectiveness of traditional fiscal and monetary policy is that the debt and income effects have sharply reduced the tax, spending, and money 'multipliers' associated with fiscal and monetary policy today. Monetary policy is mired in what is called a classical liquidity trap. In addition, cash injections of trillions of dollars into the banks have resulted in either cash hoarding or in lending to speculators and offshore investors instead of to U.S. small-medium businesses and consumers that need it most and would spend it to create jobs and recovery.

In a similar manner, today's cash hoarding by most large non-financial corporations indicates their plans not to invest in the U.S. but to invest offshore, where even greater profits are available, or to invest in speculative financial instruments (derivatives, currencies, etc.) where short-term quick profits are often possible. Globalization and financialization of the U.S. and world economy are thus major new forces mitigating against real investment in the U.S. that would otherwise create jobs. Without that investment and that job creation, recovery is increasingly difficult to achieve from normal fiscal and monetary measures. Traditional fiscal and monetary policies—that attempt to stimulate business investment spending by cutting business taxes and otherwise reducing business costs by deregulation or other measures— simply results in more cash accumulation and hoarding in the short run. Or, in the longer run, results in investing in offshore markets and/or in shorter-term financial speculative ventures.

The Obama recovery programs have failed for reasons stated throughout this book and summarized in Chapter 1: insufficient magnitude, poor composition, and bad timing, as well as the administration's loss of control of the policy agenda to Teapublicans, a wasted concern with bipartisanship, a failure to recognize and seize the historic opportunities, and so forth. But from another perspective one can argue that the Obama policies have failed due to the inability to understand that in an Epic Recession situation, there is a significant neutralization of traditional fiscal and monetary policies. Fundamentally new policies are therefore needed to achieve a sustained economic recovery. Policies that focus on debt reduction, income generation, and if necessary income re-redistribution. Policies that result in a fundamental restructuring of the tax system, the banking system, the retirement and health care systems, and of the U.S. labor market in general in order to bring about a rebalancing of income that has over the past three decades become seriously skewed in favor of the wealthiest 10% of households and the largest corporations at the expense of the remaining 90% of households and smaller businesses. As the third theme of this book noted in the introductory chapter, compared to all prior economic recoveries from recession *never has so much been received by so few at the expense of so many* as a consequence of the many economic recovery programs introduced from 2008 through 2011.'

The fundamentals of such an alternative set of policies and program for recovery are the subject of the following and final chapter.

# 10

# An Alternative Program for Economic Recovery

'Fundamentals of Economic Restructuring for the Twenty-First Century'

## FOUR REQUISITES FOR ECONOMIC RECOVERY

Any successfully economic recovery program in the future must not repeat the strategic errors of the Obama administration. A successful recovery program must satisfy a **First Principle of a Balanced Immediate–Intermediate– Longer-Run** program. While the primary emphasis must be on immediate solutions that work, it must also emphasize equally important—and adequately funded—intermediate and longer-term measures. Obama's first program was based on the recovery getting underway quickly after one year and relied on the market—i.e. the business sector—to do the heavy lifting after that year. That failed. The Obama program also relied on subsidizing a floor under consumption for a year. That worked for only a year then ran out. The Obama program emphasized a composition of tax cuts, especially business tax cuts. That ended up hoarded after a year. The first program's failure proves that a recovery strategy must be longer term and cannot rely on the market after only a year. It lacked any effective intermediate programs, and was therefore forced to add piecemeal ineffective and insufficient stop-gap measures after a year. It also proposed very long-term infrastructure projects with virtually no effect in the immediate or intermediate term. A successful program cannot rely on insufficiently funded, capital-intensive, long-run infrastructure spending. In short, the first Obama program was lopsided in terms of focus on the immediate and very long-term and insufficiently so in both cases, while lacking any real intermediate programs. When subsidies ran out and business did not spend its tax cuts after a year, the administration was left holding an empty policy bag.

Recovery Programs must also satisfy the **Second Principle of Priority Focus on Jobs, Housing, and State-Local Government.** Moreover, the measures undertaken to address these three key areas must not be token in magnitude but of sufficient massive scale and 'paid for'—i.e. funded—not by raising deficits but by new tax initiatives. That requires a fundamental restructuring of the tax system, which leads to the Third Principle of a successful future recovery.

The **Third Principle of Fundamental Restructuring of the Tax, Retirement, and Banking Systems** is no less essential for any sustained economic recovery. The priority programs identified in the Second Principle are not possible, for

170

example, without a basic reordering of the tax system, the banking system, and the retirement system in the U.S.

The *tax system* has been turned on its head in the past three decades and today is a major factor in restricting both the growth of investment in the U.S. and therefore jobs and, even more so, in undermining consumption growth that in the final analysis is necessary for investment and jobs. The U.S. is not 'broke.' It is wealthier than ever before. It's just that that wealth has been accumulated and concentrated among a growing, narrow group of corporations, investors, and the wealthiest 5% and even 1% of households. That concentration and accumulation has been made possible by several forces, but none more massive in effect than the inversion of the tax system in favor of the wealthy and their corporations, the latter functioning as the 'money conduit' to transfer wealth and income to the wealthiest households, speculators, and investors. Moreover, two important trends in recent decades have been growing within that accumulation and concentration, also enabled by the tax system changes since the 1970s. The first is the shifting of that concentrated income and wealth to offshore shelters and to investing in what are called emerging markets in Asia and elsewhere. That's investment that could have, and should have, gone into the U.S. to grow the U.S. economy and create jobs. The second is that the tax system-enabled income concentration at the top has been invested increasingly in financial instruments and markets around the globe as well—another mass diversion of money that could, and should, have been invested in job-creating projects in the U.S. This offshore flowing of capital from the U.S., now enabled and promoted by today's inverted tax system, must be reversed. And more fundamentally still, the income and wealth accumulated and concentrated by the wealthiest households and their corporations must be re transferred back to the bottom 80% of households by means of a new, fundamental restructuring of the U.S. tax system.

Not least of the required three fundamental restructurings is the *banking system*. With the rise of global speculative investing in recent decades, banks and bankers have accumulated an inordinate amount of economic and political power. This 'financialization' of the U.S. economy has had dire consequences for both the political system and the economy. One consequence of the growing negative impact of financialization on the economy has been the growing financial instability that has had a devastating effect on household, small business, and consumer credit. Households and small businesses have had nothing to do with the causes of recent and chronic financial instability precipitated by the banks and 'shadow' banks. Yet they have suffered the most from it. It is therefore necessary to create not simply a wall between the essential consumer-household credit markets and the high-risk, speculative finance that has been growing exponentially for decades. A moat must be placed between the two.

The *retirement system* established in the U.S. in the late 1940s is crumbling. There are 100 million people who directly depend on it and it is in the process of rapid decline. Social Security is inadequate to provide a reasonable retirement, yet it is under intensive attack. Medicare is eroding in terms of coverage while its costs to retirees is rising. It is under even greater attack. Private defined benefit pensions have been decimated and reduced over recent decades and employers are intensifying their efforts to dismantle what's left. Their past alternative to real defined benefit pensions—the 401k plans and other defined contribution pensions—have proved a complete failure in providing retirement income security. The last of the 1940s-envisioned 'three-legged stool' retirement system for the U.S.—personal savings—has been all but eliminated as a source of retirement as stagnating incomes in the U.S. now for decades have resulted in families spending their retirement savings just to make ends meet in the present. More than 77 million baby-boomer generation Americans are now approaching retirement and tens of millions cannot afford to do so. Most therefore must continue to 'work until they drop,' as they say, further shortening their life spans while preventing younger workers from accessing job openings in the labor force.

At the deepest level, the reason why Obama's recovery programs have repeatedly failed is that the U.S. economy has become 'system fragile.' By fragility is meant that debt levels have risen for households, most businesses and governments alike. Fragility is also a function of the terms on which debt must be repaid. However, it is more than just debt levels or terms; fragility is about the lack of adequate income growth to pay for debt principal and interest. Fragility may increase because debt levels rise, or because payment terms become more stringent. It may also rise because income stagnates or falls.

In the U.S., banks took on massive debt, especially in the last decade, which they then couldn't pay. Their collapse led to bailouts by government. Those bailouts simply transferred banks' bad debt to the federal government's balance sheet—i.e. raising the latter's deficits and total national debt. The deep recession increased government debt further, both federal and state-local. The historic tax cuts of the past decade, combined with escalating war spending and runaway health care costs, exacerbated government debt still further. Simultaneously, the recession-induced and tax cuts resulted in lower 'income' for governments, as their debt levels correspondingly rose. In other words, the big banks were bailed out, reducing their debt, and fragility was reduced, but at the expense of rising government debt and fragility.

At the same time household fragility was rising as well. The bottom 80%'s incomes were stagnating and falling for a number of reasons. As income fell, they borrowed—i.e. took on more debt—in order to offset stagnating and falling income. Mortgage refinancing meant more debt. Borrowing for major medical expenses added to debt levels. They 'borrowed' from their personal savings and from their pensions. The explosion of credit card usage represented still another source of borrowing—i.e. debt. Student loans…more debt. With falling incomes and rising debt households thus became more fragile as well. Much of the same could be said for the millions of small businesses that borrowed and increased debt as income level growth became more difficult over the decade.

In contrast, large corporations did not incur excessive debt—except for certain industries like the auto sector and the banking 'arms' of large corporations like GE credit, for example. Most big, multinational corporations do not have to borrow or take on debt. It is medium to small companies that require bank loans and other forms of credit—i.e. debt. So big banks accumulated excess debt but that was 'offloaded' to the government, while households and small businesses loaded up on debt while their income stagnated.

The point is that a successful recovery program over the longer run must address the **Fourth Principle of Reducing Systemic Fragility by Restructuring Debt and by Redistributing Income** to the bottom 80% of households, small businesses, and local government. Specific programs must also be introduced to ensure that, after sustained economic recovery has been achieved by the first three principles, the U.S. economy does not re-experience the crisis in the future again, in the longer run.

The specific proposals and measures described in the next section incorporate the above four principles in the following eight program areas:

- Program 1: Job Creation
- Program 2: Housing
- Program 3: State and Local Governments
- Program 4: Tax System Restructuring
- Program 5: Retirement System Restructuring
- Program 6: Banking System Restructuring
- Program 7: Debt Fragility Reduction
- Program 8: Income Fragility Reduction

## AN ALTERNATIVE PROGRAM FOR ECONOMIC RECOVERY

### PROGRAM 1: JOB CREATION

It is possible to create 17 million jobs without increasing the deficit. To do that, the government must directly create jobs since it is increasingly apparent that the private sector—those big corporations sitting on $2 trillion in the U.S. and another $1.4 trillion offshore—refuse to do so. It is also necessary because the big banks refuse to use their $1.7 trillion in excess reserves to lend to smaller businesses to create jobs. If banks won't loan and businesses can't or won't spend to create jobs in the U.S., then the only option is for the government to create jobs directly. The first four direct job proposals 1.1 through 1.4 include four new government programs designed to directly create the 17 million jobs. The jobs average $40,000 a year, with another $10,000 annual cost reserved for each job to cover administration of the programs. That's a fully loaded cost of $50,000 a year. One-fourth of that $40,000 would also go toward providing decent benefits for each worker as well, pensions, and health care. So we're talking about jobs that pay roughly $15 an hour, or $30,000 a year, with full medical and pension benefits similar to an average union benefit package. The funding for the four direct job programs is provided by the Tax System Restructuring described in Program 4 that follows. The first four job creation programs below represent a total cost of approximately $1.6 trillion. A direct job creation program that does not add to deficits and debt requires a fundamental restructuring of the tax system. The taxes raised from the first five proposals in Program 4 would provide the $1.6 trillion in the first year, plus an additional $900 billion in tax revenue for each of the following four years. The Jobs Program includes additional, non-direct government job programs as well.

### Jobs Program 1.1: Alternative Energy Public Investment Corporation

The first direct job creation program is called the *Alternative Energy Public Investment Corporation (AEPIC)*. It would invest directly in alternative energy infrastructure. The cost is approximately $500 billion. It would create jobs over the mid to long term.

### Jobs Program 1.2: Civilian Reconstruction Corporation

A more immediate direct job creation program is the *Civilian Reconstruction Corporation (CRC)*. It is patterned after the Civilian Conservation Corp of the 1930s. That latter program created half a million jobs in just a few months, sending young workers into the countryside to clean up rural America and build new roads, dams, water projects, and the like. The new CRC would focus, however, on non-energy infrastructure repair and maintenance in our urban areas. It is to urban renewal what the 1930s CCC was to rural redevelopment. Its cost is $250 billion.

### Jobs Program 1.3: Community Health Services Administration

A third program is the *Community Health Services Administration (CHSA)*. It would build medical clinics in communities throughout the country and pay for health service professionals to provide services to the working poor, who are now on Medicaid or are forced to over-populate the emergency rooms in hospitals throughout the economy at present. However, significant savings would also result from a reduction in the current cost of Medicaid. Its impact on job creation would be both immediate and midterm. It would cost $200 billion.

### Jobs Program 1.4: Twenty-First-Century Works Progress Administration

A fourth program, also focused on immediate job creation, is a *New Twenty-First-Century Works Progress Administration (WPA21)*. It would target direct government job creation in non-infrastructure and non-health services employment across all industries and occupations. Its cost is $600 billion.

### Jobs Program 1.5: Reverse Offshoring Incentives for Manufacturing Jobs

A fifth program, costing $25 billion in each of the first two years, or $50 billion, is designed to provide incentives to companies to reverse prior offshored investment projects and repatriate those jobs back to the U.S.

The first four Jobs Programs constitute direct government job creation. This fifth is a more traditional incentives program to restore critical jobs back to the U.S. Payments would not be made for the first six months, in order to ensure and prove that jobs were in fact repatriated back to the U.S. It would be accompanied by an offshoring penalty tax for new offshoring of jobs. Employers' incentives to repatriate jobs would be reduced by a new offshoring penalties tax.

### Jobs Program 1.6: Social Security Early Retirement Incentives

In order to create more jobs for younger workers, Social Security benefits would be increased for workers retiring at age 62, equal to 1.5 times the benefit levels they would otherwise have received at age 66–67. The extra benefits would expire at full retirement age. To receive the early expanded benefits, recipients would not be allowed to work part time while retired. This program is funded by Tax Programs 4.11 and 4.12 below.

### Jobs Program 1.7: Local Government Job Creation

Cities and municipalities would establish local agencies for the processing of consumer financing of programs provided through the new government utility banking structure described in Program 6: Banking System Restructuring. Those local agencies would create additional jobs. Jobs Programs 1.5–1.7 create an additional 2–3 million jobs over five years.

### PROGRAM 2: HOUSING

A Housing Program must first address the crisis in foreclosures. The government must undertake directly the modification of mortgages—both principal and interest payments—and reduce monthly payments to allow homeowners to avoid foreclosure. The second immediate task is to refinance mortgages for homeowners in negative equity, also reducing their principal and interest payments. The third is to stimulate the housing sector long term by providing cost of money (i.e. no profit) mortgages to consumers in the bottom 80% income households. This applies to refinancing of existing homes by providing lower mortgage rates (but not principal reduction), as well as the financing of new homes entering the market. New government agencies—a Home Owners Loan Corporation and government Utility Banking System—assume control of these measures to restabilize the housing market. The program also aids homeowners to finance broad home improvements, and prevents future speculation in single-residence homeowner mortgages.

### Housing Program 2.1: Six-Month Foreclosure-Home Seizure Moratorium

A foreclosure moratorium will not solve the housing problem by itself. However, a moratorium is necessary to provide time to enable the establishment of solutions to the foreclosure and negative equity crises noted in this Program 2. Also, no bank seizures would be permitted in the interim without a court order and decision.

### Housing Program 2.2: New Home Owners Loan Corporation (HOLC) and Purchase of Foreclosed and Negative Equity Mortgages with Principal and Interest Modifications

The U.S. government must take over conforming mortgages facing foreclosure and experiencing significant negative equity; both mortgages currently owned by the government agencies, Fannie Mae and Freddie Mac, as well as those in foreclosure-negative equity owned privately. The Federal Reserve would provide $500 billion to a HOLC. With that $500 billion to start, the HOLC would pay investors and the agencies holding the mortgages 25 cents on the dollar and tell them to go away. The ownership of the mortgages is then transferred to the Federal Reserve. The consumer agency within the Federal Reserve would then process the refinancing of the now government-owned mortgages, reducing both interest and principal for homeowners facing foreclosure as well as in significant negative equity. Principal would be modified to a three-year average for 2004–06 and interest reduced to the current 30-year Treasury bond rate fixed for a period of three years, after which it would adjust to the then 30-year rate. Should owners sell the homes within five years of refinancing, the government will realize 80% of the capital gains, declining thereafter by 10% for the next five years.

### Housing Program 2.3: Government Utility Banking System for Financing Remaining and Future Single-Residence Mortgages

All other mortgages would be refinanced, or newly financed, at prevailing 30-year Treasury bond rates. Mortgage lending would be funded through a government Utility Banking System on a cost of money, non-profit basis. That government consumer banking system would be established apart from the private banking system, based on a special division created within the Federal Reserve, administered by its consumer agency, with loan processing carried out at local government municipal levels.

### Housing Program 2.4: Home Improvement 15% Household Investment Tax Credit

To stimulate the home repair and home improvement market, all homeowners should be eligible for a 15% credit on their personal tax filings for home improvements, repairs, and upgrades. A credit for the full cost of solar, wind, and alternative energy upgrades over three years would further stimulate the housing market and housing jobs, save energy costs, and raise home values.

### Housing Program 2.5: Ban on 'Securitizaton' of Mortgages and Mortgage Bonds

Much of the problem of speculation in housing that brought on the crisis in 2007 is due to the practice of 'securitization' and reselling of mortgages in global secondary markets. Such resale of mortgages, whether in original or derivative forms, is banned.

## PROGRAM 3: STATE AND LOCAL GOVERNMENTS (SLG)

Recessions and slow economic recovery from recessions are the first and greatest cause of fiscal crisis of state and local governments. It is not spending on services or on public workers' wages and benefits. The number one cause of the fiscal crisis of state and local government is the lack of job creation and slow growth due to a declining economy.

The slash and burn programs being implemented at the SLG level today are therefore totally unnecessary. Nor is it necessary for the federal government to subsidize the states and cities with hundreds of billions of dollars more in direct assistance. What's needed is for tax increase and revenues to rise to cover the $150 billion minimum shortfalls across all the states.

### SLG Program 3.1: Government Direct Jobs Programs Benefit

Job creation programs noted in Program 1 would allocate an appropriate percentage to the public sector from the total of 17 million jobs created. The Government Utility Banking System also will add jobs to cities and municipalities. The public sector jobs created thus add to state and local income taxes, while reducing unemployment benefit payment levels. More employment results in an increase in state sales tax revenues, and also reduces foreclosures due to unemployment, raising local property tax revenues. Program 1 direct job creation thus assists state and local government fiscal stability both by raising local tax revenues and by reducing local government costs.

### SLG Program 3.2: Business-to-Business (B2B) Value Added Tax (VAT) 1% Sharing

Consumers and households pay a significant sales tax to provide states' tax revenues. Businesses buying from businesses should also pay an appropriate B2B tax on intermediate goods sales, just as households pay on final goods sales. This B2B tax is initially levied at 2%. One-half, or 1%, of the tax is allocated to states. The other 1% is allocated to a National 401k Pool, described as part of a general restructuring of the retirement system in Program 5 below.

### SLG Program 3.3: Restoration of Buy American Bonds (BABs) Program

BABs was a federal program that lowered states' costs of borrowing in municipal bond markets, to help states to borrow funds to meet budgets at a below-market cost. This program was discontinued prematurely. There is no reason why the Federal Reserve Bank cannot provide low-cost assistance funding for this program until the states and cities can balance their budgets.

### SLG Program 3.4: State-to-State Business Relocation Equalization Tax

This tax aids state budgets in terms of both the revenue and the spending. It prevents states' decline in corporate tax revenues as they, the states, increasingly compete with each other in recent years in a 'race to the bottom' to lure companies from each other. This tax would automatically offset any tax advantage to a company from moving from its existing state to another state. It thus removes the tax incentive advantage to a company relocating and slows the decline in states' corporate tax revenues. To the extent that companies relocate nevertheless, the equalization tax collected raises revenue earmarked for spending on job creation within the losing state.

### SLG Program 3.5: Medicaid and Employee Health Insurance Price Controls

To control escalating Medicaid costs, today comprising almost one-fourth of state spending costs, a price ceiling is established for services that health providers charge Medicaid patients and public employee patients. The ceiling limits price increases to no more than the annual increase in the national Consumer Price Index. If health providers refuse to provide their services to Medicaid patients or public employees as a result of the price ceiling, then Medicaid patients and state public employees denied service become eligible and 'rolled into' the Congressional health insurance plan now enjoyed by members of the House and Senate, who are themselves public employees. Medicaid patients become eligible as well for health services provided by the network of medical clinics established by the Community Health Services Corp noted in Jobs Program 1.1.

### SLG Program 3.6: Fed $500 Billion Bridge Loan to Public Pension Funds

The Federal Reserve Bank provided $9 trillion in virtually zero-interest loans to the banks during the recent financial crisis; $1 trillion of that was loaned to foreign banks. Under this program the Fed provides a temporary bridge loan of $500 billion, one-twentieth of the amount, to public sector pension funds that qualify due to a benefits funding level below 70%. Federal Reserve pension bridge loans are provided at the same 0.25% rate at which the Federal Reserve loans to member banks.

### SLG Program 3.7: Banks Repay Losses from 'Swaps Trading' to Cities

Many cities, school districts and other local government entities were lured by banks in the past decade into speculating with bank products sold to them called 'interest rate swaps,' often misleading the cities about their risks and returns. In this program, banks are required to repay cities which were similarly misled for these bad investments, with appropriate interest.

### PROGRAM 4: TAX SYSTEM RESTRUCTURING

The first purpose of the tax system restructuring is to immediately fund the four government direct jobs programs. The total cost of the four direct government job creation programs above was $1.6 trillion. The following first five tax proposals provide $1.6 trillion in the first year, and another $3.6 trillion over the next four years. Creating the 17 million jobs at $40,000 each further results in additional personal income tax revenues to the federal government in the amount of $75 billion a year and $375 billion over the five-year period.

Other tax restructuring measures 4.8 and 4.9 target restoration of SLG revenues and significantly assist the stabilizing of local government budgets. Others play a central role in retirement system restructuring and the expansion of Social Security and national retirement, as well as the stabilizing of Medicare and health service costs in the U.S. Putting a tax system back on its feet after having been, in effect, 'stood on its head' through the past three decades is central not only to job creation but also to addressing local finances—both critical for economic recovery. In addition, it is essential for retirement restructuring and for the long-run reduction in the bottom 80% of households' consumption fragility, without which sustained economy in the long run is not possible as well.

### Tax Program 4.1: Professional Investors' Tax Haven Repatriation Tax

About $4 trillion today is held in offshore tax havens by U.S. investors, individuals and institutions, in island nations like the Cayman islands, Vanuatu, the Seychelles, the Isle of Man, Cyprus, etc., and in more traditional havens like Switzerland, Lichtenstein, etc. The Internal Revenue Service (IRS) has identified 27 of these, which it calls 'special jurisdictions.' If just $2 trillion of that $4 trillion was required to be re-deposited in U.S. banks, those investors would have to pay the 35% top tax-bracket personal income tax on the $2 trillion in the first year, raising about $700 billion. Future earnings on the remainder would also be taxed in the second to fifth years, yielding another $200 billion a year. Refusal to repatriate should result in a 10% penalty after 90 days, followed by similar penalties. Countries that refused to cooperate should have their U.S.-based assets frozen, and then taxed until compliance.

### Tax Program 4.2: Multinational Corporations' Offshore Profits Recovery Tax

Multinational corporations today are hoarding between $1 trillion and $1.4 trillion in their offshore subsidiaries, refusing to pay the required 35% corporate tax rate. If they were required to repatriate that lower amount of $1 trillion, it would raise in the first year a sum of $350 billion and another $140 billion a year in each of the next four years. Refusal to repatriate should result in a 50% tariff on the re-importing of their offshore products to the U.S. until they repatriated.

### Tax Program 4.3: One-Year 15% Surtax on $2 Trillion Corporate Cash Hoard

Companies refusing to invest one-third of their current cash hoard within six months in the U.S., and create jobs as a consequence of such investment, should be taxed at a 15% surtax rate for the remaining six months of the first fiscal year. That raises another $300 billion in tax revenue for the first year.

### Tax Program 4.4: Financial Transactions Tax on Stocks, Bonds, and Derivatives

Another $150–200 billion a year, at minimum, is raised by implementing a financial transactions tax as follows: $1.00 per every common stock trade for stock value traded at $10,000 or less. Add $100.00 for stock trades valued $10,000–100,000. 1% on all trades worth more than $100,000. $1.00 per each $1,000 value for all forms of corporate bond sales, both investment and junk grade bonds. Similar charges for commercial paper transactions. And $1 per $100 notional value for all interest rate, currency, and other derivatives trades, levied on each of the counterparties, as well as 1% tax of notional value for all credit default swaps derivatives trades.

### Tax Program 4.5: Capital Gains, Dividends, and Estate Tax Restorations

This proposal raises taxes on capital gains and dividends from current 15% to the 35% rate that is currently levied on all top-bracket personal incomes. It would also tax carrying interest at the same rate and require all hedge fund managers to pay 35% instead of their current 15%. Estate tax rates and thresholds are restored to 1980 levels. These measures raise at minimum $125 billion in the first year, and potentially more, as well as $125 billion per year for the next four years.

### Tax Program 4.6: Immediate Expiration of the Bush Tax Cuts

Bush tax cuts passed in 2001–04 cost over the last decade approximately $2.9 trillion. Their extensions alone in 2010–11 cost the U.S. budget about $450 billion a year. For the next decade the cost is an estimated $4.2 trillion. Tax Program 4.5 above is included in the total Bush tax cuts. Not addressed in 4.5, however, are the additional Bush tax cuts involving top-bracket rates for individual and corporation income taxes as well as numerous additional deductions, exemptions, and credits worth collectively more than another $100 billion a year. Restoring the top marginal rates to the 2000 levels of 39.6% raises additional tens of billions of dollars a year in revenue with which to balance the budget or other uses.

### Tax Program 4.7: Restore Top Personal and Corporate Tax Rates to 1980 Levels

Top marginal individual and corporate tax rates are proposed by this program to restore to 1980 levels, which were 50% each for both individual and corporate tax rates.

### Tax Program 4.8: Business-to-Business 2% VAT

This proposal was in part addressed in Jobs Program 1.6 above, as a means to fund an increase in Social Security early retirement benefits in order to make available new job opportunities for young workers. 1.6 identified and earmarked 1% of the 2% VAT for B2B sales on intermediate goods. The other 1% of the VAT is allocated to states as a major measure for restoring their revenues and fiscal stability as well, as indicated in SLG Program 3.2 above. Once again, the justification for this 4.8 (3.2) tax proposal is that if consumer households can pay an up to 10% sales tax on final goods and services, then businesses should pay at least a 2% tax on their inter-sales to each other.

### Tax Program 4.9: State-to-State Business Relocation Equalization Tax

This program was also previously described in SLG Program 3.4 above, as a means to re-stabilize state revenues and budgets.

## Tax Program 4.10: Increase 12.4% Social Security Payroll Tax on Wages and Salaries (Earned Incomes) to $250,000 Over the Next Five Years

Currently fewer than 85% of all wage-earners pay up to the current top annual limit of $110,100 because wage income at the top wage levels above $110,100 has risen faster than the Social Security base increase. If this was adjusted to prior levels where 100% of wage income was captured by the 12.4% payroll tax, the increase would more than cover any potential shortfalls in Social Security benefits until 2085. However, this proposal recommends paying the Social Security payroll tax on all forms of income, wages, and salaries (i.e. earned income), and all other forms of income up to $250,000 a year. A large Social Security surplus would result as a consequence, and could be applied toward raising monthly Social Security benefit payments by as much as 20%, as described in Tax Program 4.11.

## Tax Program 4.11: Levy 6.7% Payroll Tax Equivalent on All Capital Incomes

An even larger Social Security surplus would result if a 6.7% tax were levied on all incomes, whatever the form and with no ceiling limit. This would transform social Security from a payroll tax, or quasi-payroll tax (4.10) to a true social insurance tax. The tax revenue raised would amount to additional hundreds of billions of dollars a year to permit a 20% raise in monthly Social Security benefit payments for the 48 million current and future retirees. That 20% income boost would enable a major improvement in household consumption fragility.

## Tax Program 4.12: Increase Medicare Payroll Tax by 0.25%

An initial 0.25% in the payroll tax for the next ten years provides all necessary funding to stabilize the Medicare system for ten years. That's a combined 0.5% for employee and employer. Starting in the eleventh year, 2022, another 0.25% each tax increase is necessary. Thereafter, the 77 million baby-boomers begin to decline as a cost factor, the costs of Medicare level off, and then decline. So a total tax increase of 0.5% over 20 years for both worker and employer totally covers the Medicare cost shortfalls. Those who consider this mere 1.0% tax for the next ten years unacceptable should consider that the typical employer-insured health care plan costs the equivalent of 25% of a worker's take-home pay today.

## Tax Program 4.13: Excess Profits Tax on the 'Big Four Parasite' Industries

There are four industries that are sucking the economic life-blood from the U.S. economy, at the expense of not only workers and the bottom 80% of households but of millions of smaller businesses as well. These industries extract super-profits out of the economy, by reducing real wages and other businesses' income through their excessive inflation. They are the banks, the oil companies, the health insurance companies and the big pharmaceutical companies. They charge excess prices that have been rising at double digits annually on average now for decades, and thereby reap super-profits at the expense of everyone else. An excess profits tax equal to a minimum 10% of gross profits of companies in these industries should be levied on the biggest of these companies. The excess profits tax revenue should be returned to consumers, workers, and small businesses as rebates to offset the excessive price they pay for health care, gasoline, gas and utility costs, and mortgage interest. The rebate to be paid in the form of credits on annual federal tax returns.

## PROGRAM 5: RETIREMENT SYSTEM RESTRUCTURING

### Retirement Program 5.1: Social Security Early Retirement Incentive

This program was previously described as Jobs Program 1.6 above. It improves Social Security monthly benefit payments for those who retire early at 62 in order to create more jobs for young workers. This retirement program is funded by the B2B VAT also noted in Tax Program 4.8 above, in the amount of 1% of the 2% tax on sales of intermediate goods and services.

### Retirement Program 5.2: Raise Social Security Monthly Retirement Benefit Payments by 20%

This program is financed by Tax Program 4.10 above, that raises annual income limits on earned incomes (wages and salaries) required to pay the 12.4% payroll tax for Social Security up to $250,000 a year; and Tax Program 4.11, that levies a new 6.7% payroll tax on all unearned capital incomes (capital gains, dividends, etc.). The extending of the payroll tax to those now not paying enables a 20% increase in monthly Social Security payments for all retirees.

### Retirement Program 5.3: Establish a National 401k Pool as Retirement Supplemental Program to Social Security

Social Security payments now provide on average barely one-third of what is necessary for retirement. When Social Security was established, it was estimated that this one-third would be supplemented by private pensions and personal savings. But the latter two sources have declined significantly. A new retirement system in the long run is required—one that improves Social Security and replaces existing private employer 401k plans with a nationalized 401k pool. Existing 401k plans would be rolled into the national pool, with employees having all the same rights as the private plans in terms of contributions and withdrawals. The pool would be administered by the Social Security system as a separate program, Part E, and a separate trust fund. The government would invest the pool on behalf of participants, including into new public investment corporations. Employees would be guaranteed against any losses, while all profits from investment would accrue to the national pool.

### Retirement Program 5.4: Repeal Provisions of the 2006 Private Pension Act Allowing Private and Public Sector Pensions to Make Loans to Hedge Funds

A major cause of pension funds' $4 trillion losses from 2006 to 2011 has been the Pension Act of 2006 which, beginning that year, allowed pension funds to loan and to partner with hedge funds speculating in subprime mortgages and other ultra-high-risk financial securities. Public pension-defined benefit funds in particular should be prohibited by law from such investing.

### Retirement Program 5.5: Ban Congressional Annual Borrowing from the Social Security Trust Fund

The Social Security Trust Fund has accumulated $2.4 trillion in surpluses since the major payroll tax hike in 1986 that provides a current 12.4% tax rate on a base of annual income that is indexed for inflation and rises each year. That surplus is estimated to increase to $3.7 trillion by 2026, providing all recent payroll tax cuts are restored by the U.S. Treasury and no further payroll tax cuts are enacted. But the entire $2.4 trillion surplus to date has been 'borrowed' by the federal government to offset its general budget deficits since 1986, and replaced with special, non-negotiable Treasury bonds. The cash surplus should be returned to the Trust Fund and it should be made a criminal offense for Congress to borrow from the Trust Fund in the future.

### Retirement Program 5.6: Federal Government Investment Authority to Allocate 25% of the Social Security Trust Fund Surplus to Public Investment

With the replaced $2.4 trillion cash to the Social Security Retirement Fund, the federal government should invest 25% in government corporations targeting alternative energy investment and other appropriate secure investments. All 'profits' from such investments then accrue to further expand the Social Security Trust Fund surplus.

## PROGRAM 6: BANKING SYSTEM RESTRUCTURING

Today's total for-profit and increasingly speculative and unstable banking system has become a major drag on the U.S. economy and a force preventing sustained economic recovery. The big banks in particular are increasingly focused more on foreign profit opportunities than on investing in the U.S. Not only is the banking system not lending to small businesses at prior historical levels during recovery from recession, but it is increasingly focused on speculative forms of financial investing that do not contribute to growth and jobs in the U.S. It now functions as a bottleneck to providing consumer credit to households, consumers, and small businesses. A major restructuring of that banking system is now in order if credit is to play a role in economic recovery. That restructuring must start with the creation of a fully government-owned Utility Banking System that provides consumer-related loans at the prevailing cost of money and thus without a profit mark-up.

### Banking Restructuring Program 6.1: Government-Owned Utility Banking System to Provide Stable Credit Flow to Consumer Markets

Money and credit is a utility. The provision of money and credit is as essential to the economy as power and energy and a skilled labor force. In particular, consumer markets are repeatedly and unnecessarily impacted negatively by periodic banking crashes and instability. A Utility Banking System providing loans on a continuing, stable basis is therefore required. This banking system would provide loans to home mortgages up to FHA-conforming loan limits, to consumers for auto loans, for student loans, and for small businesses with 50 or fewer employees. The funding is provided by a 0.25% interest loan from the Federal Reserve up to an amount of $1 trillion, through the Fed's own internal Consumer Agency. The agency in turn administers lending to local community offices: cities and municipalities for small business loans, credit unions for auto and student loans, and local branches of the Federal Reserve districts for mortgage loans.

### Banking Restructuring Program 6.2: Democratize the Federal Reserve System

From its inception in 1914 the Federal Reserve has always been a quasi-bank-controlled institution. The Great Depression of the 1930s reduced that private control only in part. It is now time to fully democratize the Fed and remove all private sector banking influence from its decision-making appointments and processes. To that effect, the twelve Districts of the Fed should no longer have private banking industry board members, nor should the national Board of Governors of the Federal Reserve. The Board of Governors of the Federal Reserve, its policymaking body, should be comprised of 18 members—six appointed by the House of Representatives, six by the president, and six elected at large for terms of fours during national elections, according to appropriate methods to be determined. The Federal Reserve must evolve from a role of 'lender of last resort' for 'too big to fail' banks and assume the more important role of 'lender of first resort' to the general public.

## PROGRAM 7: DEBT FRAGILITY REDUCTION

As described previously in this chapter, the overhang of massive debt loads throughout the U.S. economy is still functioning as a huge anchor on the recovery of consumption, investment, and now even desperately needed further government spending stimulus. Federal spending, deficits, and federal government debt causes and consequences were discussed in depth in Chapter 7 of this book. Federal deficits and the debt rose from $5.6 trillion in 2000 to more than $15 trillion today. But the even more massive increase in debt was by business, and financial and banking businesses in particular. Non-banking business debt rose from $5.4 trillion to more than $11 trillion between 1998 and 2008, nearly doubling. But banking-financial debt more than tripled, from $6 trillion to more than $19 trillion over the same period. Consumer debt also doubled over the period, from $1.4 trillion to about $2.6 trillion, not counting mortgage debt. These huge debt overhangs have not been significantly 'deleveraged' since the economic crisis of 2008. As a result, consumer household spending and many sectors of business investing have been unable to recover. Government debt in turn has accelerated since the bailouts and recession, and now is choking on itself as well. Abnormally low economic growth rates have prevented a 'growing out' of the debt load.

Thus, extraordinary measures are necessary in the longer run by government action to accelerate the processes of debt deleveraging by households and small businesses. Income stimulation policies are still necessary, but today require equal consideration to debt reduction policies as well.

Various proposals in Programs 1–6 above address the longer-run problem of debt reduction while focusing on shorter, immediate problems of jobs, housing, etc. as well. These included the above:

- Housing Programs 2.2, 2.3 and 2.5
- SLG Program 3.3, 3.6 and 3.7
- Retirement Program 5.4
- Banking Restructuring Programs 6.1 and 6.2.

It will be necessary over the longer term to identify and implement additional programs that will target excess debt reduction and even debt expunging. As discussed in Chapter 3, a choice the Obama administration faced in early 2009 was whether to establish a 'bad bank' in which to deposit all the banks' bad assets, or instead to do what Obama decided: inject massive amounts of cash into the banks but leave the bad debt on their balance sheets. The debt remains to this day, except for limited cases of asset sales by the banks. Similarly, household debt has not significantly declined (deleveraged). What debt reduction has occurred has been the write-offs of mortgages and some credit cards. It is not enough.

A good additional target for debt reduction is the huge run-up in student debt in recent years. It will simply have to be written off at some point, or millions of students when they get jobs will remain 'consumption fragile' for decades and thus inhibit economic recovery. Another would be the rewriting of government small business loans issued to date.

The argument against debt reduction by legislation, or even debt expunging, is that investor-creditors who loaned the money to borrowers will suffer losses. The answer to that is twofold: first, so what? They were at the center of the cause of the crisis and have been bailed out while the households, students, and small businesses have in the interim paid the price for something they didn't create. Secondly, it's necessary for economic recovery that they finally 'take a haircut,' as the saying goes, and assume their appropriate share of losses. Will this result in reluctance to invest? Perhaps. But they're not investing in any event, at least not in the U.S., so there's no net loss in the short term.

## PROGRAM 8: INCOME FRAGILITY REDUCTION

Debt reduction is only one half of the equation of consumption fragility in the case of households and consumers, in the case of financial fragility in businesses, and in the case of government balance sheet fragility afflicting both state-local and now federal governments. Consumption, investing, and spending cannot get going at previous rates in this recession because of income stagnation as well.

The bottom 80% of consumer households, small businesses, and state-local governments have become particularly income fragile in recent years. For households, the income problem, moreover, has been growing for decades and just accelerating in recent years.

If excess debt is not reduced, then income must be significantly increased. Or vice versa, if income is not increased, then excess debt must be significantly reduced. But it is difficult to reduce debt when income is stagnating. The best approach to reducing the more general condition of consumption fragility is to both reduce debt and increase income.

Programs 1–6 above have various elements in them to increase income as well as reduce debt. Income increase was addressed specifically in the following:

- All the Jobs Programs 1.1–1.7 increase income to the working labor force
- Most of the Tax Programs increase 'income' to governments
- Retirement Programs 5.1 and 5.2 increase income to seniors.

But this is just a shortlist of measures and programs needed to restore a balance to income distribution in the U.S. economy, without which a drag on consumption will continue. And a continual sluggish or non-recovery of consumption provides an incentive for big corporations to increase investment and thus job creation offshore, where consumption is rising.

The U.S. economy has struggled for more than three decades with stagnating real incomes by the bottom 80% of households that are the main engine of consumption growth. Conversely the top 20%—and within that mostly the top 1%—have enjoyed historic income acceleration while the rest have stagnated at best or even fallen. As noted in previous chapters, the income of the 1% wealthiest households escalated from 8% of total income in 1978 to about 24% in 2007, according to IRS data. That is an unsustainable trend. It was also roughly the trend experienced in the 1920s, when the top 1% income share rose to 22% on the eve of the great crash of 1929.

Other programs are therefore also necessary to rebalance incomes in the U.S. in the longer run and thus to ensure continued economic recovery and growth. Income stagnation is the analogue to debt increase in the determination of consumption fragility. Other programs not considered here that would help alleviate continuing consumption fragility on the income—not just the debt— side are the following:

- Raise the minimum wage to 50% of the average hourly wage and index it to inflation
- Require that all involuntary part time and all forms of temporary labor (together called 'contingent') must be provided retirement, health care, and other benefits by their employers, as well as access to all other company benefits and rights

- Revoke free trade agreements that do not result in a net increase in jobs in the U.S. and which lower the average wage of workers in import industries negatively impacted by free trade
- Allow the union wage differential to once again rise to its appropriate historical level by permitting unions a fair opportunity to organize workers by passing the Employee Free Choice Act (EFCA)
- Reduce escalating and accelerating costs for private health insurance premiums that now absorb up to 25% of an employee's typical take-home pay for family coverage. Reduce that cost amount by two-thirds by instituting a Single-Payer National Healthcare System administered through Medicare for all those households earning less than $165,000 a year (the bottom 80%).

\*      \*      \*

Some critics of this Alternative Program will no doubt argue to the contrary of these Programs 1–8 by declaring that the U.S. economy cannot afford them. Deficits and debt are already at record levels, they will likely argue.

But these programs are all funded out of a basic restructuring of the tax system, other public investment earnings, and programs that redistribute income (which today means a 're-redistribution' of income). They will argue these programs represent 'class warfare.' The reply is no, it's not class warfare, but rather defense against class warfare being waged today, and intensified monthly, by those who have concentrated the wealth, income, and political power in their hands and won't give up an iota of any of it.

So far as deficit and debts are concerned, the reader is redirected to Chapter 7 of this book, which provided conclusive data that showed that the current deficits and the $9 trillion in run-up in the federal debt total from 2000 to 2011 have been caused by just a few specific programs. To recall, the Bush tax cuts alone account for at minimum $2.9 trillion of the $9 trillion debt increase. And they will add another $4.2 trillion over the next decade if allowed to continue. The escalating cost of the Pentagon and wars accounts for another $2.1 trillion. And that's just the excessive inflation from the same, not the basic costs. Then there's nearly $1 trillion more over the past decade caused by health care inflation acceleration, with huge negative impact on Medicare, Medicaid, and private sector benefit costs as well. Throw in the $3 trillion in fiscal stimulus plans and Congressional financed (taxpayer-funded) bailouts and we're close to the $9 trillion. Add several hundred billions of dollars in interest payments on it all–and there's your deficits and debt $9 trillion total.

In conclusion, a fundamentally different approach and set of policies and programs are required if the U.S. economy ever has a chance to enter upon a sustained economic recovery. The policies employed to date by both Bush in 2008 and Obama in 2009–11 have all failed to generate a sustained recovery. And now the radical right and their corporate supporters in Congress are about to reverse what little effect the Obama policies have had to date, by introducing massive spending cuts that will only exacerbate consumption fragility as well as the financial fragility faced by millions of small businesses and state and local governments. Whether the Obama programs of the past three years 'succeeded' in preventing a depression is a debatable point. Perhaps that is so. But what is not debatable any longer is the evidence of the past three years that those programs have not succeeded in any sense in generating a sustained recovery.

With the U.S. economy, starting in 2013, facing a minimum $2.2 trillion in spending cuts—and a reversal of the Obama programs—we will soon see if Obama's claim that he at least stopped a depression is true. Those cuts may just provide the final event that does drive the current Epic Recession from the Type I Epic Recession this writer has described it as in previous works, toward a Type II Epic Recession that transitions toward a true bona fide depression. Additional spending cuts in 2013 will all but ensure a Type II.

New, fundamentally different programs are now needed and quickly, for the U.S. and global economies are now drifting from economic relapse to a potential double-dip recession and the growing possibility of another depression.

The new programs must immediately address the three key problem areas of jobs, housing, and local government—the 'crises within the crisis.' A major restructuring of the tax, banking, and retirement systems is also required to institutionalize and deepen the recovery in those three key problem areas, as well as other sectors of the U.S. economy. Not least, over the longer run the even deeper problems of debt and income must be confronted, for the U.S. and global economy remains clearly 'systemically fragile.'

The economic resources are available. It is politics as usual—politics dominated by the few that have benefited to date, while the rest of Main Street has not—that today bars the way to the potential solution and economic recovery.

# Notes

## INTRODUCTION

1. The $3 trillion is from the Congressional Budget Office baseline actuals and estimates, published as *Budget Outlook Updates* in August 2010 and August 2011. The $9 trillion Federal Reserve total represents the lending to depository financial institutions, primary dealers, other institutions, liquidity swaps with foreign banking institutions, and other lending to AIG and financial arms of non-bank companies since the banking crisis of 2008. See the 'Credit and Liquidity Programs and the Balance Sheet' reports summarized on the Governors of the Federal Reserve System online at www.federalreserve/monetarypolicy/bst.htm.

2. By 'relapse' is meant a significant slowing in the rate of growth in several major sectors of the economy (e.g. housing, jobs markets, manufacturing, etc.), or significant slowing in total output in the overall economy itself (e.g. GDP rate of growth falls by half). It may also mean a negative decline in several major sectors, and not just a slowing in the rate of growth. By 'double dip' recession is meant an official declaration of 'recession' by the National Bureau of Economic Research (NBER), the body of economists responsible for determining and announcing the starts and endings of recessions. Relapses are thus integrally related to 'double dips'. They precede the latter and may or may not transition into the latter. The relapse of summer 2010 was checked by further policy responses. It remains to be seen if the 2011 emerging relapse is also checked or if it transitions to a double dip. The current budget cutting frenzy in Congress makes it more likely a case of the latter, transition to double dip but not until cuts start taking effect in 2013.

3. Most notable among whom include Dr. Nouriel Roubini, one of the few who correctly predicted the 2007 housing collapse, the banking crash of 2008, and events unfolding in the Eurozone. Others include George Soros, global financier, and Mohamed El-Erian, Co-CIO and CEO of PIMCO, one of the world's largest bond investing companies.

4. See Chapter 1 of this book for detailed references. Similarly for the paragraphs that immediately follow.

5. Jack Rasmus, *Epic Recession: Prelude to Global Depression*, Pluto Press, May 2010.

## CHAPTER 1

1. See note 1 in the Introduction to this book for a clarification of what is meant by a 'relapse' and its relationship to double-dip recessions.

2. This 'stop–go' recovery, in which short periods of weak growth are followed by subsequent short, moderate economic contractions, and by weak recoveries once again, are what this writer has described as the defining characteristics of a 'Type I' Epic Recession, and predicted would occur in 2010 and beyond (see Jack Rasmus, *Epic Recession: Prelude to Global Depression*, Pluto Press, 2010). The predictions were made in late 2009, the quarter experiencing the strongest GDP recovery when it appeared to many that a sustained recovery from recession was underway and might continue. As this writer wrote in November 2009: "The U.S. economy, at best, and in only select segments is moving sideways. The longer term scenario is more likely another downturn or a double dip or W-shaped decline that is typical of epic recessions" (see Jack Rasmus, 'Financial Fragility One Year Later,' *Z Magazine*, November 2009, p. 22).

3. Bureau of Labor Statistics, U.S. Department of Labor, News Releases, *Usual Weekly Earnings of Wage and Salary Workers*, Fourth Quarter 2001 through Second Quarter 2011, Table 3.

4. RealtyTrac, 'Year End U.S. Foreclosure Activity Report, 2010,' and monthly Foreclosure Reports through August 2011.

5. For example, millions more have used alternatives to formal foreclosure, such as 'short sales' and other measures.

6. *Bloomberg News*, 'U.S. Home Seizures Reach Record for Third Time in Five Months,' August 13, 2011.

7. 'Shadow banks' refer to financial lending institutions that do not take deposits from the general public and were not regulated by the Federal Reserve under the 'commercial banking' system. Not regulated, they generally engaged in high debt leveraged speculative investing. For a further detailed description and definition see the glossary in this writer's book, *Epic Recession*, p. 316, or reference the official report by the New York Federal Reserve Bank, *Shadow Banking, Staff Report No. 458*, July 2010. The literature on shadow banks, however, has not fully caught up with the development of the sector. This writer argues that 'shadow financial institutions' should include many multinational corporations themselves. Their financial operations function in many ways as 'shadow banking institutions' as well as in pursuit of financial securities investing and speculation as a means for expanding portfolio profits. Thus, large corporations have three sources of profits, only one of which is reported in the U.S. National Income Accounts: normal profits from sale of goods and services; depreciation funds which are a kind of profits earmarked for future investment; and portfolio profits. For an interesting view of portfolio financial profit trends by non-banking large corporations, see Greta Kippner, *Capitalizing on Crisis*, Harvard University Press, 2011.

8. *Wall Street Journal*, April 22, 3011, p. B3.

9. *New York Times*, March 25, 2011, p. 1.

10. *Wall Street Journal*, April 11, 2011, p. 1.

11. *New York Times*, July 26, 2010, p. 1.

12. For the survey by Equilar, see *New York Times*, July 2, 2011 (online July 4, 2010).

13. Equilar study, *New York Times*, July 2, 2011.

14. For reference to the Equilar survey commissioned by the *Financial Times*, see *Financial Times*, June 15, 2011, p. 20.

15. Quoted from Dr. Emmanuel Saez, 'Striking it Richer: The Evolution of Top Incomes in the United States' (updated with 2008 estimates), faculty website, University of California, Berkeley, Department of Economics, July 17, 2010.

16. Jeremy Siegel and Jeremy Schwartz, 'The Bond Bubble and the Case for Stocks', *Wall Street Journal*, August 22, 2011, p. 13.

17. Telis Demos, 'Buy Backs Point to Growing Confidence,' *Financial Times*, August 23, 2011, p. 18.

18. See Lawrence Mishel, Jared Bernstein, and Sylvia Allegretto, *The State of Working America*, 10th edition, Economic Policy Institute, 2007, Table 5.7, p. 260.

19. Saez, 'Striking it Richer.' See also Saez's 'Income Inequality in the U.S., 1913–1998,' updated to 2008, *Quarterly Journal of Economics*, vol. 118, no. 1, 2003, updated Tables 0, 1, and 2.

20. These data are from the Saez study, 'Real Annual Income Growth by Groups, 1993–2008', Table 1.

21. These figures are for the 'bottom 99%' income families, which includes higher-earner families in the 90–99% range. That overstates the recovery data and understates the loss data since their earnings range from $127,000 to $443,000 a year. The true 'bottom 90%' earn less than $127,000 to minimum wage and below, averaging the $31,244 figure noted. Saez, 'Income Inequality in the U.S., 1913–1998,' updated Table 0.

22. Bureau of Labor Statistics, *Usual Weekly Earnings of Wage and Salary Workers*, Table 1.

23. *Financial Times*, August 13, 2011, p. 8.

24. See Federal Reserve Board, *Senior Loan Officer Opinion Survey on Bank Lending Practices*, quarterly for 2009 through second quarter 2011. For summary data, see Federal Reserve Bank, 'Flow of Funds,' Table F.1, March 2011. For business press analysis, see Emily Maltby, 'Smaller Businesses Seeking Loans Still Come Up Empty,' *Wall Street Journal*, June 30, 2011, p. B1.

# CHAPTER 2

1. National Bureau of Economic Research, Business Cycle Dating Committee, 'U.S. Business Cycle Expansions and Contractions', NBER website.
2. *New York Times*, January 15, 2008.
3. U.S. Department of Labor, Bureau of Labor Statistics, *Current Establishment Survey*, reports from February through June, 2008.
4. *Wall Street Journal*, February 25, 2008.
5. It is estimated that between 1994 and 2004 alone approximately 4.8 million U.S. jobs were lost due to free trade and related trade measures. See Robert Scott, 'Where the Jobs Aren't,' Economic Policy Institute (EPI), Economic Policy Issue Brief No. 168, March 23, 2000, and Josh Bivens, 'Shifting the Blame for Manufacturing Job Loss,' EPI Briefing paper, 2004. That rate of job loss accelerated even further after 2004 as the worst impact of China-U.S. trade on jobs began to take effect, while trade-related job loss continued to rise from NAFTA and CAFTA free trade and other bilateral free trade agreements with the U.S. Most of the 2.3 million jobs lost to China trade between 2001 and 2007 occurred after 2004. See Robert Scott, 'The China Trade Toll,' EPI Briefing Paper, July 30, 2008. That job loss from China and other free trade agreements continued to rise after 2008, costing a minimum additional 453,00 jobs lost to China trade, according to a recent study by Robert Scott, 'The Growing U.S. Trade Deficit with China Cost 2.8 Million Jobs Between 2001–2010,' EPI Briefing Paper No. 323, September 20, 2011. In late 2011 President Obama requested and Congress approved additional major free trade agreements with Korea and other countries. By 2012 more than 10 million jobs were thus lost due to free trade and trade-related causes. And that total does not even begin to include additional millions of jobs lost as a result of accelerating offshoring investment and jobs by U.S. corporations over the past 15 years
6. *New York Times*, February 28, 2008.
7. *Financial Times*, February 29, 2008.
8. *Wall Street Journal*, March 19, 2008.
9. *Wall Street Journal*, March 25, 2008.
10. *New York Times*, March 28, 2008.
11. The capital gains rate was initially raised to 28% in 1986, after it was clear that its cut to 20% under Ronald Reagan was causing major federal deficits to appear. The rate was reduced from 28% to 20% in 1997 under then President Bill Clinton, and then lowered further to 15% under Bush in 2002. That resulted, between 2002 and 2006 alone, in a surge in capital gains income to investors from $269 billion in 2002 to $729 billion in 2006. The escalation of federal budget deficits the past decade, and the accompanying $9 trillion surge in total U.S. debt, thus has a good deal to do with the deep cuts in the capital gains tax. Easily $1 trillion of the current U.S. debt level is attributable to it. Additional amounts are due to cuts in dividends, inheritance, and corporate depreciation allowances and foreign profits tax avoidance. Of course, not all the deficits and debt are attributable to tax revenue falloff. An 8.2% annual rise in Pentagon costs for a decade, runaway health care costs impacting Medicaid and Medicare, refusal of Congress to fund prescription drug plans, and the bailouts of 2008–10 all contributed as well. But studies show that no less than 58% of the run-up in federal deficits and debt is due to tax cuts and revenue falloff, not spending increases.
12. Pentagon and war spending rose at an annual rate of 8.2% over the decade 2001–10. This compared to a Consumer Price Index general inflation rate of about 2% annually for the decade. If Pentagon spending, which rose from $342 billion a year in 2001 to $698 billion in 2010, had risen only by the 2% rate, the cumulative savings to the U.S. budget over the decade amounts to $2.1 trillion. This includes the share of interest on the deficit from the amount, but excludes other 'soft' war costs as veterans' benefits, replacing war materials stockpiles, or war costs 'off budget,' for homeland security, or indirect costs for the war in other departments' budgets, such as the Energy Department, the State Department, the CIA (Central Intelligence Agency), the NSA (National Security Agency), etc. Bureau of Economic Analysis, National Income Accounts, Table 3.10.5, March 25, 2011.

13. The consensus cost of the 2001–03 Bush tax cuts over the period 2001–08, is approximately $1.7 trillion. This does not include interest on the debt costs, which add another $200 billion. For these estimates see Kathy Ruffing and James Korney, 'Economic Downturns and Bush Policies Continue to Drive Large Projected Deficits,' Center for Budget and Policy Priorities, May 10, 2011. The continuation of the Bush cuts for 2009–10 add another $450 billion to this $1.9 trillion. However, this $2.35 trillion refers only to the income tax cuts associated with the Bush tax-cut record. Another $700 billion plus in personal income tax cuts occurred in the form of the numerous Alternative Minimum Tax 'fixes' over his term, which benefited mostly the wealthiest 10% of households and up. Another $250 billion in tax cuts may also be attributable to corporate tax cuts targeted for multinational and energy companies in 2005–08 as well. Finally, $90 billion in tax cuts on Bush's watch occurred with the 2008 stimulus measures passed that spring. In all, the Bush tax cuts for the 2001–10 decade amounted to about $3.4 trillion.
14. Congressional Budget Office, *Budget and Economic Outlook: Fiscal Years 2011 to 2012*, Table 1-7, lines 49–50.
15. As reported by economist Jeff Cohen on the CommonDreams website, July 24, 2011.
16. David Brooks, 'Obama's Money Class,' *Wall Street Journal*, July 1, 2008.
17. *Wall Street Journal* editorial, July 2, 2008.
18. Austan Goolsbee and Jason Furman, 'The Obama Tax Plan,' *Wall Street Journal*, August 14, 2008, p. 13.
19. Bureau of Labor Statistics, *The Employment Situation: December 2007*, January 4, 2008, Tables A-1, A-5 and A-13.
20. Bloomberg.com, 'U.S. Mortgage Delinquency, Foreclosure Rates,' February 16, 2009.
21. For a summary of the main elements of Obama's and McCain's 'Economic Recovery Plans' at this juncture, see *New York Times*, October 15, 2008, p. 26.
22. Barack Obama, 'The Change We Need,' *Wall Street Journal*, November 3, 2008, p. 19.
23. Bureau of Labor Statistics, *Current Employment Survey*, Databases and Tables, Series Id, Total Private Employment, as of May 7, 2011.

## CHAPTER 3

1. *Wall Street Journal*, November 8, 2008, p. 3.
2. *Financial Times*, November 8, 2008, p. 1.
3. Bureau of Labor Statistics, *Employment Situation Report – December 2008*, January 9, 2009, Table A-1.
4. RealtyTrac, 'U.S. Foreclosure Market Reports,' November 12 and December 11, 2008, and January 15, 2009.
5. Elizabeth McNichol and Iris Lay, 'State Budget Troubles Worsen,' Center on Budget and Policy Priorities, December 23, 2008, p. 1.
6. As a subsequent chapter will discuss, the TARP administrator under Obama, Neil Barofsky, upon leaving office, revealed that Congress's original intent in passing the $700 billion TARP was for Paulson to commit at least half of that to foreclosures and homeowner bailouts, none of which happened.
7. *Financial Times*, November 24, 2008, p. 1.
8. Amy Belasco, 'The Cost of Iraq, Afghanistan, and Other Global War on Terror Operations Since 9/11,' Congressional Research Service, *CRS Report for Congress*, September 2, 2010.
9. See *New York Times*, January 15, 2009, p. 1.
10. *Wall Street Journal*, January 8, 2009, p. 1.
11. *New York Times*, January 16, 2009, p. 1. See also *Wall Street Journal*, January 23, 2009, p. 3.
12. Rebecca Wilkins, Senior Counsel for Citizens for Tax Justice, as reported on *C-SPAN2 Book TV*, August 6, 2011. see booktv.org.
13. Wilkins, as reported on *C-SPAN2 Book TV*.
14. This writer does not adhere to the view that Obama's errors were the consequence of bad advice from his advisors. Politicians in general, and presidents in particular, choose the

advisors that they feel share their views. The conservative, cautious, tax-centric, pro-business recommendations of Obama's advisors throughout his term are reflective of those same values in Obama himself.

15. See Krugman's column in the *New York Times*, January 9, 2009, p. 23.

16. See 'Obama Remarks on the Economy,' *Wall Street Journal Online*, January 8, 2009, for the full text of Obama's George Mason University address.

17. Christina Romer and Jared Bernstein, *The Job Impact of the American Recovery and Reinvestment Plan*, Council of Economic Advisers and Office of the Vice-President Elect, January 9, 2009, Figure 1, p. 4.

18. Romer and Bernstein, *The Job Impact of the American Recovery and Reinvestment Plan*, see Table 2, p. 6. The projected job gains in construction and manufacturing followed job declines in the previous year, 2008, of 632,000 in construction and 994,000 in manufacturing.

19. See House Ways and Means Committee and Senate Finance Committee graphic, 'Where the Money Goes,' and for a more detailed description, *Fact Sheet, 'Conference Report on American Recovery and Reinvestment Act,'* Office of Speaker Nancy Pelosi, February 11, 2009.

20. Economists refer to the relative impact of tax cuts vs. spending as the 'multiplier' effect. Even conservative economists recognize the tax multiplier is significantly less than the spending multiplier. Even business economist Mark Zandi of Moodys Inc. estimated the spending multiplier as a $1.73 boost to GDP for every $1 spending by government, while the tax multiplier was only 1.01 to $1. In other words, there was no 'multiplier' effect for the tax cuts. This writer would consider that 1-to-1 ratio as even significantly overestimated. Much of the tax cuts were in fact 'hoarded' and not spent. The tax multiplier was likely less than 0.5%.

21. The remaining roughly $113 billion was mostly miscellaneous provisions designed more to gain votes in Congress than have any meaningful impact in terms of economic recovery.

22. Douglas Elmendorf, Director of the Congressional Budget Office, letter to Nancy Pelosi, summarizing impact of the ARRA. See Table 1. The CBO at the time also predicted the Stimulus would create 3.4–4.2 million jobs and lower the unemployment rate to 7.5% by 2011. Like the CEA-Romer Jobs Report forecast of the month earlier, the CBO's February 2009 forecasts would also prove to be far off the mark.

23. And they got in trouble increasingly and deeper with each financial crisis: 1837, 1859, 1872, 1884, 1893, 1907. In 1907, the U.S. Treasury had to commit all of its funds except $5 million to bail out the New York banks after the 1907 banking panic and collapse.

24. See Tobias Adrian and Hyun Shin, Federal Reserve Bank of New York Staff Report, *The Shadow Banking System: Implications for Financial Reform*, July 2009.

25. See Nouriel Roubini, 'Run on the $10 Trillion "Shadow Banking System",' *RGE Monitor*, July 29, 2009.

26. *Bloomberg News*, February 25, 2009.

27. U.S. Treasury Press Release, *Fact Sheet on Public Private Partnership Investment Program*, March 23, 2009.

28. Gillian Tett, 'Why Public Private Plan Has Bankers Squirming,' *Financial Times*, May 22, 2009.

29. U.S. Treasury Press Release, 'Homeowner Affordability and Stability Plan: Executive Summary,' and the Plan's 'Fact Sheet', February 18, 2009.

30. The big three banks—Wells Fargo, JP Morgan Chase, and Bank of America—controlled more than half of the residential mortgage servicing market. This was up from 22% of the servicing market in 2005.

31. *New York Times*, March 4, 2011, pp. 22 and 25.

32. See RealtyTrac annual and monthly reports for years 2008 through 2010, and monthly for 2011 through July 2011.

33. *New York Times*, March 30, 2011, p. 1.

34. *RGE Monitor*, 'FASB Eases mark-To-Market Rules for Toxic Assets,' April 13, 2009.

35. Buiter blog, 'How the FASB Aids and Abets Obfuscation by Wonky Zombie Banks,' April 3, 2009.

36. Buiter, 'How the FASB Aids and Abets Obfuscation by Wonky Zombie Banks.'
37. U.S. Department of the Treasury, *Monthly Lending and Intermediation Snapshot*, January 15, 2010.
38. *Wall Street Journal*, November 25, 2009, p. 11.
39. U.S. Department of the Treasury, *Monthly Lending and Intermediation Snapshot*.
40. Jack Rasmus, *Epic Recession: Prelude to Global Depression*, Pluto Press, 2010.

## CHAPTER 4

1. Bureau of Economic Analysis, *National Income and Product Accounts*, GDP, Table 1.1.1, revised as of July 29, 2011.
2. The recovery for the next six months, i.e. the first half of 2010, would prove no better. The economy in early 2010 continued to lag earlier recession recoveries again by half despite the $787 billion stimulus and the bank bailouts. And by the summer of 2010, even that 50% of normal GDP growth rate would decline even further.
3. The U.S. Labor Department reports two unemployment rates. The U-3 is the most conservative, reporting as unemployed only those workers who are out of work but actively looked for a job in the previous four weeks. It does not pick up workers who were involuntarily reduced to part-time work, those who may have left the labor force, or those who are out of work but haven't looked for a job in the previous year. The more accurate, thorough indicator of unemployment is the U-6 rate. Even that rate, however, underestimates unemployment for various additional reasons.
4. All these statistics from Bureau of Labor Statistics, Monthly *Employment Situation Reports*, June through December 2009, Tables A-1, A-5, A-6, A-9 and A-12.
5. See Tables A-5 and A-8 of U.S. Department of Labor, Bureau of Labor Statistics, Monthly *Employment Situation Reports*, from July 2009 to December 2009.
6. Referred to as the 'JOLT' rate (i.e. job opening labor turnover rate) compiled by the Department of Labor, the JOLT rate doubled from December 2008 to December 2009, from 3:1 to 6.2:1.
7. Louise Radnofsky, 'Agency Stands Pat on Stimulus Jobs,' *Wall Street Journal*, November 23, 2009, p. 5.
8. Bureau of Labor Statistics, Monthly *Employment Situation Reports*, from July 2009 to July 2011, Tables A-12 and A-15, for this chronic 'U-6' unemployment rate statistic.
9. RealtyTrac, Monthly *Foreclosure Reports* and *Year End U.S. Foreclosure Market Report*, for 2009–10.
10. U.S. Census Bureau, *State Government Tax Collections in 2009*, revised May 2010, p. 1. See also U.S. Census Bureau, *State Government Finances Summary: 2009*, by Christopher Pece, Chrul Lee, and Nancy Higgins, January 2011.
11. Bureau of Economic Analysis, *National Income and Product Accounts*, GDP, Tables 1.1.1 for the percentages and Table 1.1.6 for real total spending, adjusted for seasonality and inflation. Data revised as of July 29, 2011.
12. Once again, see RealtyTrac and Bureau of Labor Statistics, *Employment Situation Reports*, for the indicated months.
13. Council of Economic Advisors, 'Did "Cash-for-Clunkers" Work as Intended?,' April 5, 2010.
14. Edward Luce, 'Obama Weighs Job Creation Options,' *Financial Times*, October 7, 2009, p. 3. See also, *New York Times*, October 6, 2009, p. 1.
15. Neil King, 'Obama Wrestling with Jobs Outlook,' *New York Times*, October 23, 2009, p. 8.
16. Elizabeth Williamson, 'Weighing Jobs and Deficit: White House is Unenthusiastic on Legislation that Would Raise Government Debt,' *Wall Street Journal*, November 23, 2009, p. 5.
17. Congressional Budget Office, *Analysis of H.R. 2847, the Jobs for Main Street Act*, 2010, passed December 16, 2009. The final vote was 217–212, with 38 Democrats voting with

all Republicans against the bill. That same day the House passed by wide margin the $636 billion Defense Appropriations Bill for 2010.

18. Jim Abrams, *Huffington Post*, January 3, 2010.

19. See *Political Hotsheet*, March 18, 2010, for a summary.

20. Bureau of Labor Statistics, *Current Employment Survey* database, total private jobs, seasonally adjusted, series Id.

21. RealtyTrac, *Monthly Foreclosure Reports*, October to December, 2009.

22. *Wall Street Journal*, December 17, 2009, p. 8.

23. Michael Crittenden, 'Lending Falls at Epic Pace,' *Wall Street Journal*, February 24, 2010, p. 1.

24. It is not the intent of the writer here to replicate the full explanation of what is an 'epic' recession, how it is different from 'normal' recessions as well as similar and different from bona fide depressions. For a fuller treatment of that theoretical point, the reader is referred to the writer's 2010 book, *Epic Recession: Prelude to Global Depression*, Pluto Press, 2010, especially the theoretical Chapters 1–3 of that book and the various confirming historical case examples of Type I and Type II Epic Recessions in the U.S. from 1907 to 2010.

25. As a subsequent chapter of this book will further show, Obama and the Fed's response to the first relapse in the summer of 2010—i.e. the second recovery program—was able to check the third quarter's decline somewhat. But the economy quickly weakened again in the first half of 2011. That is because the second recovery program was weaker than the 2009 recovery program. So the economy's response in terms of recovery was of even shorter term and weaker still.

26. *Wall Street Journal*, August 14, 2010, p. 4.

27. Federal Reserve Board, *Senior Loan officer Opinion Survey on Bank Lending Practices*, chart data, April 2011, online update June 7, 2011. See tables for Figures, 1 (C&I), 2 (CRE), 3 (residential mortgages) and 4 (loans to households).

28. *Wall St. Journal*, June 15, 2010, p. C8.

29. *Financial Times*, November 11, 2010, p. 14.

30. *Wall Street Journal*, September 4, 2010, p. B3.

31. Jeanine Aversa, 'As Spending by Wealthy Weakens, So Does Economy,' *Associated Press*, August 1, 2010.

32. Michael Powell, 'End of Census and for Many, End of a Job,' *New York Times*, July 12, 2010, p. 1.

33. This estimate is from data gathered by the Congressional Budget Office, Moody's Economy. com research, and the U.S. 'Recovery Accountability and Transparency Board' filings as of July 30, 2010. All reported in extensive detail, in charts and graphs, by the *Wall Street Journal*, August 16, 2010, p. 6.

## CHAPTER 5

1. General Electric in particular was a major recipient of bailout assistance, as its financial arm, GE Credit, experienced serious losses in 2008–09, but was able to avail itself of generous financial assistance from the Fed and the U.S. Treasury.

2. *Financial Times*, July 8, 2010, p. 3.

3. All the preceding data in this paragraph are from the Bureau of Labor Statistics, *Current Establishment Survey*, Table B-1, historical archived, not seasonally adjusted.

4. *Financial Times*, July 21, 2010, p. 3.

5. John Gapper, 'Obama Must Learn to Love Business,' *Financial Times*, October 28, 2010, p. 11.

6. Peter Orszag, 'One Nation, Two Deficits,' *New York Times OP-ED*, September 7, 2010, p. 23.

7. Edward Luce, *New York Times*, September 10, 2010, p. 3.

8. Luce, *New York Times*, p. 3.

9.  Monthly foreclosures had also exceeded 300,000 every month for the preceding 17 consecutive months.
10. Reported on Bloomberg News, August 13, 2010.
11. *New York Times* editorial, 'Foreclosures Grind On,' August 20, 2010, p. 18.
12. *New York Times*, July 22, 2010, p. B2.
13. Associated Press, October 20, 2010, as reported by *New York Times* online, same date.
14. MortgageDaily.com, October 2010, reporting the largest mortgage servicers by portfolio size, in trillions of dollars.
15. *New York Times*, October 14, 2010, p. B9.
16. Alan Zibel, 'Disappiontment on Home Aid,' *New York Times*, January 26, 2011, p. C3.
17. *Wall Street Journal* editorial, 'The Housing Bust Lobby,' October 19, 2010, p. 18.
18. Ellen Brown, 'QE2 Shocker: The Whole $600 Billion Wound Up Offshore,' Truthout Blog, July 6, 2011.
19. 'QE intro date' refers to the date the Fed first starts buying bonds. 'QE conclusion date' refers to when the Fed stops buying bonds, even though the formal program may not end until a later date. The Dow average typically starts rising once discussion of a likely introduction of QE begins publicly, not when QE buying actually begins. The Dow thus anticipates the intro of QE buying by several months or however long the discussion of introducing QE goes on. With QE1 there was virtually no prior discussion period. With QE2 it was two to three months. A similarly brief prior discussion period took place before the introduction of what has been called 'Operation Twist', or what is sometimes referred to as 'QE 2.5,' in the second half of 2011.
20. U.S. Bureau of Labor Statistics, *Employment Situation Reports*, December 2010 and August 2011, Table B-1.
21. For a summary of the Joint Committee's findings, see Jackie Calmes, 'Study Looks at a Lapse of Tax Cuts for the Rich,' *New York Times*, August 11, 2010, p. 12.
22. See *Financial Times*, November 5, 2010, p. 4, and *Wall Street Journal*, November 5, 2010, p. 4.
23. *Financial Times*, December 8, 2010, p. 8.
24. *Financial Times*, December 8, 2010, p. 8.
25. *Wall Street Journal*, December 8, 2010, p. 1.
26. For Biden's key role in the negotiations, see Carl Hulse and Jackie Calmes, 'Biden and GOP Leader Helped Hammer Out Bipartisan Tax Accord,' *New York Times*, December 8, 2010, p. 20.
27. Laura Meckler, 'Obama Lashes Out at Critics in his Base,' *Wall Street Journal*, December 8, 2010, p. 6.
28. Dean Baker, 'Obama's Tax Deal: Read the Small Print,' *Guardian News & Media*, reprinted from CommonDreams.org, December 21, 2010.

## CHAPTER 6

1.  Bureau of Economic Analysis, *National Income and Product Accounts*, Table 6.4A, updated and revised as of July 16, 2011.
2.  For these indices data, see Basil Rausch, *The History of the New Deal 1933–1938*, Capricorn Books, 1963, pp. 93–103, whose source is primarily *The Statistical Abstract for the United States, 1934* and *The American Yearbook 1933*.
3.  For this account, see Rausch, *The History of the New Deal*, p. 129.
4.  Rausch, *The History of the New Deal*, p. 138.
5.  It is useful to note that the deficit-cutting agenda is largely focused on social programs and excludes most defense spending. Similarly, the tax-cutting is focused primarily on business and investor taxes and not broad consumer taxes. Republicans driving the agenda in 2011 have succeeded largely in 'ring-fencing' defense from all but token cuts mostly from attrition of personnel and programs. They have further opposed extending tax cuts for middle-class programs like child care and education credits.

6.  Bureau of Economic Analysis, *National Income and Product Accounts*, Table 1.1.1, revised May 29, 2009.

7.  Bureau of Economic Analysis, *National Income and Product Accounts*, Tables 6.2A, 6.4A, revised August 20, 2009.

8.  Bureau of Economic Analysis, *National Income and Product Accounts*, Table 1.1.1, revised May 29, 2009.

9.  Bureau of Economic Analysis, *National Income and Product Accounts*, Table 6.4A, revised August 20, 2009.

10. Krugman, 'The Mistake of 2010,' *New York Times*, June 3, 2011, p. 19.

11. Krugman, '1938 in 2010,' *New York Times*, September 5, 2010.

## CHAPTER 7

1.  *Wall Street Journal*, January 8, 2009, p. 1.

2.  *Federal Register*, 75 FR 7927, February 23, 2010.

3.  Paul Krugman, 'The Hijacked Commission,' *New York Times*, November 12, 2010, p. 23.

4.  All quotes from John McKinnon, 'Deficit Panel Stresses Spending Cuts,', *Wall Street Journal*, July 1, 2010, p. 6.

5.  Kathy Ruffing and James Horney, 'Critics Still Wrong on What's Driving Deficits in Coming Years,' Center on Budget and Policy Priorities, June 28, 2010, p. 10.

6.  *Medicare Trustees 2011 Annual Report*, Table III.A1, p. 45.

7.  Federal Reserve, 'Flow of Funds,' March 10, 2011.

8.  See OASI Trust Fund, 'Old-Age and Survivors Insurance Trust Fund, 1937–2010', Social Security Administration, at www.ssa.gov/oact/STATS/table4a1.html.

9.  Peter Orszag, "Safer Social Security," *New York Times*, November 15, 2010, p. 23.

10. Co-Chairs Report, *11-10-10 Draft Document* (Powerpoint Presentation), November 2010.

11. See the Tax Policy Center's analysis of the Bowles-Simpson Deficit Commission, November 15, 2010, Table T10-0247, at www.taxpolicycenter.org.

12. Peter Wallsten, 'Deficit Plan Gets Mixed Review,' *Wall Street Journal*, November 18, 2010, p. 8.

13. For details of the Schakowsky plan see 'Schakowsky Deficit Reduction Plan: Fiscal Responsibility That Protects the Lower and Middle Class', online at Schakowsky.house. gov, November 16, 2010.

14. For summary details of the budget, see *Wall Street Journal*, Associated Press, and *New York Times* feature articles on February 15, 2011, both front-page feature articles.

15. Jackie Calmes, 'Obama Concedes Budget Failings,' *New York Times*, February 16, 2011, p. 1. The 'group of senators' refers to the formation of the so-called Gang of Six.

16. Carol Lee, 'Obama's Budget Aim,' *Wall Street Journal*, April 9, 2011, p. 4.

17. *Path to Prosperity*, House Fiscal Year 2012 Budget Resolution, House Committee on the Budget, April 5, 2011, at www.budget.GOP.gov.

18. That projected $1.8 trillion was actually an underestimation of the cost of making the Bush tax cuts permanent. That more accurate cost was closer to $3 trillion from 2011 through 2021.

19. Robert Greenstein, 'Statement on Chairman Ryan's Budget Plan,' Center on Budget and Policies Priorities, April 20, 2011.

20. See Table S-4, Summary Tables, *Path to Prosperity*, House Fiscal Year 2012 Budget Resolution, House Committee on the Budget, April 5, 2011, at www.budget.GOP.gov.

21. Congressional Budget Office, 'Long Term Analysis of a Budget Proposal by Chairman Ryan,' see www.cbo.gov/ftbdocs/Ryan_letter.pdf.

22. Reed Abelson, 'Health Insurers making Record Profits as Many Postpone Care,' *New York Times*, May 13, 2011.

23. *The People's Budget*, Budget of the Congressional Progressive Caucus, Fiscal Year 2012, U.S. House of Representatives, p. 2. For a detailed analysis of this budget, see Andrew Fieldhouse, 'The People's Budget: A Technical Analysis,' Economic Policy Institute, Working Paper, April 13, 2011.

24. Thea Lee, chief economist of the AFL-CIO, *New York Times*, April 18, 2011, p. 14.

25. *Financial Times*, June 30, 2011, p. 1.

26. That higher target for Medicare-Medicaid cuts was 'signaled' earlier by Obama in April, when he publicly noted that his ideas for Medicare and Medicaid would save $340 billion over ten years and $500 billion by 2023. It should also be noted that Obama's July offer for health care spending cuts were in addition to the Medicare and Medicaid payment cuts already specified in his 2010 Health Care Act, which some estimate amount to as much as $400 billion over the decade. So the $340 billion to $500 billion offered in July 2011 most likely represented an additional amount. See Robert Pear, 'Administration Offers Health Care Cuts as Part of Budget Negotiations,' *New York Times*, July 4, 2011.

27. Mark Landler and Carl Hulse, 'Still "Far Apart" on Debt, 2 Sides Will Seek Broader Cuts,' *New York Times*, July 7, 2011.

28. Executive Summary, 'A Bipartisan Plan to Reduce Our Nation's Deficits', released July 2011.

29. See OMB Watch, 'The Budget Control Act of 2011 (Debt Ceiling Deal),' August 2011, www.ombwatch.org, and for details, see August 1, 2011, letter by Douglas Elmendorf, director of Congressional Budget Office, to Boehner and Reid, with accompanying Tables 1–3 on the deficit and other impact of the final Budget Control Act of 2011.

## CHAPTER 8

1. *Wall Street Journal*, August 7, 2010, p. B4.

2. See Bloomberg, 'Retail Sales Discount Index' and 'Retail Sales Luxury Index' trends for the first half of 2011 compared to 2010. For Walmart, Barclays Capital, *Wall Street Journal*, May 18, 2011, p. C1.

3. Stephen Roach, 'How Zombie U.S. Consumers Menace the World Economy', *Financial Times*, June 16, 2011, p. 26.

4. Ben Casselman and Justin Lahart, 'Companies Shun Investment, Hoard Cash,' *Wall Street Journal*, September 17–18, 2011, p. 2.

5. The rating agency Standard & Poor's estimated that the 500 companies in its S&P Index at year-end 2010 were parking 'north of $1 trillion in undistributed foreign earnings, or profits...overseas to avoid U.S. tax' (see Jason Zweig, *New York Times*, February 19, 2011, p. B1, and James Politi, *Financial Times*, May 12, 2011, p. 4). The amount of all foreign corporate offshored profits was certainly much larger. And in 2011 this amount of cash hoarded offshore undoubtedly rose further. The corporate-Congressional response to this massive corporate tax avoidance was the introduction of a bill in May 2011 to lower the corporate tax rate on all past offshored earnings to 5.25% instead of the normal 35%, to entice the return of the sheltered offshore profits. This very same maneuver had been done successfully in 2005. In that earlier year, $312 billion of a potential offshored $700 billion was repatriated to the U.S. by reducing the corporate rate on foreign profits to 5.25%. The argument was that it would be used to create jobs. It wasn't—92% of it was used to buy back corporate stock and increase dividends. In October 2011 Democratic Senator Kay Hagan and Republican John McCain joined forces once again to introduce a bill to tax all foreign corporate earnings—this time not just past profits but all future profits as well—at the attractive rate of 8.75% instead of the normal 35%.

6. Richard Milne, 'Rivers of Riches,' *Financial Times*, May 23, 2011, p. 9.

7. Jackie Calmes, 'Obama Asks for Review of Rules Stifling Jobs,' *New York Times*, January 19, 2011, p. B1.

8. Barack Obama, 'Towards a 21st Century Regulatory System,' *Wall Street Journal*, January 18, 2011, p. 17.

9. See various blog articles by this writer during this period, including: 'Why March–April's Job Gains will Collapse this Summer,' *Truthout*, May 22, 2011; 'Obama and Corporate Responses to the May Jobs Report,' *Znet*, June 6, 2011; 'The Predicted Job Collapse Now in Progress,' *Znet*, July 10, 2011; 'Look Again, July Jobs Declined by 198,000,' *Znet*, August 9, 2011; 'Way Worse Than Zero,' *Truthout*, September 8, 2011.

10. Laurie Segall and Catherine Clifford, 'Jobs Picture Remains Fuzzy', CNNMoney.com, October 5, 2011.

11. RealtyTrac, *Foreclosures Activity Reports*, June through August, 2011.
12. Quoted from *Daily Finance*, August 11, 2011.
13. RealtyTrac, *Foreclosure Activity Report*, August 2011.
14. Shahlen Nasiripour, 'U.S. Mortgage Woes Soar as Banks Offer Fewer Loan Modifications,' *Financial Times*, September 30, 2011, p. 5.
15. *The Niche Report*, 'Zillow Predicts True Bottom in Home Values in 2012,' online, August 9, 2011.
16. *The Niche Report*, quoted from the Zillow press release of August 9, 2011.
17. For details of state-by-state cuts planned in budgets for various areas see Erica Williams, Michael Leachman, and Nicholas Johnsons, 'State Budget Cuts in the New Fiscal Year are Unnecessarily Harmful, Hitting Hard at Education, Health Care and State Economies,' Center on Budget and Policy Priorities, updated July 28, 2011.
18. Bureau of Labor Statistics, *Employment Situation Report* for September 2011, Table 8, October 7, 2011.
19. Bureau of Labor Statistics, 'A' and 'B' archived tables, *Current Establishment Survey* (manufacturing jobs) and *Current Population Survey* (labor force statistics), October 6, 2011.
20. Williams et al., 'State Budget Cuts in the New Fiscal Year are Unnecessarily Harmful'.
21. *Financial Times*, September 29, 2011. p. 6.
22. Reuters news agency, reported by Fidelity.com, September 29, 2011.
23. Vipal Monga, 'Companies' $2 Trillion Conundrum,' *Wall Street Journal*, October 5, 2011, p. B5.
24. Emily Malty, 'Tale of Two Loan Programs,' *Wall Street Journal*, October 6, 2011, p. 9.
25. Jack Ewing, 'On Horizon, Debt Squeeze of $5 Trillion for Banks Around the World,' *New York Times*, July 12, 2010, p. B3.
26. Ben Casselman, 'Americans Tap Savings to Keep Up with Prices,' *Wall Street Journal*, October 1, 2011, p. 2.
27. Conor Dougherty, 'Income Slides to 1996 Levels,' *New York Times*, September 14, 2011, p. 1.
28. Bureau of Economic Analysis, *Personal Income and Outlays: August 2011*, September 30, 2011.
29. William Horobin, 'OECD Slashes Forecasts for Growth,' *Wall Street Journal*, September 9, 2011, p. 13.
30. Norma Cohen and Jim Pickard, 'Increase in Jobless Fuels Fears for UK Recovery and Leads to Call for "Plan B",' *Financial Times*, August 18, 2011, p. 3.
31. David Wessel, 'Tracking Missteps Behind World's Economic Slump,' *Wall Street Journal*, August 25, 2011, p. 4.
32. Michael Pettiss, 'China's Economy is Headed for a Slowdown,' *Wall Street Journal*, August 10, 2011, p. 13.
33. Chetan Ahya, 'India's Economy is Souring, Too,' *Wall Street Journal*, August 23, 2011, p. 11.
34. John Paul Rathbone, 'Recession Fears Loom in One of the Few Global Bright Spots,' *Financial Times*, October 6, 2011, p. 2.
35. Linday Whipp, 'Effects of Japan's Disasters Linger as Economy Contracts Again,' *Financial Times*, August 16, 2011, p. 1.

## CHAPTER 9

1. Jackie Calmes, 'Obama to Press Committee on Jobs,' *New York Times*, August 18, 2011, p. 13.
2. Bureau of Labor Statistics, *Employment Situation Report*, September 2, 2011.
3. *Financial Times*, September 7, 2011, p. 7.
4. Jackie Calmes, 'Obama Confirms New Hard Stand with Debt Relief,',*New York Times*, September 20, 2011, p. 1. See also Carol Lee and Naftali Bendavid, 'Obama Yokes Benefit Cuts to New Taxes,' *Wall Street Journal*, September 20, 2011, p. 1.
5. Reported by Stephanie Kirchgaessner and James Politi, 'Obama Set to Signal Big Cuts to Healthcare Costs,' *Financial Times*, September 14, 2011, p. 8. In April the president had proposed $480 billion in Medicare-Medicaid cuts.

6. Donna Smith and Richard Cowan, "Republicans Seek $2.2 Trillion Budget Savings,' Reuters, October 27, 2011. For Democrats' recommendations, see Robert Pear and Jennifer Steinhauer, 'Democrats' First Offer: Up to $3 Trillion for Debt,' *New York Times*, October 27, 2011, p. 16.

7. *Wall Street Journal*, September 19, 2011, p. 4.

8. That measure would raise $886 billion, plus another $410 billion by eliminating itemized deductions from their taxes for the same over-$250,000 group. That's a potential $1.276 trillion in tax savings and deficit reduction.

9. One favorite way to game the payroll tax system, that has been expanding for decades, is to simply reclassify employees as temporaries or contractors. The company does not pay payroll tax for workers in that category, which has converted more than 10 million workers in recent decades from what were once regular, full-time, non-contract direct employees.

10. Part of the additional $50 billion in transport spending might also be considered state subsidization, since the states received some of the money and allocated its spending at the state level.

11. Recall once again the point made in prior chapters that all the contending parties, from Obama to the Teapublicans to the original Simpson-Bowles Commission to the Gang of Six and others, agreed from the beginning on the target deficit-reduction goal of about $4 trillion. The only differences were how to pay for it and what would be the 'mix' between tax increases versus program spending cuts and the 'mix' between defense spending and entitlement spending cuts. Also agreed among all was that there would be more cuts in spending than in tax-hike revenue generation. The differences ranged from 60–40% to 87–13% for larger spending cuts.

12. Jon Hilsenrath, 'Fed Launches New Stimulus,' *Wall Street Journal*, September 22, 2011, p. 1. See lead p. 1 stories in the *New York Times* and *Financial Times* as well for that same date.

13. Bloomberg News, interview of September 1, 2011.

14. Nouriel Roubini, 'Mission Impossible: Stop Another Recession,' *Financial Times*, August 8, 2011, p. 9.

15. David Reilly, 'High Stakes get Higher for the Federal Reserve,' *Wall Street Journal*, September 19, 2011, p. C1.

16. Public release announcing new report, 'U.S. Economy Tipping into Recession,' ECRI, September 30, 2011. For the full report see ECRI's *U.S. Cyclical Outlook*, September 21, 2011.

17. 'An Ugly Forecast that's Been Right Before', reported on ECRI's website, October 9, 2011.

18. George Soros, 'How to Stave Off a Second Great Depression,' *Financial Times*, September 30, 2011, p. 11.

19. See this writer's *Epic Recession: Prelude to Global Depression*, Pluto Press, 2010, and specifically Chapters 5 and 7 for examples of Type I Epic Recessions in the U.S. in the twentieth century and the last decade; and see Chapter 6 for a Type II Epic Recession.

20. 401k pensions in the U.S. are private, personal pension plans that are offered and administered by companies and/or banks. They are unlike typical collective pensions, called defined benefit pensions, which are typically union pensions, public pensions, Social Security, etc. With 401ks, companies make a flat contribution to the 401k on behalf of the worker. The worker may add more as well. The worker then decides where to invest the money, usually in stocks and bonds. Not being very financially savvy, he usually loses money. 401ks collapsed by $4 trillion in savings after 2007. Regular pensions' funds are invested by professional pension fund managers and the company is liable to pay the worker a benefit whether or not the pension fund made money from its investment decisions. Banks love 401ks because they can charge large fees for managing them and the contributions can be directed to their stock and bond trading operations where they make money as well.

# Index